D1453881

Eros in
the Mind's Eye

Recent Titles in
Contributions to the Study of Science Fiction and Fantasy
Series Editor: Marshall Tymn

EROS IN
THE MIND'S EYE

Sexuality and the Fantastic in Art and Film

EDITED BY
DONALD PALUMBO

CONTRIBUTIONS TO THE STUDY OF
SCIENCE FICTION AND FANTASY, NUMBER 21

GREENWOOD PRESS
New York • Westport, Connecticut • London

Library of Congress Cataloging-in-Publication Data
Main entry under title:

Eros in the mind's eye.

(Contributions to the study of science fiction and
fantasy, ISSN 0193–6875 ; no. 21)
Bibliography: p.
Includes index.
1. Sex in moving-pictures—Addresses, essays,
lectures. 2. Horror films—History and criticism—
Addresses, essays, lectures. 3. Science fiction films—
History and criticism—Addresses, essays, lectures.
4. Erotic art—Addresses, essays, lectures. 5. Fantasy
in art—Addresses, essays, lectures. I. Palumbo,
Donald, 1949–   . II. Series.
PN1995.9.S45E68 1986   700   85-24777
ISBN 0-313-24102-3 (lib. bdg. : alk. paper)

Library of Congress Catalog Card Number: 85–24777
ISBN: 0-313-24102-3
ISSN: 0193–6875

First published in 1986

Greenwood Press, Inc.
88 Post Road West, Westport, Connecticut 06881

Printed in the United States of America

The paper used in this book complies with the
Permanent Paper Standard issued by the National
Information Standards Organization (Z39.48–1984).

10 9 8 7 6 5 4 3 2 1

Copyright Acknowledgments

The author and publisher are grateful to the following for granting the use of
their material:
Lyrics from *The Rocky Horror Picture Show* are reprinted courtesy of Lou Adler,
Malibu, California.
Excerpt from *The Ship of Fools* by Sebastian Brant, Edwin H. Zeydel,
translator, copyright 1944, Dover Publications, New York.
Every reasonable effort has been made to trace the owners of copyright
materials in this book, but in some instances this has proven impossible. The
publisher will be glad to receive information leading to more complete
acknowledgments in subsequent printings of the book and in the meantime
extend their apologies for any omissions.

To my sons, Anthony and David

Contents

Contents

Illustrations

Preface

DONALD PALUMBO

A companion volume to Greenwood Press's *Erotic Universe: Sexuality and Fantastic Literature*, this collection of eighteen scholarly essays explores the depiction of sexuality in fantastic artworks employing visual media, primarily two-dimensional art and film. The collection attempts as thorough a consideration of this subject as can be attained in a single volume. It covers the Western art of six centuries, from Medieval woodcuts to contemporary poster art, and the cinema of six decades, from horror classics of the 1930s to recent slasher films. In all, these essays discuss over 100 fantastic woodcuts, prints, paintings, drawings, and illustrations by seventy-five artists, from Hans von Aachen to Boris Vallejo, and nearly 100 science fiction, fantasy, and horror films, from *Alien* to *Werewolf of London*, as well as seventy-eight "Star Trek" television episodes. Yet, while the works considered range from high art to mass entertainment, from Medieval to postmodern, and from the celebrated to the obscure, this study reveals a surprising consistency of interests, concerns, symbols, and themes—and of interrelationship between artworks and their social contexts—that affirms an undeniable unity suffusing the interpretation of sexuality through the fantastic in visual media.

Paul Grootkerk's "Occult Eroticism in Fantastic Art of the Fifteenth and Sixteenth Centuries" is an encyclopedic discussion of the Germanic and Netherlandish art of the early Renaissance that depicts sexual aspects of northern Europe's Medieval traditions of witchcraft and demon worship. Death, the Devil, and the occult world of witchcraft became primary artistic subjects in fifteenth-century northern Europe; and as sexual intercourse with demons was believed to be an important aspect of the witches' sabbat, artists of the period treated eroticism both explicitly and symbolically in their frequent depictions of occult practices and themes. A complementary study, Liana Cheney's "Disguised Eroticism and Sexual Fantasy in Sixteenth- and Seventeenth-Century Art," discusses the more sublimated treatment of erotic subject matter in the depiction of mythological scenes in the art of sixteenth-century southern Europe, which grounded its tradition in its Classical rather than Medieval past, in seventeenth-century Italian religious art, and in the work of seventeenth-century Dutch realists. Due to the more repressive religious environment of southern Europe, the artists of sixteenth-century Italy, France, and Spain employed allegory as a vehicle for depicting sexual fantasy, particularly fantasies involving aberrant sexual desires, in addition to interpreting the wedding celebrations, abductions, and metamorphoses of Classical myth, especially the amorous exploits of Jupiter or Zeus, as erotic subjects. After the Counter-Reformation, disguised eroticism almost disappeared in southern European mythological paintings only to appear again in Italian religious paintings; and, while eroticism still appeared in seventeenth-century northern European mythological paintings, which offered a Puritan revision of the ancient myths, it also began to appear more frequently and explicitly in Dutch genre scenes of seventeenth-century lower- or middle-class life, realistic art that adopted a tone of Puritan morality in portraying sexuality.

Kathleen Russo's "Henry Fuseli and Erotic Art of the Eighteenth Century" traces artistic depictions of sexuality from the early 1700s, when the works of Fragonard mirrored elite society's frivolous attitudes towards sex, through a period of melancholy despair at innocence lost typified by Hogarth's paintings, to the romantic eroticism of Fuseli and Blake at century's end. As the eighteenth century progressed and sexual activity came more and more to be seen again as something immoral and forbidden, artists again turned towards fantastic subjects to express the tensions this social climate created in their consideration of the erotic. Gwendolyn Layne's "Mum's the Word" explores the expression of erotic themes and subjects during Great Britain's golden age of fantasy illustration, 1860–1920. This explosion of artistic activity managed to produce illustrators who treated sexuality with both wit and shocking frankness, in addition to artists whose eroticism was more subliminal, despite the repressive Victorian values of the time. Although relatively liberated from such moral restraint, contemporary comic book artists are these illustrators' heirs, not only in their fusion of word and image, but also in their infusion of a subtle eroticism into their work.

Francine Koslow's "Sex in Surrealist Art" and Sylvie Pantalacci's "Surrealist Female Monsters" examine the nature and nuances of twentieth-century Surrealism's preoccupation with sexuality. With roots in the women's emancipation movement as well as in Freudian psychology, surrealist thought ironically replaced the dichotomous Victorian view of woman as either virgin or whore with an equally reactionary dichotomous view of woman as either child-woman or *femme fatale*. But it is the negative pole of this second dichotomy that was most often portrayed by surrealist artists, who tried to interpret the eroticism of the subconscious, of dreams, in their works; thus, they evoked repressed psychic material, often making sexuality their subject matter, and depicted an eroticism of distortion, dislocation, and irrationality that shares the pervasive misogyny that has permeated the treatment of sexuality in fantastic art from the end of the Middle Ages to the present. Layne's "Subliminal Seduction in Fantasy Illustration" discusses the use of subliminal techniques to convey erotic content in contemporary fantasy illustration and compares this phenomenon to similar uses of subliminal embeds in contemporary advertising as well as in works by sixteenth-century European and Persian artists and twentieth-century surrealists. A complementary essay, Sarah Clemens's "And Now, This Brief Commercial Message" analyzes the erotic imagery in contemporary movie poster art to argue that sex sells fantasy overtly as well as subliminally.

Theorizing generally that horror films attempt to confront and master the audience's inevitable dread of two related unknowns, sex and death, Leonard Heldreth's "The Beast Within" argues specifically that the unbidden metamorphoses of the werewolf film symbolize the physical changes and psychological consequences of puberty. Extending this "beast within" thesis, Anthony Ambrogio's essay on "Horror Films' First Sex Symbol" chronicles the film career of Fay Wray to demonstrate that the monster in horror movies is often the hero's ignoble "double" or doppelgänger, a base version of the hero who conspicuously exhibits the hero's repressed sexual urges. Thus, the monster characteristically occupies the apex of a love triangle composed of hero, monster, and heroine; and sometimes, as in *Dr. Jekyll and Mr. Hyde* as well as in all the werewolf films, is the hero himself transformed into his secret, lustful counterpart. While the Monster in *Frankenstein* forms such an eternal triangle with Victor and Elizabeth, Martin Norden's "Sexual References in James Whale's *Bride of Frankestein*" argues that this sequel offers not only love triangles but also a variety of potential love parallelograms—among other amorous aberrations of the geometrical kind—involving Victor, Elizabeth, both monsters, and Dr. Pretorious in numerous bisexual, homosexual, incestuous, necrophilic, and Oedipal (in addition to heterosexual) permutations. From psychoanalytic and philosophical perspectives, respectively, John Kilgore's "Sexuality and Identity in *The Rocky Horror Picture Show*" and Raymond Ruble's "Dr. Freud Meets Dr. Frank N. Furter" examine the implications of the Freudian model that permeates *Rocky Horror*, a spoof of both horror and science fiction films that comically exhumes the subtext of Freudian dynamics and symbolic sexual aberration usually buried in films of both genres.

Ambrogio's exhaustive analysis of *Alien*, "In Space, No One Can Hear Your Primal Scream," is another Freudian interpretation that views this film as an Oedipal psychodrama in which the phallic, child-molesting other/father (the Alien) displaces the children (the crew) in their mother's (the ship's) affections and then attempts to violate and kill them. Jim Holte's "Pilgrims in Space" examines four American science fiction/fantasy films in which sex is markedly absent to demonstrate that America's Puritan heritage and its ethic of sexual repression or denial is, sometimes in combination with the Freudian model, another subtext that informs many science fiction, fantasy, and horror films. Andrew Gordon's "The Power of the Force" sees the *Star Wars* trilogy as another Oedipal psychodrama, a "family romance" that exhibits a preoccupation with fear of castration and flirts with homoeroticism in exploring familiar rite-of-passage themes. Mary Jo Deegan argues in "Sexism in Space" that the "Star Trek" television series and films portray the future as yet another Freudian fantasy in which patriarchal domination of women by men mirrors contemporary sexual attitudes. And Sam Umland's "Sexual Freaks and Stereotypes in Recent Science Fiction and Fantasy Films" compares movies from the 1950s with those released in the past few years, some of them remakes of the vintage originals, to demonstrate that contemporary horror and science fiction films tend to ridicule heterosexual relationships or undermine their legitimacy rather than to offer, as did their predecessors, the possibility of wholesome "romance" as an acceptable alternative to unearthly terror.

Collectively, these essays indicate that a surprising continuity, extending from the beginnings of the Renaissance to the present, exists in the depiction of sexuality through the fantastic in visual media: in the consistent use of specific symbols, in repeated returns to the fantastic as an acceptable vehicle for communicating erotic subjects during periods of social or religious repression of sexuality, and in an underlying current of misogyny evident in all media and periods. While the depiction of musical instruments and certain foods, such as specific fruits, oysters, liquor, and wine, commonly symbolized sexual license or excess in the art of the fifteenth, sixteenth, and seventeenth centuries, but less frequently thereafter, the use of animals as symbols of repressed or debased sexuality has persisted from Medieval woodcuts and the paintings of Bosch, through Fuseli's *The Nightmare*, Victorian illustrations, and Surrealism's monstrous imagery, to classic horror movies such as *The Most Dangerous Game* or *The Wolfman* and such contemporary werebeast films as *An American Werewolf in London* or Paul Schrader's remake of *Cat People*.

Fuseli's *The Nightmare*, an image of repressed sexuality, hung in Freud's office, and some nineteenth-century illustrators freely employed Freudian images in their work prior to the surrealists' wholesale adoption of Freudian symbolism in their attempts to represent the subconscious visually. While some, like Delvaux, refused to acknowledge Freud as a source, many, like Dali, who was an acquaintance of Freud's, openly expressed fascination with Freudian psychology. Such horror film spoofs as *An American Werewolf in London*, *The Rocky Horror Picture Show*, and *Young Frankenstein* playfully exploit Freudian symbols and models for comic effect, and in doing so call attention to a coherent psychological model and symbol system that has been used as a subtext in a phenomenal number of horror, science fiction, and fantasy films, from *The Wolfman* and *Bride of Frankenstein* to *Forbidden Planet*, *Alien*, and the *Star Wars* and *Star Trek* movies. While art tends to make use of Freudian symbols as images, films have an even greater tendency to use Freudian models to inform them as narrative: While Kilgore argues that all movie monsters and aliens are emblems of the submerged id or libido, Oedipal conflicts seem to be epidemic in science fiction and horror film plots, as Heldreth, Ambrogio, Norden, Ruble, Holte, Gordon, and Deegan demonstrate.

Much as artists from the sixteenth century to the early twentieth century sublimated the erotic content of their work in depictions of mythological scenes and animals, contemporary fantasy illustration, like advertising, employs subliminal embeds to enhance its sometimes explicit sexual content. Such embeds occur too in movie poster art, which also still uses the classic helpless-beauty-menaced-by-lascivious-beast/monster/alien image to suggest the existence of sexual content in films that may contain no overt sex at all. Sexuality most often appears in sublimated guise as violence, as well as explicitly, in the horror film: Big game hunting appears as a substitute for sex in *King Kong* and *The Most Dangerous Game*, and random murder complements promiscuous sexuality in the glut of 1980s slasher films. Similarly, on a subliminal level *Alien*—a science fiction film with numerous horror movie antecedents—is a tale of attempted rape/murder in outer space.

Such insistent use of sexual subtexts in films that have little or no superficial erotic content may be a vestige of the Puritan morality that infected the tone of seventeenth-century Dutch genre painting. Kilgore and Ruble argue that the triumph of the superego (represented by Dr. Scott and Riff Raff) in *Rocky Horror* is a reassuring victory for compromise between complete sexual license and sexual repression. Holte demonstrates that America's Puritan heritage reveals itself in the subtext of sexual repression that informs numerous American science fiction, fantasy, and horror films. And Umland suggests that a resurgence of Puritan morality is evident in *Halloween* and other recent slasher films in which sexually active teenagers are, in effect, punished for their promiscuity with violent death.

An underlying fear and hatred of women is conspicuous in those films that exhibit echoes of Puritan morality, but the expression of misogyny is also the single most salient characteristic consistently evident in the depiction of sexuality through the fantastic in visual media from the fifteenth century to the present. Fantastic art of the early Renaissance commonly portrayed women as witches, succubi, prostitutes, and seducers to reflect the Medieval belief that women were primarily responsible for carnal lust and man's concomitant fall from grace. Women were the subjects of violence in sixteenth- and seventeenth-century depictions of mythological abduction scenes, which often portrayed the artist or patron as an abductor, just as they are favorite subjects of violence in twentieth-century horror films. Fuseli's works, many of which portrayed women in a negative, sexually explicit and aggressive manner, reveal an unconscious hatred of women. And Dali, who was obsessed with the perverse and as fascinated by the writings of the Marquis de Sade as by those of Freud, exhibited an apparently conscious fear of women in his paintings, which often took masturbation and sadism as themes. That surrealist artists far more frequently portrayed the *femme fatale*—sometimes in the form of female monsters—than the child-woman in their works suggests, as does that dichotomy itself, that a misogynous undercurrent subtly pervaded the ostensibly pro-feminist surrealist movement, just as a misogynous subtext is evident in some contemporary films, like *Alien*, that appear to have superficial feminist sympathies.

The Alien in *Alien* is a *penis dentata*, a male organ with teeth, but a fear of women manifested as fear of castration by the female is evident in the appearance of the *vagina dentata* image in both surrealist paintings and contemporary science fiction, fantasy, and horror films. Pantalacci argues that the *vagina dentata* is depicted in Magritte's *The Rape* as well as in Dali's *Minotaure*. Gordon points out that the Sarlacc in *Return of the Jedi* is the largest, most voracious *vagina dentata* ever to appear on film, and that it appears in a film series that is ambivalent at best in its treatment of women and preoccupied on a symbolic level with fear of castration. Umland notes that the *vagina dentata* is a prominent image in Schrader's *Cat People*, in which the female protagonist literally devours her lovers after having intercourse with them.

Ambrogio argues in "Horror Films' First Sex Symbol" that the sexual molestation of women is the nexus of all horror films, which as a genre explicitly associate sex with violence, just as Clemens demonstrates that the promise of sexual molestation of women is the favorite advertising ploy for all those movies featuring beasts, robots, aliens, creatures, or Bug Eyed Monsters: King Kong symbolically threatens Fay Wray with miscegenous rape. But, despite the abduction of Elizabeth and lots of female bondage imagery, Norden argues that the locus of misogyny in *Bride of Frankenstein* is the film's "understated degradation of women and indictment of their role in reproduction." This trivialization of the role of women is a more subtle signal of misogyny apparently more characteristic of science fiction than of horror films, however. Holte argues that American science fiction traditionally ignores women and sublimates sexuality in placing emphasis on masculine dedication to the great mission or cause, as in *Star Wars*; moreover, *Outland* demonstrates that real men don't need women, and *2001* (somewhat like *Bride of Frankenstein*) suggests that mankind can evolve beyond the need for biological reproduction. Deegan sees in the "Star Trek" movies and television episodes further evidence that, in outer space, attention to women is subordinated to a masculine loyalty to the quest and to other men: In the patriarchal world of "Star Trek," women want men, but men want power; women are tempting distractions, but are secondary to the male mission; and, as in the surrealist view of the child-woman, the female role is dependent on the male. Perhaps misogyny begets androgyny: The contempt for heterosexuality and infatuation with androgyny Umland discovers in recent films may be merely the latest wrinkle—like the "spiritualized eroticism" of the Pre-Raphaelites, which legitimized androgyny in the nineteenth century—in a "trend" of at least 500 years' duration, as well as a reflection of contemporary social trends.

The depiction of sexuality in fantastic art and film is a subject that cannot be exhausted in one volume. I refer interested readers to the secondary sources in the List of Artworks, Filmography, and Bibliography in this book. Also, the companion to this volume, *Erotic Universe: Sexuality and Fantastic Literature*, contains essays that investigate in science fiction and fantasy literature many of the same interests, concerns, symbols, and themes discussed here. *Erotic Universe* also contains some discussion of the treatment of sexuality in artworks and science fiction, fantasy, and horror films not discussed in this volume. I recommend it.

Acknowledgments

I would like to recognize and thank those individuals and organizations instrumental in producing this book and determining and preparing its contents. Marshall Tymn gave the initial concept his benediction, and his and James Sabin's advice helped shape the volume. Most of these essays were first presented as papers in sessions on sexuality in fantastic art and film at the 1982 and 1983 International Conferences on the Fantastic in the Arts and National Popular Culture Association Meetings; Robert Collins, Allen Greer, Joy Schwab, Ernest Weiser, and Howard Pearce, at Florida Atlantic University, and Ray Browne, Peter Rollins, and Thomas Remington, of PCA, scheduled and helped organize these sessions. Fran Griffiths, with the assistance of Patsy Swegard, typed the manuscript with admirable imperturbability. Those whose advice contributed to the compilation of the List of Artworks, Filmography, and Bibliography are mentioned in that section.

John Kilgore would like to thank Doug and Ginny Dibianco for help in locating source materials. Anthony Ambrogio would like to acknowledge the graciousness of the editors of *Cinemacabre* and *Cinefantastique* in granting him permission to cite extensively from their periodicals. Although she, like Captain Kirk, assumes final responsibility for her work, Mary Jo Deegan would like to thank Terry Nygren, her classmates in the "Wimmin in the Mass Media" course, and Michael R. Hill (for his numerous editorial comments).

Eros in
the Mind's Eye

1

Occult Eroticism in Fantastic Art of the Fifteenth and Sixteenth Centuries

PAUL GROOTKERK

In fifteenth-century Europe a new concept of the world arose, one that no longer echoed the etherealized universe of the early Gothic era but instead wailed of pessimism and cruelty. One of the major themes in fifteenth-century art, as depicted in the most explicit detail by the Netherlandish artist Hieronymus Bosch, was the portrayal of the tortures of the damned. Johan Huizinga describes the fifteenth century as a period in a "continual state of anxiety . . . constantly under the threat of injustice and violence, with the fear of hell and the Last Judgement, of plague, fire and famine, and devils and witches."[1] Evil became the concern of late Medieval man. No longer was the spiritual emphasized; rather, malevolence dominated. Death, the Devil, and the occult world of witchcraft became primary artistic subjects.

The Germanic and Netherlandish artists displayed the strongest fascination with the macabre and the occult, but some art with these themes was also produced in Italy and France. After the break with Rome in the sixteenth century, the Germanic and Netherlandish countries returned to their Medieval past, considering this rather than the Latin spirit their national tradition. Thus, artists like Hans Baldung Grün, Albrecht Dürer, Quentin Massys, Joachim Patinir, and Bosch continued the Medieval discourse between the living and the dead. With their contemporaries, they created macabre portrayals of an unknown world of spells, incantations, queer animals, the Devil, and both grotesque and beautiful witches.

Many of the portrayals contain a strong erotic element that is sometimes, as in the work of Grün, quite graphically expressed. In the Middle Ages, sexuality was commonly considered an aspect of the occult because indiscriminate sexual intercourse was thought to be a major part of the witches' sabbat. However, while Grün was quite explicit in his depictions of fantastic sexuality, most artists of the late Middle Ages expressed such sexuality more symbolically. The numerous symbols they employed to represent occult eroticism can be classified into four major categories: depictions of musical instruments, dances, women, and animals.

Among the most famous of Bosch's fantastic paintings is *The Haywain* (c. 1485, Prado, Madrid), an allegorical illustration of man's greed and its worthlessness in which men and women fight and kill to possess a cartload of hay. But avarice is only one of the seven deadly sins depicted in Bosch's painting. Lust, a sin associated with avarice in Medieval thought, is represented by two pairs of lovers. While one couple is kissing in the bushes growing out of the haystack, the other is making music, the man playing a lute.

In a copy of a painting after Bosch, *The Concert in the Egg* (Palais des Beaux Arts, Lille), a group of people singing in a broken egg are accompanied by an elegantly dressed demon playing a lute. A lute player is also included among a group of devil, satyr, and hobgoblin musicians in a woodcut illustration from the 1555 Roman edition of Olaus Magnus's *Historia da Gentibus Septentrionalibus*, a history of the Netherlandish and Germanic people that discusses their witchcraft practices. Another demon in the Olaus Magnus woodcut is playing a bagpipe, and at the bottom of Bosch's *Haywain* a fool is blowing this instrument. The Olaus Magnus woodcut probably represents a gathering of demons preparing for the witches' sabbat; for the demons are dancing around a large circle, the "magic circle" of Satan, which was believed necessary for safe communication with the Devil. At these occult gatherings some witches provided music as accompaniment for the wild dancing that would precede indiscriminate sexual intercourse.

The depiction of the lutes and bagpipes signifies that lust, termed the "music of the flesh" by Medieval moralizers, is a preeminent subject in both Bosch's *Haywain* and the Olaus Magnus woodcut. During the Medieval period the bagpipe was considered an emblem of the male organ, and playing the lute symbolized making love. A more explicit instance of the bagpipe's symbolic significance is seen in *The Pool of Youth* by the Master of the Banderoles, a German engraving of about 1460 depicting a fool in a garden playing a bagpipe while one young man nearby fondles his female companion and another puts his hand under his maiden's elevated dress.

The bagpipe was considered the instrument of fools and suggests the foolishness of lust. The harp and lute, however, though also symbolic of lust, suggest a higher social class than the bagpipe, which was associated with the peasant and is depicted in several of Pieter Bruegel's paintings of peasants dancing and feasting. Bosch makes this distinction in *The Haywain*; the more elegant couple has the lute. However, in the Olaus Magnus woodcut no such distinction is made: Demons play both the bagpipe and the lute. This visual portrayal of equality reflects the belief that all social classes attended the witches' sabbat. At the 1611 witchcraft trial of Sister Madeleine de Demandolx, the nun confessed that all classes of men and women, from "people of sordid and base condition to gentlemen," attended.[2]

At these gatherings the witches usually were nude. This is clearly depicted in Hans Weiditz's sixteenth-century woodcut titled *Witches Celebrating*; in *Witches' Brew*, a woodcut illustration from Abraham Saur's *Ein Kurtze Warning* (Frankfurt, 1582); and in Grün's woodcut titled *Witches' Sabbat* (Figure 1, 1514). The nudity of these participants parallels the nudity of Bosch's figures in the Hell panel of *The Garden of Earthly Delights* (Figure 2, c. 1500, Prado, Madrid), in which an oversized bagpipe is prominent. This nudity signifies also the debased equality of all men and women in the world of lust, which the punishments suffered by the lusty souls in Bosch's triptych indicate is the domain of the Devil.

The demonic implications of the harp are also especially evident in Bosch's *The Garden of Earthly Delights*, in which one of the lust-driven creatures is eternally crucified on an oversized harp that represents his sin. This vision is repeated in a triptych from Bosch's workshop, *The Last Judgement* (Groeninge Museum, Bruges), which contains both the harp-crucifixion detail and a group of nudes dancing briskly around a massive bagpipe, almost as if in worship. This vignette again calls to mind the frenzied dancing of the witches' sabbat, which preceded not only sexual intercourse but also the traditional sabbat homage to the Devil.

Next to the amorous couple with the lute in *The Haywain* is a devil piping some lascivious tune through his nose, which is shaped like a long trumpet. The music of the devil has lured the lovers' attention from the angel next to them, who is praying for their salvation. The theme of the trumpet-nosed devil is repeated in the central panel of Bosch's *The Temptation of St. Anthony* (Figure 3, c. 1500, Museu Nacional de Arte Antiga, Lisbon). In late Medieval art the representation of devils with wind instruments is a very common motif. Among the numerous examples of this subject is a woodcut illustration from Ludovicus Caelius Rhodiginus Ricchierius's 1517 Basel edition of the *Lectionum Antiquarum* depicting the Devil blowing a cornetto.

Sister Madeleine de Demandolx also testified at her trial that "there is a sabbat every day . . . the witches are gathered together by the cornet which is winded by a devil."[3] In Agostino Veneziano's sixteenth-century engraving titled *Lo Stregozzo*, a young follower of the Devil, seated on a goat, blows a cornetto while leading a procession to the sabbat. The concept of a devil calling followers together by blowing a cornet appears to be a corruption of the idea of the Last Judgement, at which time trumpets will awaken the dead (I Corinthians 15:52). The diabolical implications of wind instruments are also clearly depicted in the musical Hell of *The Garden of Earthly Delights*, in which a damned male carries an enormous flute on his back and has another flute eternally protruding from his rectum. This punishment too may allude to the witches' sabbat, for sodomy was but one of the sexual acts performed at these occult assemblies.

Sebastian Brant's *Ship of Fools* (1494) warns

1. Hans Baldung Grün, *Witches' Sabbat*, 1514. Reprinted with permission of The Metropolitan Museum of Art, Joseph Pulitzer Bequest, 1917. (17.50.46)

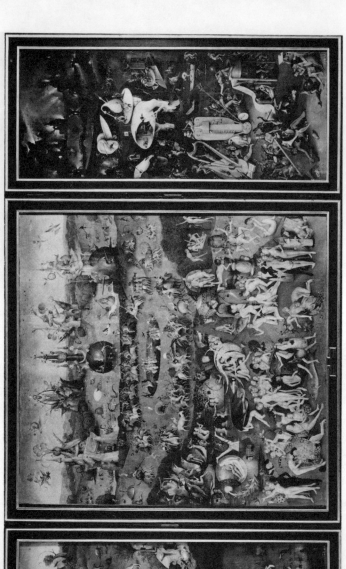

2. Hieronymus Bosch, *The Garden of Earthly Delights*, c. 1500. Courtesy of Museo del Prado, Madrid.

3. Hieronymus Bosch, *The Temptation of St. Anthony*, c. 1500. Reprinted with permission of MUSEU NACIONAL DE ARTE ANTIGA—Lisboa.

7

> That dance and sin are one in kind
> That very easily 'tis scented:
> The dance of Satan was invented.

Between 1566 and 1568 Pieter Bruegel and his followers produced a number of paintings and engravings that represent the
sinfulness of dancing. Among these works are two paintings by
Bruegel, *Peasant Wedding Dance* (1566, Institute of Art, Detroit)
and *The Peasant Kermis* (c. 1567, Kunsthistorisches Museum, Vienna), as well as a sixteenth-century engraving by Pieter van
der Borcht titled *Peasant Kermis*. Symbolically, *Peasant Wedding
Dance* is another condemnation of lust, as is indicated by the
presence of the bagpipe, the two visibly aroused men in the
foreground, and the amorous couple in the center right. This
painting recalls Brant's comments on the relationship between
dancing and lust:

> They dance about like fools insane.
> . . . Whom Cupid strikes, Amour ignites,
> So that the fire his vitals bites
> And he cannot put out the flame.

The kermis is a Netherlandish/Germanic peasant carnival noted
for its drinking and brawling. About the kermis Brant wrote:

> There's naught more evil here on earth
> Than giddy dancing gayly done
> At Kermess, first mass, where the fun
> Is shared by priests and laity,
> Where cowls can flap in zephyrs free.

This carnival was usually held on holy days and was looked
upon by contemporary moralizers as a blasphemy due to the
licentiousness and unruliness that usually accompanied it. Van
der Borcht's engraving depicts a woman vomiting and a lustful
couple as well as peasants dancing.[4]

The fact that priests too danced at the kermis, noted by Brant,
is revealed also in an engraving by Bruegel titled *The Feast of
Fools* (Figure 4, c. 1568), in an etching of the same title (c. 1550–
1560) by Frans Hogenberg, and in a woodcut entitled *The Nose*

4. Pieter Bruegel, *The Feast of Fools*, c. 1568. Copyright Bibliothèque Royale Albert Ier, Brussels.

Dance at Gumpelsbrunn (1534) by Sebald Beham. Keith Moxey explains that

The religious Feast of Fools was an institutionalized ritual that constituted an integral part of ecclesiastical life in the southern Netherlands from the thirteenth to the sixteenth centuries. The festival, which was a characteristic part of the communal life of cathedral chapters, consisted in an inversion of the clerical hierarchy. The lower clergy took control of the cathedral and proceeded to hold mock services as well as drunken revels at which scandalous and indecent behavior was given free rein. At Tournai, a mock bishop was elected who was baptized with buckets of water and paraded about town, sometimes in the nude.[5]

The Feast of Fools demonstrates the concept of the "world upside down" that was a characteristic of the black mass. The ceremony itself was infamous for its desecration of the Catholic mass, and often involved sexual blasphemies. In 1335 the Inquisitor at Carcassonne found a naked shepherd parodying the Catholic mass, and in 1458 the French inquisitor Nicholas Jacquier described a priest copulating in a church and collecting his semen in order to mix it with the holy chrism oil.

The dancers depicted both in the prints portraying the Feast of Fools and in Bruegel's *Peasant Wedding Dance* are dancing in a ring. Such a circular dance is even more clearly evident in the background of a 1559 engraving after Bruegel, *Kermis at Hoboken*. In the 1626 edition of the *Compendium Maleficarum*, Francesco-Maria Guazzo describes the dancing at the witches' sabbat: "Following the banquet came dances which are performed in a circle but always to the left. . . . Sometimes they dance before eating and sometimes after the repast. . . . All the rites are performed with the utmost absurdity in a frenzied ring with hands joined and back-to-back."[6] Back-to-back dancing, though considered indecent, was one form of Medieval folk dancing often practiced by the rougher elements in towns. The couple in the lower right-hand corner of Bruegel's *Peasant Wedding Dance* is dancing back to back, and the man is in a very visible state of arousal; this again recalls the sexual activities of the witches' sabbat.

Circle or ring dancing is also evident in the Olaus Magnus woodcut of demonic musicians dancing around the "magic circle" of Satan and in Jacob Cornelisz. van Oostsanen's *The Witch of Endor* (1526, Rijksmuseum, Amsterdam), which depicts a witches' sabbat. That circular dancing was an act of the Devil and symbolic of lust is most clearly seen in Bosch's *Garden of Earthly Delights*, where in the central panel a "cavalcade of men" circles the so-called "pool of women." According to some authorities this vignette is based upon the morris dance, an old fertility game in which young men wildly pranced around a young maiden. In *Kermis at Hoboken* the circular dance group is dancing around a young couple; and in Bruegel's *The Feast of Fools* the fools are dancing in a ring around an orchestra of fools, a detail that recalls the group of nudes dancing around a massive bagpipe in the Hell panel of *The Last Judgement*. At a witches' sabbat participants commonly ring-danced around the Devil, who often sat in the center of the circle in the form of a goat.

In the Middle Ages women were seen primarily as sexual objects and considered responsible for the bedevilment of man and the discovery of carnal lust. It is thus little wonder that Brant wrote,

> A temporal pleasure's like unto
> A brazen, sensual woman who
> Infests the street and plies her trade
> Inviting every amorous blade
> To come and practice fornication. (ch. 50; p. 178)

Erasmus reiterates this viewpoint in stating that women exist for no other "purpose than that of pleasure."[7]

Women as seducers are quite literally represented in a number of fifteenth- and sixteenth-century artworks. Among these is the central panel of Bosch's *Garden of Earthly Delights*, in which a circular pool of nude women beckon to a circle of men riding around them. This idea and image reflects the Medieval concept of woman as the initiator of sin and lechery, a precedent set by Eve.

Similarly, Bosch's two versions of *The Temptation of St. Anthony* (original: Lisbon; copy and variation: Rijksmuseum, Amsterdam) both depict an alluring nude young woman tempting the saint. This detail is repeated in the left panel (representing St. Anthony) of Bosch's *Hermit Saints* triptych (Palace of the Doges,

Venice). In all three paintings the beautiful nude is standing in a body of water, perhaps a river. The bathing nude is the Devil-Queen, the seductive guise assumed by Satan in his encounter with Anthony.

These details are repeated again in *The Temptation of St. Anthony* by Patinir and Massys (Figure 5, c. 1520, Prado, Madrid), which shows Bosch's influence. The background contains two seductive nudes enticing the saint from the river while a third nude toasts him from a banquet table in a rowboat at which a well-dressed woman, a demon, and a hooded oarsman (possibly Charon) also are seated. The three nudes in the river are repeated in a 1522 woodcut of the same subject by Jan Wellens de Cock. In the Lisbon version of Bosch's *Temptation of St. Anthony*, the Devil-Queen is behind a banquet table at which demons pour some liquid refreshment. This devilish feast, including the liquor, is repeated in the Patinir/Massys boat scene. These scenes recall the banquet at the witches' sabbat. Sister Madeleine de Demandolx testified that at the sabbat "The drink which they have is malmesy, to provoke and prepare the flesh to luxurious wantoness."[8]

In every one of these works the women stand in a body of water as they entice their male counterparts because in the Middle Ages love and lovemaking were associated with water. Often in astrological prints "the children of Venus" were shown as mixed couples bathing in the nude; to "swim in the Bath of Venus" was a sixteenth-century Netherlandish expression for being in love. In none of these paintings or prints are couples in a body of water, however; instead, the women are always enticing the men to join them, as if to baptize them in the "river" or "pool" of lust. This is analogous to the Devil's rebaptism at the sabbat of those individuals newly indoctrinated into the realm of Satan; only by participating in this ceremony could individuals join the sabbat orgies. A woodcut from the 1626 edition of Guazzo's *Compendium Maleficarum* depicts such a rebaptism. All the seductive women in these works represent succubi, devils in female shape who specialize in seducing men.

The *Temptation of St. Anthony* by Patinir and Massys also contains in the foreground three elegantly attired women who are being goaded to seduce the saint by a hag with prominently

5. Joachim Patinir and Quentin Massys, *The Temptation of St. Anthony*, c. 1520. Courtesy of Museo del Prado, Madrid.

exposed breasts. These three women, as well as the attired female in the boat, may be prostitutes, and the hag might be their
madam. The theme of prostitution is very common in Medieval
art and literature, as Brant's verses illustrate. Examples in art
include the house of prostitution in Bosch's *The Wayfarer* (c. 1500,
Boymans-van Beuningen Museum, Rotterdam), in which a couple embrace in the doorway; Quentin Massys's *Ill-Matched Lovers*
(c. 1520, National Gallery of Art, Washington, D.C.), which shows
an elderly lecher paying a fool for the pleasures of a young
woman; and Lucas van Leyden's 1519 woodcut titled *The Prodigal
Son*, in which the young harlot in the center seduces the "son"
as the elderly madam at her side drinks a glass of wine. The
prostitutes in the Patinir/Massys *Temptation of St. Anthony* might
also be succubi, and vice versa. Johannes Nider's *Formicarius*,
written in 1435 and first published in Augsburg in 1475, relates
that many harlots offered their services to those attending the
Council of Constance (1414–1418) but that the most sought-after
prostitute was a succubus. In 1468 a man in Bologna was con-
demned to death for running a brothel staffed by succubi, who
were reputedly more desirable than mortals due to their pur-
ported sexual prowess.

The three elegantly attired young women and the old hag in
the Patinir/Massys *Temptation of St. Anthony* may also be witches.
The elderly hag is the stereotype of a witch—"an old weather-
beaten crone," as Samuel Harsnett describes one in his 1599
Declaration of Popish Impostures.[9] The iconology of the witches'
prominently exposed breasts is seen in a great many other portrayals of witchcraft. Among these numerous works are Grün's
engraving titled *The Bewitched Groom*, in which a half-nude, hag-
gard wretch waves a sheath of burning wheat through the stable
window; Dürer's engraving titled *Witch Riding on a He-Goat*, which
depicts a long-breasted nude witch riding a goat to the sabbat;
and Abraham Saur's woodcut illustration titled *Witches' Brew*, in
which two elderly wretches, one with long, exposed breasts,
prepare some diabolical brew for the sabbat.

Witches were also thought to have supernumerary breasts in
unnatural locations that were used for "giving suck" to familiars.
The "Lungtuttin," a giant, hair-covered female spirit of the Ty-

rol, supposedly offered small children her long breasts to seduce them. From one breast flowed milk; from the other, venom. In Austria an old witch sitting naked in the cornfields, a corn spirit, reputedly preyed on small children by forcing them to drink tar from her long, black, iron breasts. Witches seduced or stole children either to cook and eat them at the sabbat or to offer them to incubi, devils in male shape who would sexually molest them there.

Though most witches are old and ugly, some are young and beautiful. Like their aged cronies, these are most commonly portrayed naked. Nude young witches are depicted in Dürer's 1497 engraving titled *Four Witches*, whose only diabolical implication is the Devil in the doorway of the room, and in Grün's 1514 woodcut titled *Witches' Sabbat*, which depicts six nude witches of various ages, among them a very young witch arriving at the sabbat seated on a goat. Grün often rendered young witches as explicitly erotic, extremely licentious beings. In one of his drawings three excited nude witches, one old and two young, are portrayed playing leapfrog so that the derriere of one of the young witches is prominently and enticingly displayed as if in expectation of sexual penetration.

In *Tableau de l'inconstance des mauvais anges et demons* (Paris, 1612), Pierre de Lancre relates that the Devil's bifurcated penis "was generally sinuous, pointed, and snake-like, made sometimes of half-iron and half-flesh, at other times wholly of horn, and commonly forked like a serpent's tongue; he customarily performed both coitus and pederasty at once, while sometimes a third prong reached to his lover's mouth." In another erotic drawing, Grün represents a devil in the form of a hideous monster performing cunnilingus on a young witch. Bestiality was yet another common form of demonic sexuality; de Lancre also notes that "The devil in the form of a goat, having his member in the rear, had intercourse with women by joggling and shoving that thing against their belly." Various writers on witchcraft (such as Alphonso de Castro, 1547) maintained that many women become witches due to the voluptuous pleasures of the sabbat despite the sexual abuses. Since women in the Middle Ages were considered to be more licentious than men, male incubi appear much more frequently than do succubi in literature on demonology. Incubi were believed to outnumber succubi nine to one, suggesting the strong affinity between women and the Devil.[10]

As de Lancre's description of demonic bestiality would suggest, the goat (in particular the he-goat) is the most common animal form associated with sexual aspects of the occult in fifteenth- and sixteenth-century art. According to an anonymous twelfth-century Latin manuscript, *The Bestiary*, the he-goat is "a lascivious and bunting animal who is always burning for coition."[11] The transvection of witches to the sabbat on goats is represented in numerous artworks, including an illustration in Guazzo's *Maleficarum* of a nude witch airborne on a goat with bat wings; Grün's *Witches' Sabbat*, which contains a young nude witch seated backwards on a flying goat; Dürer's *Witch Riding on a He-Goat*, which repeats Grün's image but with an old witch; and Bruegel's 1565 engraving titled *St. James and the Magician Hermogenes*, which depicts a nude witch departing for the sabbat astride a flying billy goat. The image of witches seated backwards on airborne goats may be related to the circle dances of the sabbat, in which dancing proceeded always to the left or back-to-back. Paulus Grillandus mentions in the *Tractatus de Herecticies et Sortilegiis* (Lyons, 1536) that these reversals may indicate a "reversal of customary Christian procedures, similar to making the sign of the cross from right to left or jumbling the words of consecretion at the mass ('hoc est corpus') into hocus-pocus."[12]

Having arrived at the sabbat, witches and sorcerers alike customarily paid homage to the Devil in the form of a goat sitting atop a throne. Sometimes this homage was likewise performed backwards. However, the most infamous act of homage was the ritual kiss on the Devil's buttocks, known as the "osculum infame" or "osculum obscoenum," the celebrated kiss of shame, which symbolized the epitome of degradation. Jean Bodin wrote in *De la demonomanie des sorciers* (Paris, 1580) that "There is no greater disgrace, dishonour, or villainy than that which these witches endure when they have to adore Satan in the guise of a stinking goat, and to kiss him in that place which modesty forbids writing or mentioning."[13] This act of obeisance is graphically shown in an illustration from a fifteenth-century French manuscript on witchcraft (Bodleian Library, Oxford) representing a young witch on her knees bending over to kiss a goat's derriere. This scene is repeated in an illustration in Guazzo's *Maleficarum* (Figure 6) that contains a devil with a goat's head and bat wings, his tail elevated in a predatory manner, and a young witch on her knees about to kiss his clearly exposed posterior. Behind the young witch stand other witches and sorcerers awaiting their turn.

Another, similar form often assumed by the Devil is the satyr, a mythological creature that is a man with the ears, horns, tail, legs, and feet of a goat. In mythology the satyr is known for its lasciviousness and lechery, and for often participating in nighttime orgies that parallel the nocturnal events of the sabbat. The Devil is portrayed as a satyr in the Olaus Magnus woodcut of demonic musicians, in Ricchierius's illustration of a devil blowing the cornet, and in an engraving titled *The Devil Tempting St. Jerome* from Pierre Boaistuau's *Histoires prodigieuses* (Paris, 1597). One of the most significant attributes of devils absent from these depictions of demonic goats and satyrs is the reputed enormity of their penises. Nicholas Remy asserts in *Demonolatreiae Libri Tres* (Lyons, 1595) that "The female witches also all maintain that when they are laid by their demons, they can admit, only with the greatest pain, what are reputed their tools, because they are so huge and rigid."[14]

The bird is also symbolic of occult eroticism because its realm, the air, is traditionally ruled by devils, a belief reflected in the many images of witches being borne through the air to the sabbat. The most significant bird form assumed by the Devil is the owl—"notua" in Latin since it flies only by night, the traditional time of the Devil and the sabbat as well as of human sexuality. The owl is a symbol of both evil and lust in Bruegel's *The Feast of Fools*; the fool in the center foreground has an owl perched on his arm and is making an obscene gesture suggesting the sex act. The owl is a symbol of lust is especially common in the paintings of Hieronymus Bosch. In *The Ship of Fools* (c. 1485, Louvre, Paris) Bosch includes a monk and a nun among a group of peasants carousing in a boat whose mast is a full-grown tree containing an owl in its branches. The idea that the owl represents lust is reinforced by other symbolic objects in the painting: On the table between the nun and monk is a bowl of cherries,

6. Anonymous, *Kiss of Shame*. In *Compendium Maleficarum* by Francesco-Maria Guazzo (Milan: 1626). Courtesy of the Collections of the Rare Book and Special Collections Division, Library of Congress.

another traditional Medieval symbol of lust, and the nun is playing a lute. In the lower right-hand section of *The Garden of Earthly
Delights* is a large owl seated above a platter scattered with cherries; below this platter a man and a woman dance madly in a
"twine" of cherries.

Numerous other birds depicted in Bosch's *Garden of Earthly
Delights* also represent evil or sexuality as these concepts are
related to the occult. Included in this group are blackbirds, crows
or ravens, and spoonbills carried on the heads of the nude women
in the central pool. Ravens and crows were associated with hanging and bad luck. The raven was also believed to be a form the
Devil would assume when he wanted intercourse with a witch.
The blackbird suggests the evil connotations of the color black;
sometimes an amorous devil would appear to a witch as a Moor.
The spoonbill and the ibis are waterfowl that represent evil and
lust due to the Medieval association of sexuality with water.
Patinir and Massys's *Temptation of St. Anthony* includes an ibis
sitting in the river by the three succubi. Left of center in the
central panel of Bosch's *Garden* sit a group of gigantic birds,
many with human riders, bogged down in a large body of water.
The entire image represents man caught in the mire of his own
lusts. Prominent among this group of birds are the kingfisher,
known for its sexual incontinence and brutality, and the wood-
pecker, another symbol of the Devil. Directly below this group
of birds is a man embracing an owl.

The depiction of monkeys also symbolized lust. In Bosch's
Last Judgement (c. 1500, Akademie bildenden Kunste, Vienna) a
monkey squatting on the roof in the central panel plays a lute
above his head while watching a demon violate a conceited,
nude young woman. Some scholars have suggested that the
monkey is actually another demon serenading the woman to
further degrace her. In the Patinir/Massys *Temptation of St. Anthony* a monkey is pulling the hood of Saint Anthony's robe as
the saint is being taunted by four harlots/witches. The demonic
aspect of the monkey is vividly portrayed in Bruegel's *St. James
and the Magician Hermogenes*: Monkeys warm themselves by the
fireplace as Hermogenes confronts St. James with a vision of
hell and a glimpse of witches flying up the chimney to the sabbat
on broomsticks.

Perching on the floor directly behind the monkeys in Bruegel's engraving is a cat, one of the most traditional symbols of demonology. According to *The Bestiary*, the cat resembles the Devil in its habit of catching and gobbling things. This conception of the cat is literally represented in Dürer's engraving titled *Adam and Eve* (1504), in which the image of the cat about to capture and eat the mouse parallels the image of Eve about to offer the apple to Adam and thereby "capture" him. Similarly, a woodcut representing adultery in Brant's *Ship of Fools* depicts a woman tickling a fool with a reed while on the floor a cat eats a freshly captured mouse. The cat is supposedly another form sometimes assumed by the Devil. An intently watching cat is included in a drawing ascribed to Grün that depicts a naked, elderly witch waking an erotically posed, nude young witch to take her to the sabbat. Another staring cat appears in Grün's *Witches' Sabbat*.

The horse too was a form sometimes assumed by the Devil. In Teutonic folklore the nightmare, "Mahr," often appears in the shape of a horse. Grün's *Bewitched Groom* depicts a half-nude, elderly witch looking through a window into a stable containing the prone groom, who appears to have been thrown by the large horse standing in the rear and staring at his attendant. The groom is lying in a vulnerable position that would allow either the witch, as a succubus—or possibly the horse, if it is indeed the Devil—to "ride" him. The theme of "riding" is repeated in the central panel of Bosch's *Garden of Earthly Delights*, in which many naked men ride various animals, including horses, around the pool of nude women. In discussing this painting Walter Gibson notes that "Animals traditionally symbolized the lower or animal appetites of mankind and personifications of the Sins were often depicted on the backs of various beasts; the act of riding, finally, was commonly employed as a metaphor for the sexual act."[15]

The fantastic art of the fifteenth and sixteenth centuries, especially that of the Germanic and Netherlandish nations, is inordinately complex. Musical instruments, dance, women, and animals are only four of the many categories of symbols it employs to suggest occult eroticism. Many other symbols are likewise related to the concepts of the "world upside down." Scholars disagree about the exact meanings of these symbols; however, their omnipresence is one indication that witchcraft was an important aspect of Medieval man's reality, a worldview that incorporated and associated the occult and the erotic.

NOTES

1. Johan Huizinga, *The Waning of the Middle Ages* (London: E. Arnold and Co., 1924); cited in *Larousse Encyclopedia of Renaissance and Baroque Art*, ed. René Huyghe (New York: Prometheus Press, 1964), p. 24.

2. Rossel Hope Robbins, *Encyclopedia of Witchcraft and Demonology* (New York: Bonanza Books, 1981), p. 419.

3. Ibid., pp. 20–25.

4. Sebastian Brant, *The Ship of Fools*, trans. Edwin H. Zeydel (New York: Dover Publications, Inc., 1962), ch. 61, pp. 204–205; ch. 13, p. 89; ch. 61, p. 205. Further references to this work appear parenthetically in the text.

5. Keith P. F. Moxey, "Pieter Brueghel and The Feast of Fools," *Art Bulletin* 64, no. 4 (December 1982): 640–646.

6. Robbins, p. 421.

7. Desiderius Erasmus, *The Praise of Folly*, trans. John Wilson (Ann Arbor: University of Michigan Press, 1971), p. 28.

8. Robbins, p. 421.

9. Ibid., p. 541.

10. Ibid., pp. 466, 463, 420, 490.

11. Terence Hanbury White, ed. and trans., *The Bestiary, A Book of Beasts* (New York: Putnam's, 1960), p. 74.

12. Robbins, pp. 421–422.

13. Ibid., p. 420.

14. Ibid., p. 466.

15. Walter S. Gibson, *Hieronymus Bosch* (New York: Praeger Publishers, 1973), p. 86.

2

Disguised Eroticism and Sexual Fantasy in Sixteenth- and Seventeenth-Century Art

LIANA CHENEY

Mythological subjects provided a wealth of erotic inspiration for many sixteenth- and seventeenth-century painters.[1] Manuals on sex, particularly Ovid's *Ars Amatoria*, a guide to seduction that incorporated the extant Eastern sex manual of Paxamos's *Twelve Acts for the Action of Love*, were increasingly popular throughout this period. Numerous books were also written on the virtues and vices of women and on the merits of educating women to be good courtesans, wives, or nuns; examples are Pietro Aretino's *Dialogues* and the Dutch poems and sayings of Jacob Cats in *Spiegel*. In depicting love and sex, sixteenth- and seventeenth-century artists made reference to ancient and contemporary historical sources as well as to literary sources. These painters disguised the life of their own time and sublimated it into a realm of fantasy and imagination. Mythological paintings thus became the visual vehicle for their erotic desires and sexual fantasies.

Such mythological episodes as wedding celebrations (Frans Floris's *Feast of the Gods*, 1546), abductions (Titian's *Rape of Lucretia*, 1570), and metamorphoses of the gods in pursuit of their sexual objects (Correggio's *Danae*, 1530) were among the favorite themes portrayed by sixteenth- and seventeenth-century artists. Mythological love scenes, like *Feast of the Gods* (Figure 7), usually take place in an Arcadian landscape; most seduction scenes, like *Rape of Lucretia* (Figure 8), occur indoors. Artists could, through these subjects, express their passions and erotic fantasies in the personages of Zeus or Jupiter, Aphrodite or Venus, Eros or Cupid, Dionysus or Bacchus, Adonis, Leda, Danae, and others. The voyeur in these paintings is not only the artist, but also the viewer. In some scenes, however, the artist is not only an observer, like the viewer, but also one of the protagonists. In Correggio's *Danae* (Figure 9) and *Jupiter and Antiope* (also 1530), for example, the artist and viewer are merely spectators; but in Titian's *Rape of Lucretia* and Correggio's *Jupiter and Io* (1532), the artists may have depicted themselves as the violator.

Italian painters of the sixteenth century, known as the Cinquecento or "fifteen hundreds," reveal their erotic fantasies in the depiction of nude women from the more daring mythological legends. Specifically, the metamorphoses of Jupiter provided an extensive repertoire for these painters. According to Ovid, Acrisius, King of Argos, imprisoned his daughter, Danae, in a bronze tower because an oracle had predicted that her son would kill her father; eventually, Jupiter visited Danae as a golden shower, and Danae subsequently gave birth to Perseus. Jupiter loved Antiope, a Theban princess, in the shape of a satyr; Antiope bore Jupiter two sons, Amphion and Zenthis. To pursue Io, a priestess of Hera at Argos, Jupiter transformed himself into a cloud of smoke. Ovid and Livy agree that it was Sextus, son of Tarquinius Superbus, who raped Lucretia, wife of Tarquinius Collatinus. But Jupiter turned himself into a jovial, sturdy bull to abduct Europa (Titian's *Rape of Europa*, 1562) and seduced the beautiful Leda, wife of Tyndareus, King of Sparta, in the shape of a swan (Rosso Fiorentino's *Leda and the Swan* after Michelangelo, 1530).

Cinquecento painters also used allegory as a vehicle of disguised sexual celebration, to arouse and seduce viewers into experiencing a visual sexual fantasy. This arousal created by the artist's image is personal as well as universal, since the painted fantasy manipulates the spectators' imaginations and stimulates their recollections and associations with other images from the erotic feast of sexual fantasies. Bronzino's *Allegory of Luxuria* (Figure 10, 1545), also entitled *Venus, Cupid, Time and Folly*, is an example. It depicts the sexual desire between Cupid and

7. Frans Floris, *Feast of the Gods*, 1546. Courtesy of Statens konstmuseer, National Swedish Art Museums, Stockholm.

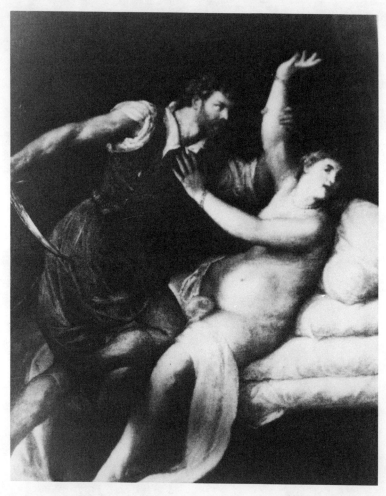

8. Tiziano Vecellio Titian, *The Rape of Lucretia*, 1570. Courtesy of the Musée des Beaux-Arts, Bordeaux.

9. Antonio Allegri da Correggio, *Danae*, 1530. Reprinted with permission of Alinari/Art Resource 7966 Correggio, Danae, Rome, Borghese.

10. Agnolo Bronzino, *Allegory of Luxuria*, 1545. Reprinted with permission of The National Gallery, London.

Venus, his mother. The figures in the painting are distressed at what is revealed by Time, jealousy and despair; the Sphinx smiles falsely while plotting revenge; and the dancing Cupid in his inexperience does not recognize the pitfalls and perversities of erotic love. The cold, porcelain treatment of the lovers' bodies emphasizes their sensuality. *Allegory of Luxuria* is one of the clearest examples among Italian paintings of the Cinquecento of the changes from the earlier depiction of disguised eroticism, as in Rosso's *Leda and the Swan* or Correggio's *Jupiter and Antiope*, to eroticism manifested as overt sexual fantasy. The allegorical meaning of the painting is subordinated to a sexual fantasy experienced by both artist and viewer.[2]

Outside Italy, other European painters of the sixteenth century also portrayed sexual fantasies in their mythological paintings. Bartholomeus Spranger's *Hermaphroditus and the Nymph* (1580), Hans von Aachen's *Bacchus, Ceres and Cupid* (1585), Joseph Heintz's *Adonis Leaving Venus* (1590), and the School of Fontainebleau's *Venus at her Toilette* (1535) all serve as examples.[3] Flemish, Dutch, German, French, and Spanish artists were influenced by Italian Cinquecento painters and became interested in depicting mythological scenes and in portraying the nude. The volatile political situation in Europe at this time caused many artists to leave their own countries: Italians went North, and Northern artists moved to Italy. After the sack of Rome in 1527, Giulio Romano left Rome to establish himself as a court painter in the Duchy of Mantua. Rosso Fiorentino and Primaticcio took refuge at the court of Fontainebleau under the patronages of Francis I of France. Both artists brought the Italian Cinqencento manner of painting to France. Moreover, the intellectual and artistic patrimony of Italy drew foreign artists to visit and work there: like Dürer in Venice, Karl van Mander in Rome, or Stradanus in Florence.[4]

Floris, van Mander's pupil, painted the *Feast of the Gods* in 1546. This picture interprets an ancient celebration in Flemish artistic terms.[5] The eroticism is subdued, and the fancifulness of the occasion is revealed by the interaction of the gods. The reputedly aphrodisiac food and drink—wine and oysters—emphasizes the sexual nature of the event. Spranger's *Hermaphroditus and the Nymph* (Figure 11), von Aachen's *Bacchus, Ceres and*

Cupid, and Heintz's *Adonis Leaving Venus* show a closer interaction between two mythological figures rather than Floris' large
gathering of gods. These painters depict an intimate seduction
scene in which the lovers come together in a secluded and idyllic
landscape. The elongated nude bodies of the females and their
placement in relation to their male companions overtly demonstrate the erotic nature of the meeting. In Spranger's painting,
as in Bronzino's, aberrant sexual desire is conveyed through the
use of a mythological theme. In one work, a nymph seeks the
love of a hermaphrodite but realizes the incongruity of her desire; and Venus allows her own son to arouse and pursue her
in the other. These artists express personal fantasies through
perversely inappropriate mythological sex.

In the depiction of mythological feasts and weddings, the
artist, viewer, and participants in the action are jointly involved
in the conviviality and celebration of the event; but in the abduction scenes, in which the female is subjected to violence, the
artist identifies himself as the abductor. The viewer or patron
who has commissioned such a work may also identify with the
protagonist; he might even be sexually aroused by feeling his
possession of the painting is the metaphorical equivalent of pos-
sessing the woman depicted, as well as by the visual scene.
Cinquecento painters and patrons, in their still-religious environment, employ mythological narratives to sublimate their erotic
fantasies, as in *Rape of Lucretia, Danae*, and *Leda and the Swan*.
Abduction scenes such as Titian's and Bronzino's appear to be
more common in Italian paintings of this period.

In addition to the grouping of mythological figures taking part
in bacchanalian or abduction scenes, there are also depictions
of individuals. The solitary figure represented is usually a goddess performing some activity in a boudoir. At times the female
figure may be reclining on a bed or sofa, as in the School of
Fontainebleau's *Venus at her Toilette* or *After the Bath* and Vasari's
Venus at her Toilette (1555). Rarely, if at all, is a male depicted as
an object of eroticism or sexual fantasy in this period.

The Cinquecento artists portrayed a female figure entertaining
the viewer with her action and the display of her nude body.
The viewers and artists are spectators. But this seductive representation in Cinquecento art is camouflaged by the title of the

11. Bartholomeus Spranger, *Hermaphroditus and the Nymph*, 1580. Reprinted with permission of Kunsthistorisches Museum, Vienna.

painting, which identifies it as a mythological story or allegory. The disguised eroticism in these mythological paintings of the Italian Cinquecento almost disappears in seventeenth-century Italy. Perhaps as a result of the religious impact of the Counter-Reformation, the themes depicted by artists were subject to censorship. The disguised eroticism is transferred from the settings of classical mythology to religious settings, as in Bernini's *The Ecstasy of St. Theresa* (1645), an instance of artistic representation of the lives of the saints.[6] In Flemish, Dutch, and Spanish paintings of the seventeenth century, however, eroticism disguised as mythology continued to be a vehicle of sexual fantasy, as in Rubens' *Abduction of the Daughters of Leucippus* (1617), Velázquez's *Venus at her Mirror* (1651), and Rembrandt's *Danae* (Figure 12, 1636). Still, most Dutch seventeenth-century painters replaced the disguised eroticism in mythological stories with genre scenes, as did Jan Steen in *The Dissolute Household* (1661). This change added a new dimension to the paintings, which now not only expressed covert sexual desire but also moralized on it.[7]

The mythological love scenes in landscapes of the sixteenth century give way to the merry company scenes of gatherings in interior settings in seventeenth-century art; *The Dissolute Household* replaces *Feast of the Gods*. The allegorical grouping changes into a duet scene; *Hermaphroditus and the Nymph* gives way to Frans van Mieris's *Oyster Meal* (1661). The elegant, artistocratic, artificial figures of the earlier period are now, in the seventeenth century, replaced by middle-class figures; Jacob Ochtervelt's *The Oyster Meal* (1667) supplants *Allegory of Luxuria*. This is particularly noticeable in Dutch art. Two pictures with the same mythological subject but painted over 100 years apart, Correggio's and Rembrandt's *Danae* (1530 and 1636), illustrate the change from the sixteenth-century's sexual fantasy and disguised eroticism to the seventeenth century's Puritan version of an ancient myth.[8] Correggio depicts a shower of gold coins descending into Danae's lap; Rembrandt's less provocative interpretation transforms the rain of coins into rays of light, which are not only perceived by the servant, but are also eagerly received by the nude mistress. In contrast to Correggio's classical setting, Rembrandt's Dutch interior lends immediacy and realism to the action. The androgynous quality of the servant suggests that Rembrandt has depicted himself in the role of voyeur in order to experience the moment of bliss vicariously. But Correggio not only is an onlooker at the scene in his painting, but also participates in the sexual delight of Danae through the figure of Eros seated at the edge of her bed. Overt sexual desire is expressed in the seventeenth-century painting, whereas the sixteenth-century work retains the fantasy of the myth. Both works disguise the actual act by recourse to a metaphor: erotic love for a shower of golden coins or light.

In later Dutch paintings, such as Steen's *The Dissolute House-hold* (Figure 13) and van Mieris's *Oyster Meal* (Figure 14), the representation of mythological stories is transformed into genre scenes depicting a lower- or middle-class, contemporary (i.e., seventeenth-century) setting. The variations on genre scenes of merry company and duet themes offer crowded interiors and figures who carry on in a relatively uninhibited manner. Chaos supplants decorum. The floors are covered with scattered kitchen utensils, pieces of clothing, and food, including oyster shells and pitchers of wine. The subtlety of the moralizing in these merry company paintings and scenes is characteristic of Dutch art. The preponderance of emblem books circulated in the Netherlands during the seventeenth century, paradoxically, guides and adds complexity to the interpretation of these paintings. Books by Alciati, Valeriano, Ripa, Cameraii, Visscher, and Cats contained emblems, poems, inscriptions, and mottos that were generally familiar to the public and borrowed by the artist in his paintings.[9] Thus is sexual fantasy transformed into down-to-earth reality, and the disguised eroticism is commented on, with moral overtones, in contemporary visual language. The sexual fantasy merges with the disguised eroticism. Aphrodisiacal props, such as wine, oysters, musical instruments, and gambling implements, indirectly but clearly emphasize the debased nature of sexual behavior.

A new sense of intimacy, with its focus on the duet lovers scene, is exemplified in van Mieris's *Oyster Meal* and Ochtervelt's *The Oyster Meal.*[10] Van Mieris's painting adroitly captures the emotional nuances of seduction. Only a man and woman are depicted in this scene. Partially visible behind them is a Dutch

12. Rembrandt van Rijn, *Danae*, 1636. Reprinted courtesy of the Hermitage Museum, Leningrad.

13. Jan Steen, *The Dissolute Household*, 1661. Courtesy of the Victoria & Albert Museum, London.

14. Frans van Mieris, *Oyster Meal*, 1661. Reprinted with permission of the Mauritshuis Museum, The Hague, Netherlands.

bed. The jovial woman sits next to a table; holding a crystal glass filled with wine, she selects an oyster from a tray offered to her by her attentive admirer. The gentleman is unable to disguise his passion: He offers the oysters with a satisfied, seductive smile. The maiden looks at him coyly while exposing her voluptuous breasts. It is obviously an amorous scene.

In Ochtervelt's painting the intimate and erotic quality of the duet scene is refined and heightened. While a man and woman are again drinking wine and eating oysters, oysters are no longer displayed on a table, nor are their shells scattered about on the floor. Rather, the man selects an oyster and offers it to his mistress, who offers a glass of wine in exchange. As both wine and the oyster are considered aphrodisiacs, the offered foods may be considered symbols of sensual, coveted, subliminal desire— aphrodisiac aperitifs to precede the feast, as foreplay precedes intercourse. Ochtervelt's *Oyster Meal* presents a crescendo of the romantic mood. The closeness of the figures, the blocking out of the background, and the focus on the erotic exchange of aphrodisiacs accentuates the intimate quality of the scene. The pairing of attributes (wine and oyster) with romantic feelings is the visual vehicle for a personal celebration between a man and a woman. Any moral message is either too subtly presented or simply absent.

In the duet scenes the elements of frivolity, gregariousness, debauchery, and overindulgence are accentuated, and the moral message appears to fade away. The sexual fantasy has lost its whimsicality and playfulness, but not its direct expression. The camouflaged sexual pursuit in mythological scenes of the Cinquecento becomes an overt, direct, casual, and sometimes humorous encounter between two lovers. The mystical quality of the allegories and the romantic past evaporate into amusing vignettes and visual double entendres. The invitation to conviviality and tryst in the paintings of the sixteenth century has evolved into the realization of sexual desires in the seventeenth century. The previously disguised eroticism is now openly revealed, but a moralistic overtone is usually added. The once playful mythological scene is transformed into a didactic representation of commonplace behavior. Thus eroticism is fused with sexual fantasy, and the result is a visual image of seduction conveying a message of sexual restraint.

NOTES

1. Lionello Puppi, "Eroticismo e osismo nella produzione artistica del Manierismo," *Rivista Internazional di Architettura* 8–9 (Fall 1976): 142–146.

2. Charles McCorquodale, *Bronzino* (New York: Harper and Row Publishers, 1981), pp. 87–90.

3. Arnold Hauser, *Mannerism* (London: Routledge and Kegan Paul, 1965), pp. 240–271; André Chastel, *La Crise de la Renaissance, 1520–1600* (Geneva: Skira, 1968), pp. 65–120.

4. Sydney Freedberg, *Painting in Italy, 1500–1600* (Baltimore: Penguin Books, 1971), pp. 114–116, 165–169, 234.

5. Carl van de Velde, *Frans Floris* (Brussels: Paleis der Academien, 1975), vol. 1, pp. 187–188; A. Blankert, ed., *Gods, Saints and Heroes* (Washington, D.C.: National Gallery of Art, 1980), pp. 55–98.

6. G. Bauer, *Bernini in Perspective* (Englewood Cliffs, N.J.: Prentice-Hall, Inc., 1976), pp. 77–89.

7. Jochen J. Becker, ed., *Incogniti Scriptuis Nova Poemata* (Soest, Holland: Davaco, 1972). This book, originally published in 1624, is a seventeenth-century emblem book with poems containing a double meaning. Another study that elaborates on the double entendre of some seventeenth-century genre subjects is E. de Jongh, "Erotica in volgenperspectief," *Simiolus* 3 (1968–1969): 22–74.

8. J. Rosenberg and S. Slive, *Dutch Art and Architecture* (Baltimore: Penguin Books, 1972), pp. 94–95.

9. E. de Jongh, ed., *Die Sprache der Bilder* (Braunschweig: Herzog Anton Ulrich Museum, 1978); Mario Praz, *Studies in Seventeenth Century Imagery* (Rome: Edizioni di Storia e Letteratura, 1964); John Landwehr, *Emblem Books in the Low Countries: 1554–1949* (Utrecht: Haentjens, Dekker and Gumbert, 1970); Arthur Henkel and Albrecht Schöne, *Emblemata* (Stuttgart: J. B. Metzler, 1967); Roemer Visscher, *Sinnepoppen* (Amsterdam: Willem Iansz, 1614); Jacob Cats, *Howelich* (Amsterdam: M. de Groot, 1661); and Jacob Cats, *Silenus Alciabiadis, Sive Proteus* (Middleburg: I. Hellenij, 1618).

10. O. Naumann, "Frans van Mieris as a Draughtsman," *Master Drawings* 16, no. 1 (Spring 1978): 3–34; S. D. Kuretsky, *The Paintings of Jacob Ochtervelt: 1634–1682* (London: Phaidon, 1979).

3

Henry Fuseli and Erotic Art of the Eighteenth Century

KATHLEEN RUSSO

Henry Fuseli (1741–1825), who became an artist after moving from his native Switzerland to London in 1764, has long been considered one of the most original and bizarre painters of the eighteenth century. He was described by his contemporaries as intense, fiery, and extremely erudite, characteristics strongly reflected in his paintings. His demonic and horrific visual interpretations of literary themes, folklore, and occasional narratives of his own invention typically highlight a particular moment of fear, passion, and intensity that is often highly erotic. This fascination with powerful sexual imagery makes consideration of Fuseli's *oeuvre* pertinent to any discussion of sexual fantasy in the visual arts.

Fuseli's prominent role in the English art world as a teacher and a first-class member of the Royal Academy did not prevent a great deal of criticism from being directed towards aspects of his work that were considered immoral, if not dangerously demonic. In 1806 Edward Days called him "the principal hobgoblin painter to the devil."[1] Such statements amused Fuseli, who delighted in commenting sarcastically on his good relationship with the Devil. Fuseli's works clearly illustrate why he was the target of such criticism, and also why he was lauded as one of the most imaginative painters of the period.

Fuseli painted numerous works dealing with dream images. His most famous is *The Nightmare* (Figure 15). The original version, painted in 1781, gained such notoriety that he subsequently painted a number of other versions on request. Much has been written about this well-known, enigmatic painting.[2] The subject is thought to have been inspired by local folklore about witches and demons who rode around at night seeking to invade the dreams of women who slept alone. The woman is shown lying on her back, a posture that was believed at the time to encourage nightmare images. This obviously erotic pose has been related to many earlier paintings, all of which seem to have been inspired by the *Vatican Ariadne*.

The other figures in the painting include a gruesome-looking incubus, who sits on the chest of the sleeping woman, and a powerful horse's head, whose eyes flame as he peers through a red curtain. Both the incubus and the horse are associated historically with the Devil and sex. Both have been linked by Powell to prior artworks—the incubus to Classical Selinus figures, and the horse to paintings by Leonardo da Vinci and Veronese and to a woodcut by Hans Baldung Grün.[3] Fuseli's very learned background in theology and the humanities suggests that any number of artistic and literary sources may be the potential inspiration for these figures, but it is the painting's overall mystery, sensuality, fearfulness, and psychological intensity that generate its popular appeal.

The personal and psychological aspects of this work have not been overlooked. Two years prior to painting *The Nightmare*, Fuseli fell in love with Anna Landholt while visiting Zurich on his way back from Rome to London. He was not permitted to marry her due to her father's disapproval, but returned to London still infatuated with Anna, who does not appear to have entirely reciprocated his feelings. Janson suggests that this unrequited love inspired *The Nightmare*; this idea is supported by the fact that there is an unfinished portrait, believed to be of Anna Landholt, on the back of this picture.[4] Thus, *The Nightmare* may be a very personal portrayal of suppressed passion as well as a universally terrifying depiction of a nightmare image. This painting was considered to be so representative of sublimated

15. Henry Fuseli, Swiss, lived 1741–1825. *The Nightmare*, 1781. Oil on canvas, 40″ × 50′ (101.6 cm. × 127 cm.), 55.5A. Gift of Mr. and Mrs. Bert L. Smokler and Mr. and Mrs. Lawrence A. Fleischman. Reprinted with permission of the Founders Society, Detroit Institute of Arts.

sex, and of the fantastic dreams produced by this sublimation, that Freud had a copy hanging in his office.

Although *The Nightmare* is his best-known work, Fuseli conjured up numerous other visions that involve the same powerful, emotional approach to women and sex. *Ezzelin Bracciaferro Musing Over Meduna, Slain by Him for Disloyalty During His Absence* (Figure 16, 1779) portrays a crusader who has killed his wife for real or imagined infidelity while he was away. This work was particularly admired by Lord Byron, who futilely searched Italian literature for the origins of the theme only to discover, on finally asking Fuseli, that the artist had made it up.[5] As in *The Nightmare*, there is great emotional tension and a feeling of madness directed against a female victim. As Schiff and Hofmann have theorized, the negative and aggressive attitude toward women revealed in Fuseli's work resulted from the artist's unconscious fear and hatred of women.[6] However, Fuseli's misogyny did not prevent him from having numerous mistresses as well as a wife, Sophie Rawlins, whom he married in 1788, when he was forty-seven.

Fuseli's negative attitude toward women prompted him to portray them in a very aggressive, often sexually explicit manner. His drawings in particular abound with witches, courtesans, and other women reputed to be of bad or evil character. In *Half Length Figure of a Courtesan* (Figure 17, c. 1800–1810), he portrays a bare-breasted female as a hard and wickedly sensual figure. The meticulous attention given to this courtesan's hairstyle is characteristic of the artist, who had a fascination with women's coiffures and fashions. In this work he has adorned the elaborate hairstyle with ribbons and ostrich feathers, and used a phallic symbol decorating the arm band to direct attention to bare breasts supported by a ruffled bodice.

Many of Fuseli's works pass from the realm of the erotic to that of the pornographic. His *Symplegma of a Man With Two Women* (Figure 18, c. 1770–1778) is one of a number of works in which he depicts two or more women satisfying one man's sexual desires. Typically, the women perform this task in an aggressive, almost menacing manner; here the man's feet, and apparently his arms also, are bound. A more menacing, even perverse attitude is evident in a number of Fuesli's works depicting cour-

16. Henry Fuseli, *Ezzelin Bracciaferro Musing Over Meduna, Slain by Him for Disloyalty During His Absence*, 1779. Reprinted with permission of The British Library, London.

17. Henry Fuseli, *Half Length Figure of a Courtesan*, c. 1800–1810. Courtesy of the Kunsthaus Zurich, Graphische Sammlung.

18. Henry Fuseli, *Symplegma of a Man With Two Women*, c. 1770–1778. Courtesy of the Fondazione Horne, Florence.

19. *The Great Red Dragon and the Woman Clothed with the Sun*; William BLAKE;
National Gallery of Art, Washington; Rosenwald Collection.

tesans maiming children or lesbians performing various sexual acts.[7] B. R. Haydon wrote, "The engines in Fuseli's mind are blasphemy, lechery and blood. His women are all whores and his men all banditti."[8] The works of William Blake and Johan Tobias Sergel, Fuseli's contemporaries, met the same accusations of decadence and moral turpitude.

Blake (1757–1827) was a poet and mystic who imbued even his religious themes with a passionate sensuality the public did not fail to notice. In his *The Great Red Dragon and the Woman Clothed with the Sun* (Figure 19), he illustrated a scene from the book of Revelations. Here, a woman who has just given birth is pursued by a dragon with a masculine physique and a lengthy, coiled snake's tail (a generous symbol of male sexuality). Although the woman escapes by sprouting wings and flying away, the sexual tension in the painting is evident. This type of powerful, quasi-erotic fantasy is seen in many of Blake's biblical interpretations. Although no sexual relationship is directly expressed in Blake's work, there are strong erotic overtones. Robert Hunt attacked Blake's works for indecency in the August 7, 1908, issue of *The Examiner*, observing that "An appearance of libidinousness intrudes itself upon the holiness of our thoughts."[9]

While the sexual fantasy in Blake's works is certainly tame, almost naive, when compared to that in the works of his friend, Fuseli, other artists associated with Fuseli were less subtle, particularly those with whom he became acquainted during his 1770–1778 stay in Rome.[10] Sergel (1740–1814), a Swedish sculptor who became a good friend of Fuseli's at this time, executed a number of sepia drawings that rival Fuseli's in overt fantastic eroticism. In a series of drawings based on the theme of satyrs attacking numphs, Sergel displays a thoroughly explicit sexuality.[11] Like Fuseli, Sergel was influenced by the Classical tradition in Rome, which can be seen in the choice of satyrs and nymphs as subjects even though the style of these drawings is more Romantic than Classical. Other drawings by Sergel, such as *Abduction Scene* (Figure 20, c. 1770–1780), also display Romantic stylistic elements in the aggressive and explicit treatment of an erotic theme.

Sergel, like the rest of Fuseli's circle in Rome, was well aware of the erotic art of the Roman Classical period. He was also influenced by subjects of this type incorporated into the work of such artists as Giulio Romano, the sixteenth-century painter and architect who depicted sexual intercourse in his illustrations of scenes from Aretino's sonnets. Artworks employing themes of this nature continued to be executed in Italy during the seventeenth and eighteenth centuries, but were particularly popular in France. In fact, French art of the Rococo period (c. 1700–1750) is known for its unabashed delight in sensual pleasures. The treatment of sexual themes during this period displays a very different attitude from the more somber treatment revealed in the works of Fuseli, Blake, Sergel, and other artists working at the end of the century, however.

To the Rococo artist sex was fun, a game to be well played for the mutual enjoyment of both men and women. The actual games played by early eighteenth-century courtiers were rife with sexual symbolism and became popular themes with painters of the period. Blind man's bluff and swinging were considered preludes to or symbolic of the act of love and were depicted in this way by the artists of the time. Jean-Honoré Fragonard (1732–1806) painted many works illustrating this aspect of French aristocratic life. His most famous work is *The Swing* (Figure 21, 1766), in which his patron, Baron de Saint-Julien, is placed in a position that enables him to "admire the graces of this comely young lady."[12] The work is charmingly and elegantly risqué; the flirtatiousness of the lovers is enhanced by the beauty of the pastel colors and lush landscape.[13] This painting communicates a thoroughly different attitude than do the fantastic visual dramas of Fuseli and his contemporaries.

Even when the Rococo artist chose a much more explicit approach in portraying sexual themes, the attitude is still one of a playful conspiracy between the participants. This is demonstrated by the popularity during this period of the theme of adolescents, often in groups of threes, experimenting with sexual intercourse. In a work attributed to François Boucher (1703–1770) called *The Boyish Prank*, a teenage boy displays his handkerchief-draped masculinity to two young, giggling girls.[14] In an untitled drawing by Fragonard (Figure 22), a similar escapade is depicted. Here, a very young man offers instruction to a slightly older youth regarding what action to take with a naked and

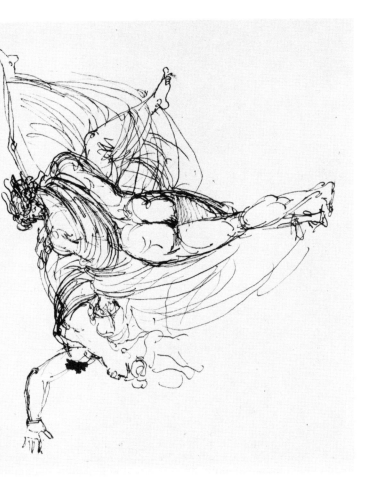

20. Johan Tobias Sergel, *Abduction Scene*, c. 1770–1780. Reprinted with permission of Statens konstmuseer, The National Swedish Art Museums, Stockholm.

21. Jean-Honoré Fragonard, *The Swing*, 1766. Reproduced by permission of the Trustees of the Wallace Collection, London.

22. Jean-Honoré Fragonard, untitled, n.d. In the Contes de la Fontaine. Courtesy of VILLE DE PARIS, Musée du Petit Palais.

23. Jean-Baptiste Greuze, *The Broken Pitcher*, 1773. Courtesy of Musée du Louvre, Paris.

obviously willing young girl. The conviviality of Boucher's and Fragonard's *ménage à trois* is quite frivolous, even silly, especially when compared to Fuseli's starkly humorless treatment of the same subject in *Symplegma of a Man with Two Women*. The difference in approach between the earlier works by Boucher and Fragonard and those created later by Fuseli was precipitated by the rise in power of the middle class. This resulted in a suppression of the overtly erotic in favor of a usually more demure depiction of sensuality that conveyed moralistic overtones.

Jean-Baptiste Greuze (1725–1805) is the best-known French practitioner of this genteel approach to sexual themes. His concern for what was called *sensibilité* was inspired by the philosophies of Locke and Rousseau as well as by the popular literature of the period. The theme in Greuze's *The Broken Pitcher* (Figure 23, 1773) is the loss of innocence and the remorse that follows.[15] This meaning would have been well understood by contemporary viewers, for a broken pitcher was a popular visual metaphor for the loss of virginity; the attitude and placement of the figure's hands reinforce this moralistic interpretation of the painting's symbols. The sense of fun and intrigue portrayed by Boucher and Fragonard is replaced here by a melancholy sadness at the loss of virtue. These strongly middle-class sentiments reflect the fact that an idealized bourgeois morality was gaining influence in the late eighteenth century over the liberal attitudes of the aristocracy. The work of Greuze and other artists who incorporated the same sentiments in their paintings was championed by Diderot and like-minded intellectuals who provided critical support for this "purity" of direction.

English artists at this time promoted the same moralistic attitudes in an even more literal fashion. William Hogarth (1697–1764), the self-proclaimed father of English painting, became famous for engraved and widely circulated narrative serials that stressed the depths of despair and degradation to which one may fall in straying from a virtuous path. His well-known *Harlot's Progress* and *Rake's Progress* are only two examples of his numerous visual sermons. In *Before* (Figure 24, 1798) and *After* (Figure 25, 1798) the message is clear: A woman who succumbs to a man's sexual advances will be used and then abandoned.

The earlier, playful and frivolous attitude towards sex, ex-

24. William Hogarth, *Before*, 1798. Reproduced by Permission of the Syndics of the Fitzwilliam Museum, Cambridge.

25. William Hogarth, *After*, 1798. Reproduced by Permission of the Syndics of the Fitzwilliam Museum, Cambridge.

55

emplified in the works of Fragonard and Boucher, evolves into a melancholy despair at the loss of innocence, seen in the works of Greuze and Hogarth, and then into a romantic eroticism characterized by passion and intensity. Once sex is viewed as something immoral and forbidden, its depiction requires and assumes a heightened tension and power. These complex qualities ultimately find expression in fantasy, as the romanticized works of Fuseli, Blake, and Sergel demonstrate.

NOTES

1. Nicholas Powell, *The Drawings of Henry Fuseli* (London: Faber & Faber, Ltd., 1951), p. 21.

2. Janson, Powell, Schiff, Moffitt, and Allentuck are among those who have attempted an analysis of this painting; see this volume's bibliography.

3. For an in-depth discussion of the sources for this work, see Nicholas Powell, *Fuseli: The Nightmare* (New York: Viking Press, 1972), pp. 70–75.

4. Horst Woldemar Janson, "Fuseli's Nightmare," *Arts and Sciences* 2, no. 1 (Spring 1963): 28. Reproduced in *Sixteen Studies* (New York: Harry N. Abrams, Inc., 1974), pp. 77–82.

5. Peter Tomory, *The Life and Art of Henry Fuseli* (New York: Praeger Publishers, 1972), p. 92.

6. Gert Schiff and Werner Hofmann, *Henry Fuseli 1741–1825* (London: Tate Gallery, 1975), p. 19.

7. See Gert Schiff, *Johan Heinrich Fuseli*, vol. 2 (Zurich and Munich: Verlag Berichthaus and Prestel-Verlag, 1973), pp. 123–125.

8. Powell, p. 64.

9. See Patrick Keane, "The Human Entrails and the Starry Heavens: Some Fantasies in the Visual Arts as Patterns for Yeats' Mingling of Heaven and Earth," *Bulletin of Research in the Humanities* 84 (Autumn 1981): 381.

10. For information on this period of Fuseli's career and many of the artists with whom he was associated in Rome, see Nancy L. Pressly, *The Fuseli Circle in Rome: Early Romantic Art of the 1770's* (New Haven: Yale Center for British Studies, 1979).

11. Reproduced by Per Bjurstrom in *Drawings of Johan Tobias Sergel* (Chicago: University of Chicago Press, 1979).

12. Nietta Apra, *Eighteenth Century French Art*, trans. Terry Peppiott (Milan: Arti Grafiche Ricordi, 1963), page facing Plate XII.

13. For further information on the swing motif in eighteenth-century art, see Donald Posner, "The Swinging Women of Watteau and Fragonard," *The Art Bulletin* 64 (March 1982): 75–88.

14. This work is reproduced in Guiseppi Von Lo Duca's *Die Erotik in der Kunst; die Welt des Eros* (Munich, Vienna, and Basel: Verlag Kurt Desch, 1965), p. 238.

15. For more information on Greuze, see Anita Brookner, *Greuze* (London: Paul Elek, Ltd., 1972).

4

Mum's the Word: Sexuality in Victorian Fantasy Illustration (and Beyond)

GWENDOLYN LAYNE

We are not amused.

Queen Victoria

The Victorian period has exceptionally strong resonances for modern fantasy illustrators. During her sixty-four–year reign (1837–1901), Queen Victoria—Britain's quintessential "mum"—established industriousness, temperance, piety, and virtue as her nation's recognized values in an era when religious orthodoxy, middle-class ideals, and social complacency were being challenged by Charles Darwin, Matthew Arnold, and Oscar Wilde. Still, Eros walked side by side with repression: Euphemism and ambiguity cloaked the often daringly subversive messages and images of literature and art.

Advances in printing techniques, specifically the shift from block printing to photographic reproduction, freed illustrators from the vagaries of engravers while subjecting them to the merciless precision of the camera. Half-tone printing, perfected around the turn of the century, was followed by the development of full-color reproduction. The new technology heralded the publication of a plethora of illustrated books and magazines.

Suddenly there was an enormous market for artistic talent, and some of the world's finest illustrators were there to fill that need.

If the golden age of illustration occurred between 1860 and 1920, as Brigid Peppin opines,[1] then the 1860s are both its springboard and its zenith. A partial list of artists working during this golden age reads like a *Who's Who* of illustrators: Edward Burne-Jones, Harry Clarke, Walter Crane, Gustave Doré, Edmund Dulac, Arthur Hughes, William Holman Hunt, John Everett Millais, Kay Nielsen, Arthur Rackham, Charles and William Heath Robinson, Dante Gabriel Rossetti, Frederick Sandys, and John Tenniel. In the 1860s an explosion of talent expressed the best, most imaginative features of the illustrator's art and, despite the strictures of Victorian mores, limned an eroticism that ranged in theme and subject matter from the subdued to the shameless.

Aubrey Beardsley (1872–1898), who in the 1890s became the standard-bearer of Victorian illustration, owed his status to other attributes besides his being "almost the only illustrator able to penetrate the [period's] dense barrier of sexual evasion and euphemism."[2] All the qualities of exquisite craftsmanship, daring experimentation, and open challenge to Mum's social rule were exhibited in the art of this consumptive who died at the age of twenty-six. While those artists who worked in or were influenced by the 1860s pursued decorative beauty in all its forms, from the lush sensuality of Rossetti to the cool Persian designs of Dulac, Beardsley gave style to the unspeakable and provided a forum for the forbidden. Never have genitals been so playfully displayed as in his outrageous drawings for *Lysistrata*. Even when required to censor his illustrations, Beardsley managed to suggest their erotic intent by depicting frantic swarms of sexual curiosities and social misfits engaging in various licentious activities.

While Beardsley practiced variations on the sexuality of the grotesque, his contemporaries developed more subtle expressions of Eros. If the eighteenth century was the "period of graceful indecency," as Robert Ross terms it,[3] then the nineteenth century might be called the era of witty innuendo. And the illustrated book monopolized much of the artists' erotic attention. In fact, as David Bland notes, "A tendency to eroticism has dogged the illustrated book, particularly the luxury type, through the ages."[4] Master of the illustrated book and precursor of the artistic innovators of the 1860s, William Blake (1757–1827), poet and engraver, both wrote and illustrated his own volumes. A visionary who has no true peers save, perhaps, the best contemporary comic book artists, he transformed the printed page into a finely tuned blend of text, illustration, and decoration. Not essentially concerned with the erotic, Blake's drawings reveal man's nature as a duality: the painfully human and savagely angelic. His nineteenth-century legatees include Edward Lear, the master of the illustrated limerick, and Richard Doyle, whose "Brown, Jones and Robinson" adventures anticipated the modern comic strip.[5]

Doyle was a contributor to *Punch* as well as an illustrator of "fairy pictures," some of which presented subliminally otherwise bowdlerized sexual material. An illustration from *The Doyle Fairy Book*, published in 1890, shows a girl startled awake in bed by a commotion. Her face is clearly that of the young Queen Victoria, such depictions having been a permissible practice in the early years of Mum's rule. But she is being straddled by a "purposeful looking gnome," and her bed curtains are crawling with other gnomes while still others have built a fire in the middle of the floor in obvious preparation for a party. Although no genitals are displayed, many of these night visitors are nude, and it is clear that they are up to some kind of sexual mischief.

Comic book graphics are obvious twentieth-century heirs to Blake's and Doyle's work. Blake's contribution is the inextricable fusion of text and illustration, and Doyle's is the infusion of subtle eroticism. Of course, many of today's comic graphic artists need not be so subtle in their depictions of sexuality; a cursory examination of any *Conan* adventure or of *Heavy Metal* reveals how liberated illustrators have become, even though their mass audience still will not permit them some liberties Beardsley took. But during the golden age of comic strips in the first decades of this century, an artist such as Winsor McCay would pack some rather innocent-appearing sequences with a subliminal eroticism. In one *Little Nemo* strip, vertical segments depicting an elephant advancing on the dreamer evolve into a final image, thrusting itself at the viewer, of a decidedly sexual-looking object that inserts itself into and disturbs Little Nemo's never-peaceful slumber.

The erotic depiction of animals easily predates the cunning artistry of Winsor McCay, however. Darwin had planted the idea that man and ape were relatives, and the artists of the Victorian age transported that speculation to the arena of fantasy. Animals were no longer mere beasts of burden or simple Aesopian symbols of human attributes. Anthropomorphized further, they were bedecked in the manner of man. Randolph Caldecott, Walter Crane, Rackham, and Louis Wain depicted fully clothed animals. So did Rossetti, in illustrations for his sister Christina's *Goblin Market and Other Poems*. One scene in this book depicts a girl buying goods with a curl of her golden hair from a crowd of clothed animals. A tress coils around the neck of an obviously ecstatic cat, who blissfully fondles the hair that is soon to be sheared off into his waiting paws. The other creatures crowd around, greedily looking on, while a rat tries to flag down another girl. The scene is simultaneously erotic and disturbing.

Another specialist in depicting animals, Beatrix Potter, wrote and illustrated her own books for children, but she clothed her woodland creatures only from the waist up and, undoubtedly subconsciously, then put them in situations where they had to shed their attire. Beatrix Potter's American heir, Walt Disney, chose to dress one of his more famous characters similarly. Although Donald Duck kept on his middy blouse and his sexuality was denied by context, Disney's fondness for sight gags focusing on the derriere made the fulminating duck the butt of many a joke. The resonances reach maturity in the notorious *Realist* poster, a parody in which, among many other outrages, Donald Duck peeks under Daisy's dress to discover that she is a fully anthropomorphized sexual creature.

Eroticism was conveyed in other ways as well by the Pre-Raphaelites—Rossetti, William Holman Hunt, and the prolific John Everett Millais. Their illustrations for a Tennyson poetry anthology published in 1857 set the 1860s in motion, and subsequent adherents of the style were numerous and equally talented. Intensity was the style's hallmark—in line, chiaroscuro, mien, gesture, and use of space.[6] And the focal image of most

Pre-Raphaelite illustration was that of Rossetti's wife, Elizabeth Siddell. Her features became the paradigm for a peculiarly seductive beauty—a "spiritualized eroticism."[7] Idealized and generally passive, the Pre-Raphaelite woman is a mysteriously asexual yet alluring figure usually found lolling about a lush Medieval landscape. She represents and legitimizes androgyny, abhorred yet secretly desired by the Victorians.

A century later, in a Manhattan loft, four of the best-known fantasy illustrators in America formed their own version of a brotherhood of artists; their purpose was also to produce "exquisite paintings," as "aids to contemplation or revery."[8] Known as the Studio, the collective consisted to Jeffrey Jones, Michael William Kaluta, Barry Windsor-Smith, and Berni Wrightson. Their style is a romanticism laced with the symbolic and anachronistic. It is no accident that some of their exemplars worked during the golden age of illustration, for their paintings not only glow with rich sensuality but also contain titillating humor and wit. A comparison of pieces by Victorian illustrator Vernon Hill—one of the more obvious imitators of Blake—and by Studio artist Kaluta shows both the similarities that transcend and the differences wrought by time and technology.

Vernon Hill's illustrations for the verse collections *Ballads Weird and Wonderful* and *The New Inferno* are considered to be his best work. Figure 26, *The Personality*, is from *The New Inferno* (1911). As is the case in Blake's works, the image is symmetrical and the figure sculpted. The highly stylized body has none of the heightened realism favored by the Pre-Raphaelites; yet the black-and-white block print is, due to its subtle yonic imagery, innocently suggestive. This arresting moment might be an instance of purity of intent colliding with subliminal effect. In Figure 27, *Why He Doesn't Sleep at Night* (1976), Kaluta appears to have taken the same fellow and incarnated him into an equally fantastic but less symbolic situation.

While some illustrators present the human form in stylized or idealized representations, others get down to bare facts. Nude is one thing, however, and naked quite another. During Queen Victoria's reign, another catchword might have been "naughty but nice." In Figure 28, a Reginald Knowles illustration for *Tales from the Norse* (1910), the female form is displayed but does not

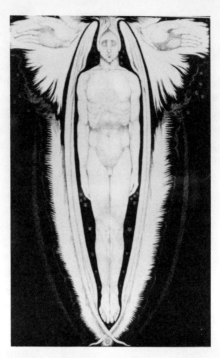

26. Vernon Hill, "The Personality." From *The New Inferno* by Stephen Phillips (London: John Lane, 1911). Courtesy of The Bodley Head, London.

intrude on the picture's focus. The border has strong affinities with the innocent nudity and fluid interaction between nature and man that typify Arthur Rackham's fantasy designs. Here Knowles reveals his predilection for Art Nouveau in avoiding questionable or objectionable displays of the female figure by tactfully positioning hands, vines, and postures.

Such tact is also evident in Figure 29, a 1956 illustration for Robert Heinlein's *Door into Summer* by Frank Kelly Freas, which recalls Knowles while anticipating the pneumatic torsos of Frank Frazetta and Boris Vallejo. Rather than cavort in the bushes, this patently nakedized woman floats in an ocean of stars. She is at once discreetly screened and ominously threatened by the silhouetted apparatus. The stars and interstellar dust serve the same function as the creepers in Knowles' illustration: They cover the bare essentials. However, while she is sensuous, Freas's full-lipped lass has less erotic appeal than Knowles's nymphs. It would seem that seven nude women amongst the ivy are worth more than one naked lady in the sky.

Freas and other early twentieth-century fantasy artists were primarily employed creating science fiction illustrations for pulps. Today, the field is much broadened, encompassing "fantasy" illustration involving dungeons, dragons, star warriors, and alien worlds of every imaginable ilk. What began in the nineteenth century as "fairy" illustration for children has obviously come of age. Certainly, John Dickson Batten's illustration for *More English Fairy Tales* (Figure 30) contains more than a passing resemblance to certain erotic man-and-serpent fantasies by Frazetta or to the dragons in a dungeon by the Hildebrandt brothers.

Batten and H. J. Ford were two leading illustrators of fairy tales. The former specialized in creating realistic fairies and monsters in naturalistic environments and, with Ford, "succeeded in transposing the sexual metaphors of original folklore into his own imagery."[9] Hobgoblins with phallic tongues and knights hacking away at serpents with which they are intimately interlaced were delineated with the emphasis on line and the sensitive observation that were canons of the Pre-Raphaelite tradition. Sexuality might be in the eye of the beholder, who might well see something Freudian in the frame; but, as with much of the Pre-Raphaelites' work, it was usually there to behold.

Virgil Burnett is a modern "fairy tale" illustrator whose work does not have the look of current popular art but more clearly shows direct influences from the golden age. Figure 31 demonstrates the serene, subtle style of his expert black-and-white drawings. His illustrations for *Sir Gawain and the Green Knight* are elegant statements of the poem's erotic qualities. Burnett's precise, highly detailed style is reminiscent of the Pre-Raphaelites as well as of Beardsley, who immediately comes to mind when a Burnett illustration is seen.

An obvious counterpoint to Burnett's Medieval coquette is a Beardsley drawing for *Lysistrata*, which appeared in an edition that could not be publicly distributed although, as Ross observes, Beardsley's *Lysistrata* designs "are as frank, free, and outspoken as the text."[10] Figure 32 (1896) is Beardsley at his most reckless and amusing. Whereas Burnett eschews the obvious or the pruriently erotic representation, Beardsley and, later, Harry Clarke made shockingly explicit sexual imagery the focus of much of their work. Both Beardsley and Clarke were inventive, accom-

27. Michael William Kaluta, *Why He Doesn't Sleep at Night*, 1976. From Jeffrey Jones, Michael William Kaluta, Barry Windsor-Smith, Berni Wrightson, *The Studio* (Holland: Dragon's Dream, Ltd., 1979). Courtesy of Michael William Kaluta.

28. Reginald Knowles, *Tales from the Norse* (London: George Routledge and Sons, Ltd., 1910). Courtesy of Routledge & Kegan Paul PLC, London.

29. Frank Kelly Freas, for "Door into Summer" by Robert A. Heinlein, in *Magazine of Fantasy and Science Fiction* (October 1956). From *Frank Kelly Freas: The Art of Science Fiction*, published by The Donning Company/Publishers.

30. John Dickson Batten, "The Lambton Worm." In *More English Fairy Tales* (London: David Nutt, 1890). Courtesy of Studio International, London.

31. Virgil Burnett, illustration for *Sir Gawain and the Green Knight; A Comedy for Christmas*, translated by Theodore Silverstein. Chicago and London: The University of Chicago Press, 1974. Copyright © 1974 by The University of Chicago Press. Reprinted with permission of The University of Chicago Press.

LYSISTRATA.

32. Aubrey Beardsley, frontispiece for *The Lysistrata of Aristophanes*, 1896.

plished draftsmen; both explored sources of inspiration and style that ranged from Medieval illumination to Rococo decoration to, in Beardsley's case, Oriental effects. Clarke's sexy Satan, a "sexually ambiguous creature with cloven high-heeled boots,"[11] traversed the same dangerous ground as Beardsley's eunuchs and transsexuals.

Shocking, unsettling, anarchistic illustrators of today certainly have a mentor in Beardsley; students of his style appear in underground comics and effect the stylish sexual humor of *Heavy Metal*, *Epic*, and other such lavishly produced "comic" books. It might be noted, however, that much of Beardsley's greatness resides in his superb skill as a draftsman combined with his clever satire. He was distinct from the 1860s tradition, never staying with one style and forgoing chiaroscuro, tones, and values for the purity of line.[12]

Another concern of comic books that involves the special skill of exaggerated realism is the depiction of gore, which was typical especially in American comic graphics before the ground swell for censorship that precipitated the Comic Code of 1955. No strangers to the subject of Eros and death, Victorian artists explored the same terrain, but with a more seriously satiric eye. In Clarke's "wonderfully grisly illustration" of the final moments in Poe's "The Facts in the Case of M. Valdemar," the loathsome, detestable putrescence is almost gleefully portrayed as a "disintegrating body, from which part of an arm has detached itself and from whose eyes and mouth blood and gore run."[13] It is no wonder that Clarke's work is said to resemble that of Hieronymus Bosch.

More pointedly illustrative of the consequences of sensuality is Sandys' "Amor Mundi." This illustration for Christina Rossetti's poem shows a pair of lovers blithely wandering through a meadow. "Oblivious of the writhing snakes and the emaciated corpse beneath their feet,"[14] they cannot see that the decaying body lies in the future of the young woman who so heedlessly revels in her lover's song. To the Victorian mind, the price of sin and sexuality was the lurking horrors of inevitable, all-tooprevalent death.

A final form of erotic expression in Victorian illustration is inspired by the Orient, a frequent source of Western man's sexual fantasies. Beardsley and Crane experimented with the "Japanesque," while Dulac embraced as well the delicate, intensely colored Persian and Indian miniature paintings. Except for Beardsley, who considered and then rejected the project, almost every major Victorian illustrator undertook the task of illustrating that most popular of Oriental fantasies, *The Arabian Nights*. Amazingly, during the golden age over forty artists embellished this text. The best-known edition was *Dalziels' Illustrated Arabian Nights*, to which Arthur Boyd Houghton, Millais, and Tenniel contributed their talents. Batten illustrated *Fairy Tales from the Arabian Nights*, and Ford *The Arabian Nights Entertainment*. Dulac, exploiting technical advances in color reproduction, designed his rendition of the Oriental classic so that his illustrations are almost indistinguishable from the Persian miniatures he so carefully studied.

The erotic aspects of these efforts, as well as those of the illustrations for Edward FitzGerald's *Rubaiyat of Omar Khayyam*, generally consisted of portraying partially or wholly undressed women in sumptuous Oriental settings. However, the Oriental association itself held libidinous connotations for the Victorians. Of course, Orientals had a long tradition extending into the nineteenth century of exploring the expression of Eros; however, Oriental erotic art was intended only for the eyes of astute and discreet collectors. Figure 33, dated 1830, is a Mughal miniature based on a favorite Indian theme, love on a swing. Only mildly erotic, the painting is a tame example of the genre.

Sexuality in Victorian illustration could be represented subliminally, overtly, allegorically, and androgynously, nudely, nakedly, gorily, or in the Oriental manner. Whether the subject was fairies or Greeks, the burgeoning audience hungry for illustrated weeklies and books could feed upon offerings from dozens of talented artists who explored and exploited the outer limits of the Victorian tolerance for erotica. Of course, not all illustrations involved sexuality. Charles Ricketts, Kate Greenaway, and Rackham, to name just a few, were elegant of line and pure of content. But those who did challenge the order of the day did so with wit and humor. And they have sent a clear message to today's artists: The golden age of illustration is dead, but the late twentieth century is illustration's renaissance!

33. Indian Miniature painting, Bazaar style, c. 1830. Courtesy of Victor Lownes.

NOTES

1. Brigid Peppin, *Fantasy: The Golden Age of Fantastic Illustration* (New York: Watson-Guptill, 1975), p. 8.

2. Ibid., p. 14.

3. Robert Ross, *Aubrey Beardsley* (New York: Jack Brussel, 1967), p. 48.

4. David Bland, *A History of Book Illustration: The Illuminated Manuscript and the Printed Book* (Cleveland & New York: The World Publishing Co., 1958), p. 23.

5. Peppin, p. 9.

6. Ibid., p. 11.

7. George P. Landow, "And the World Became Strange: Realms of Literary Fantasy," *Georgia Review* 33, no. 1 (1979): 7–42.

8. Jeffrey Jones, Michael William Kaluta, Barry Windsor-Smith, and Berni Wrightson, *The Studio* (Holland: Dragon's Dream, Ltd., 1979), p. 10.

9. Peppin, p. 19.

10. Ross, p. 47.

11. Peppin, p. 22.

12. Ross, p. 37.

13. Landow, p. 40.

14. Peppin, p. 11.

5

Sex in Surrealist Art

FRANCINE A. KOSLOW

Surrealism began as a literary movement in Paris in 1924, when poet André Breton (1896–1966) published his *First Manifesto of Surrealism*. Breton, a former student of psychiatry, defined the movement as "dictated by thought, in the absence of any control exercised by reason, exempt from any aesthetic or moral concern."[1] Surrealism, as defined by Breton, was based on belief in the omnipotence of dreams and the unconscious. The active collaboration between surrealist artists and literary figures that followed Breton's manifesto resulted in visual works that deal with hitherto unexplored phenomena, including enigmatic sexual fantasies. Eroticism in art has been around since prehistory. Fertility goddesses and Greek phalluses were common early art objects. Yet these images were extensions, however explicit or exaggerated, of objects in the real physical world. Surrealists deal specifically with distortions and the irrational. Their eroticism, however explicit, explored subconscious, uncontrolled realms, bizarre domains that were almost uninvestigated prior to the advent of Freudian psychology.

The surrealist painters and poets centered their activities in the late 1920s around Paris and Breton. Their art was based on humor, subversion, and dream. Confronting a postwar world of disintegrating social, cultural, and economic mores, the surrealists were rebels who embraced the absurd, the accidental, and the illogical in order to open doors of preception previously closed by rational thought. Among their heroes was Isadore Ducasse (who used the pseudonym "the Comte De Lautremont"), a late nineteenth-century symbolist writer who promoted the juxtapostion of disparate objects. Lautremont's symbolic image of the chance meeting between a sewing machine and an umbrella on a dissection table stimulated the surrealists to place unrelated objects together on the picture plane. The impact of the surrealist image lies in this dissociation of objects from their familiar contexts.

The surrealists also chose to embrace the illicit and often dark side of human nature. Under Breton, they canonized the Marquis de Sade and invented a cult of love that elevated libertinism. They employed Sigmund Freud's method of evoking repressed material through free dream association and took greatest interest in the psychiatrist's theories on sex (Eros) and death (Thanatos). The surrealists expressed their opinions freely on such matters as female orgasm, onanism, and sadomasochism and other sexual perversions, and often made sex the subject of their work. Artists like Max Ernst (1891–1976), René Magritte (1898–1967), Salvador Dali (b. 1904), and Paul Delvaux (b. 1897) created artworks that shocked on two levels, the candor with which they depicted sexuality and the odd juxtaposition of subjects and objects that do not belong together in the rational, real world.

Alfred Barr states in his pivotal 1936 exhibition catalogue titled *Fantastic Art, Dada and Surrealism* that Surrealism grew out of the ashes of Dada. Dada, an anti-art movement, claimed the German artist Max Ernst as one of its leaders. Ernst made the transition from Dada to Surrealism when he moved to Paris in 1921 and met Breton and his followers. A leader of the Hanover Dada group that had held the infamous Cologne International Exhibition in a men's urinal, Ernst appealed to the rebel surrealist spirit. He had studied psychiatry and philosophy at the University of Bonn and, having shared quarters with Breton's close collaborator, Paul Éluard (b. 1895), was immersed in the world of dreams and the unconscious. As an artist Ernst became fascinated with the collage technique of cutting and pasting objects together in unusual combinations. His collages anticipated Surrealism in their subject matter and technique. When Breton chose Ernst as a welcome member of his Paris coterie, he was well aware of the impact of such works as Ernst's 1923 oil painting titled *Men Shall Know Nothing of This*.

Men Shall Know Nothing of This is an enigmatic coital image in which the two sexes balance each other in curious symmetry. The dreamlike composition appears to have been pasted together and linked with strings. The space is that of another dimension of reality reminiscent of the metaphysical paintings of Giorgio de Chirico, an artist revered by Ernst and the surrealists in the early 1920s. The upper region of the composition is dominated by two sets of amputated lower extremities locked in the sex act. Two female legs, spread in a froglike pose, are penetrated from above in what appears to be the anal or abdominal region by the male legs, which are joined at the thighs. The erotic legs are pierced at the feet by the umbrellalike arch of a new moon. They float above a disembodied hand that penetrates a ring and a whistle. Geometric configurations resembling a concentric ring of planets or the phases of the moon surround the hand. These seemingly unrelated parts exist in a landscape dominated by two large trapezoids topped with circles, possible symbols of the male and female. The ground beneath exudes visceral, biomorphic forms. The disembodied, floating images are images of metaphysical, interplanetary sexuality. The title indicates that ordinary men shall know nothing of Ernst's metaphysical fantasy, which exists only in the recesses of the unconscious mind. Ernst's painting forms a solid link between the metaphysical art of de Chirico and surrealist illusionism. It is an abstract dream image of obscure meaning.

In late 1925, the Belgian painter René Magritte created a surrealist image based on dreamlike illusionism. The originality of Magritte's image lies in the secret affinities between seemingly dissociated objects. Magritte's style is consistently that of precise, magic realism—the realistic presentation of what appears to be an ordinary scene, without any strange or monstrous distortion, that nevertheless contains fantastic juxtapositions of elements or events that do not normally exist together. Magritte painted *The Rape* (Figure 34, 1934) in Brussels, and Breton chose

Magritte's drawing of the same subject for the cover of the 1934 surrealist publication *Qu'est-ce que le surréalisme*.

The painted version of *The Rape* was included in the 1934 surrealist Minotaure exhibition in Brussels, where it was hung in a private room at the back and shown only to initiates. The exquisitely detailed painting is a highly Freudian sexual metaphor that combines a female head and nude female torso in a visual pun. The face's features are replaced by breasts, belly, and pudendum. Breasts and nipples replace the eyes, the navel becomes a nose, and the pudendum is the figure's mouth. This comical monster rises sphinxlike against a blue sky and sea. Magritte habitually appended unrelated titles to his works, and this title has no apparent relation the the comical *trompe l'oeil* image; there is no rape or violence in *The Rape*. Magritte's initial artistic concern is to reconstruct the female torso with absolute fidelity to anatomical detail inside the frame of the female head.

Metamorphosis and the constant fluctuation of objects from their ordinary contexts characterize the good-humored sexuality of Magritte's art. In another visual pun, *La Dame*, Magritte places a nude blonde inside a bottle of wine. Magritte's carefully rendered portraits of nude women isolated from their normal ties with the rest of the visual world are bewildering and beguiling erotic compositions.

Salvador Dali, more than any of the other surrealists, relied on Freud and the Marquis de Sade in his erotic art and writings. This master of publicity and propaganda has made sexual perversities the subject of much of his art. According to Dali, art is "a spontaneous method of irrational knowledge based upon the interpretive-critical association of delirious phenomena."[2] His surrealist images were allegedly induced by the "paranoic-critical method"[3]—a delirious interpretation of the world and of the ego, which assumes exaggerated importance. His images of obsession with castration, putrefaction, voyeurism, onanism, and impotence are painted with meticulous realism. Although Dali's technique is precise in terms of modeling and perspective, he converts details, colors, and forms of the material world into images of the obsessions of a madman. His paintings are bizarre combinations and transformations of optical reality.

Many of Dali's paintings deal with autoeroticism and deep

34. René Magritte, *The Rape*, 1934. Reprinted with permission of the Menil Foundation, Houston, Texas.

sexual anxiety. His art and life read like a texbook of Freudian
sexual deviations. Born at Figueras, near Barcelona, Dali claims
he has been obsessed since early childhood with masturbation,
death, and decay. The young Dali was fascinated with Freud,
who recognized the literalness with which Dali used Freudian
symbols. Dali, who was inspired toward an art of free fantasy
by reading Freud's *Interpretation of Dreams*, first met Freud while
a student in Madrid. Later, in 1938, he was reintroduced to Freud
in London. The psychiatrist acknowledged Dali's obsession with
the unconscious but wondered where the rational world existed
in Dali's domain. He told Dali, "It is not the unconscious I seek
in your pictures, but the conscious."[4]

Breton welcomed Dali, and his outrageous behavior and
shocking symbolism, when Dali first joined the surrealist movement in 1929. During the next five or six years he remained in
Paris, Dali managed to intimidate his colleagues, who eventually
repudiated him. However, Dali continued to practice Surrealism,
and made the movement live in his art, for the next fifty years.
Dream images were essential to Dali, who claims that his painted
images were waking dreams that arrived already formed and
had to be translated on the canvas.

His most prevalent dreams were masturbatory in nature. Dali
created *The Great Masturbator* in 1929—the year he stole Gala
Éluard from her husband, Paul—to release what he called his
"heterosexual anxiety"[5] over his passion for Gala. *The Great Masturbator* is dominated by the profile of a distorted, fleshy head
in a desert landscape. The head is Dali's, and a couple embrace
in a sexual pose below the head. A female figure grows from
the nape of Dali's profile; her eyes closed, she reaches with her
nose and lips for the genitals of an adolescent boy. A key to
understanding the artist's intent is the praying mantis that serves
as Dali's mouth: The female praying mantis devours the male
immediately after the sexual act. When asked about the theme
of *The Great Masturbator*, Dali stated, "The fantasy of being de-
voured in the sexual act leads to the solipsistic safety of onanism."[6] Dali's fear of women complemented his fascination with
autoeroticism and sadism.

The Marquis de Sade coupled sexual love, not with tender-
ness, but with cruelty; sexual pleasure resulted from humiliation

and the infliction of fear and pain. Dali composed one of literature's most sadistic texts, "Reverie," which was by far the most
complex and detailed of the essays to appear in the December
1931 issue of *Le Surréalisme ASDLR*, in a section entitled "Me-
diations." "Reverie" begins with a description of Dali's state of
mind and behavior one October afternoon in his house in Spain
as he was wavering between intellectual work and masturbatory
practices.[7] Dali's obsession with sodomy, masturbation, and excrement are evident in this long text, as the following excerpts
illustrate:

. . . lying amid the excrement and rotting straw of a very dark cow shed,
and greatly excited by the stink of the place, I sodomized the woman
I love. . . .

I sit on the wet stone bench with my two hands I raise my penis with
all my might, then I go to the cow shed were Dulita and the two women
are lying naked among excrement and rotting straw . . . and Dulita is
changed into the woman I love.[8]

Dali's daydreams construct a sequence of disturbingly sadistic
events that lead Dulita, an eleven-year-old girl, into his cow
shed fantasy. The power of the overly graphic essay lies in the
reader's confusion over which images are meant to be real and
which are fantastic.

Young Virgin Auto-Sodomized by Her Own Chastity (1954) recalls
Dali's "Reverie" in oil. The figure of a nude female wearing
high-heels dominates the painting. She is shown from the rear,
looking out a window onto the Mediterranean. Her buttocks
spread and metamorphosize into two phalluses. Below her buttocks is what appears to be a third phallus, ready to sodomize
the "young virgin." Two additional, missile-like phalluses shoot
above the virgin's head.[9]

Unlike Magritte's, Dali's erotica is frightening rather than comic;
and Dali's works are a visual diary of his perverse fantasies. His
titles are meant to relate to the images. What is so powerful
about Dali's work is the quality of his technique and the freedom
of his imagination. Dali is a master of metamorphosis who has
made a career of painting images of fear and paranoia. "The

only difference between me and a madman," Dali once stated,
"is that I am not mad."[10]

Paul Delvaux creates dreamlike erotic fantasies that are more
charming than disconcerting. Delvaux categorically refuses to
acknowledge Freud and recognizes only memory and imagination as specific sources for the formation of his images. The
transposition and exposition of the female nude have been fundamental elements of Delvaux's painting since 1934, but there
is no evil lurking in these poetic images of nude women.

Delvaux completed *Pygmalion*, one of his most important
paintings, in 1939. Here Delvaux reverses the well-known theme
by exchanging the masculine and the feminine roles: A nude
sculptress embraces a male sculpture. The male is a partial figure,
truncated at the thighs and upper arms; however, he appears
to be metamorphosizing in his abdominal and genital area into
living flesh at the sculptress's touch. She gazes at her creation
with obvious desire, anxious to place her belly next to his. The
feminization of the Pygmalion myth, which ended in Galatea's
liberation from stone, has turned the female figure into the creator. The man is the ideal figure projected by the woman: He
has no arms or legs, but is equipped with a beautiful face and
a substantial phallus. Juxtaposing eroticism with poetic and highly
romantic dream imagery, Delvaux's *Pygmalion* exists in a surreal
space outside the sculptress's studio. A nude female who is
becoming a tree, or a vine in the process of becoming a human,
appears in the right side of the composition. A gentleman with
derby and cane walks past a two-story building toward dunes.

Sex in surrealist art, as these examples illustrate, is linked with
daydreams, dreams, and nightmares. Surrealism's power lies in
the strangeness of its encounters, and the surrealists' erotic art
emphasizes the chance encounter. Surrealism's genesis entailed
a powerful exploration of the unconscious through the negation
of as many as possible of the psychological defenses of control,
suppression, and active intervention. The preoccupation with
sexual imagery in much surrealist art is an affirmation of this
elevation of the poetic imagination. Imagination, memory, and
obsession prevail over current, mundane preoccupations in the
surrealist realm.

NOTES

1. André Breton, "Manifesto of Surrealism" (1924), in *Manifestoes of Surrealism*, eds. Richard Seaver and Helen R. Lane (Ann Arbor: University of Michigan Press, 1927), p. 26.

2. Maurice Nadeau, *The History of Surrealism*, trans. Richard Howard (New York: Macmillan, 1965), p. 67.

3. Paul H. Walton, *Dali/Miro* (New York: Tudor Publishing Company, 1967), p. 8.

4. Dawn Ades, *Dali and Surrealism* (New York: Harper and Row, 1982), p. 74.

5. Ibid., p. 59.

6. Gert Schiff, *Images of Horror and Fantasy* (New York: Abrams, 1978), p. 90.

7. Marcel Jean, *The Autobiography of Surrealism* (New York: Viking Press, 1980), p. 272.

8. Ibid., pp. 272 and 275, citing Dali's "Reverie."

9. Dali expert Paul Walton identifies the phallic projectiles as rhinoceros horns. He writes, "Dali maintains that this combination of a female nude with rhinoceros horns creates an image of innocence, because he associates the rhinoceros horn with the horn of the unicorn, a medieval symbol of chastity." *Dali/Miro*, p. 28.

10. Sarane Alexandrian, "Introduction," *Dali Paintings* (New York: Tudor Publishing, 1969).

6

Surrealist Female Monsters

SYLVIE PANTALACCI

According to Gerard Durozoi and Bernard Charbonnier, surrealist ethics are based on two phenomena that gathered momentum as world movements at the beginning of the twentieth century, the emancipation of women and the continuing development of a science of the unconscious.[1] Since either had the potential to change the established moral and social values of their contemporary society, the surrealists viewed both phenomena as revolutionary. And both had other common elements: Women's demands included the right to sexual freedom, and psychoanalysis was the first intellectual movement to stress the importance of erotic desire in everyday life. The combination of these two revolutionary ideas led the surrealists to a new view of women. The traditional dichotomy, virgin or prostitute, was replaced by another dichotomy, child-woman or *femme fatale*.[2]

According to surrealist theory, the child-woman is a wonderful fairy, a mediatrix whose essential function is to lead man to a higher state of knowledge and happiness. But she cannot fulfill this function unaided: Unaware of her power, intuitive (a female quality) but not analytical (a male quality), she must wait for the man in her life who will reveal to her her extraordinary capabilities.[3] Xavière Gauthier notes the contradiction inherent in a so-called revolutionary theory that considers a woman to be a child, and thus places her in such a traditional state of dependency.[4] In this male vision of the cosmic roles of man and woman, man is the instigator of woman's emancipation, which is to serve his ends, effect his salvation. Another reactionary aspect of this surrealist concept is a complete sacralization of women reminiscent of the Catholic concept of the Virgin Mary.[5]

The negative side of this surrealist dichotomy is the *femme fatale*, the woman whose sexuality attracts and destroys men. This image too remains almost identical to one view of women held for centuries by the Catholic church, and reveals the same fear of a female behavior that does not fit the established patriarchal pattern of right and wrong. In theory, as in artworks springing from this theory, the image of woman is a dichotomy whose opposite sides each reveal a deeply reactionary perception of sex roles.

While the "positive" image of the child-woman is elaborated more frequently in theoretical and poetic works, the *femme fatale* is more often portrayed in surrealist paintings.[6] René Magritte's *La Gâcheuse* and *L'Esprit de la géométrie*, Salvador Dali's cover for *Minotaure* No. 8, and Joan Miro's *Tête de femme* similarly demonstrate the surrealists' negative image of the *femme fatale* by depicting frightening, monstrous heads appended (usually) to attractive female bodies. These paintings were created in the 1930s—when, after several years of internal conflicts and crises, the surrealist movement attained a theoretic stability and established more widely accepted definitions with the second *Manifeste du Surréalisme*, the departure of such dissident members as Robert Desnos, Jacques Prévert, and Louis Aragon, and the arrival of Dali, Louis Buñuel, and others. Such expression of fear and hatred of woman in art is not limited to this decade; it is an age-old, recurrent theme that will be developed or reused later by the surrealist painters and other artists. But the essential strength of the surrealists of the 1930s lay in their innovative and conscious depiction of desires and phantasms identified as such by the artist—and presented as such to the viewer—through the application of psychoanalytic theory to the work. Similar material up to that time had been considered relevant only to the analysis of dreams and madness. The surrealists intended through their imagery to send a message from their unconscious to that of their audience through such a well-controlled, technically refined artistic vehicle as, for example, Dali's paranoiac-critical method.

For this reason, reference to the Freudian method of dream interpretation is appropriate for the analysis of these surrealist works. The monstrosity of the women represented in these paintings lies in the simultaneous presence of contradictory elements, some attractive—nude breasts or legs, seductive poses—and others repulsive and/or threatening. Freud notes that it is the "custom" of dreams "to take both members of an alternative into the same content, as though they had an equal right to be there," and to ignore "antithesis" and "contradiction."[7] In applying the same principle visually, surrealist art can illustrate a mechanism operating exclusively within the domain of the unconscious, one whose rules allow for an irrational twisting of meanings and the violation of classically accepted logical formulations; thus, for example, contrary to Aristotle's law of the excluded middle, a depicted object could have both female and nonfemale elements at the same time.

A common detail among these selected paintings, the representation of nude breasts, emphasizes woman's maternal aspect; some works do not even show the full body, but truncate it under the chest (Magritte's *La Gâcheuse* and *L'Esprit de la géométrie*, Miro's *Tête de femme*). Magritte's *L'Esprit de la géométrie* (Figure 35, 1937) represents a typical mother and baby composition, the woman holding her infant in her arms. However, the painting shocks the viewer by placing the heads on the wrong bodies; the concomitant inversion of proportions (the juxtaposition of the enormous, bald baby's head and the small, long-haired mother's head) also suggests an inversion of roles, that the child protects and nurtures the helpless adult. This radical inversion corresponds to another inversion recognized in psychoanalytic theory, the transformation of the powerful, good, nurturing mother (the good phallic mother) into a terrifying mother who overfeeds her baby (the bad phallic mother).[8] This inversion could also express a phantasm of reversed orality in which the nurturing mother is transformed into a monster who will eat her child, a recurrent theme in mythology.

Another element common to these pictures and related to the

35. René Magritte, *L'Esprit de la géométrie*, 1937, © Georgette Magritte 1985.
Reprinted with permission.

motif of orality is the emphasis Miro, Magritte, and Dali give to teeth. Teeth may symbolize different phantasms depending on their contexts. For a child in the oral phase, they can be reassuring within the context of the phallic mother, who is perceived as phallic because the child assimilates the tip of the breast as a penetrating penis during lactation. The phallic mother can also be perceived negatively, as distressing, when she overwhelms by force-feeding her baby; the child can then use teeth as defensive weapons to stop this unpleasant situation. Teeth may sometimes be phallic symbols of fertility, but they are usually associated with fear of castration. The skull's teeth in *La Gâcheuse* (Figure 36, 1935) look as sharp as a guillotine. The title of this painting ("the spoiler," "the troublemaker") suggests that Death, the despoiler, supplants beauty and love; but it could also imply that destruction is a corollary of love, that there is a castrator in every woman.[9]

In Miro's *Tête de femme* (Figure 37, 1938), as in Dali's *Minotaure*, the phallic shape of the threatening mouth (beak or muzzle) can evoke fear of castration. Miro's painting recalls Max Ernst's *L'Ange du foyer* (Figure 38, 1937), which represents a monstrous creature dancing. Her mouth is another beak with teeth, and her arms are raised in the same movement. Either figure would probably grab and devour an unfortunate passerby. Dali's monster is even more terrifying. Even though the body's attitude is seductive, the image's central point of focus, the groin, is guarded by a castrating, snappish lobster that hangs above the genital area to forbid any sexual approach. This is a representation of a common phantasm, the *vagina dentata*: Robert Gessain notes that some are fearful that sexual penetration can lead to castration because of teeth (or razor blades, etc.) concealed within a woman's genitialia.[10] The *vagina dentata* is also suggested by the interchange of higher and lower parts of the body, such as a mouth with teeth for a vagina. In Magritte's *The Rape* (Figure 34), parts of the female body constitute the woman's face: Breast, navel, and pubic hair represent the eyes, nose, and mouth.

The image of woman in these paintings is neither flattering nor original. The paintings convey to various degrees a common *vagina dentata* phantasm, a particular aspect of the castration complex. Yet such paintings sometimes present a temporary

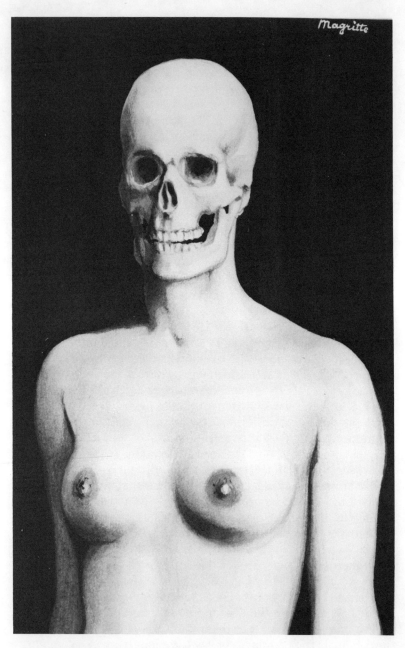

36. René Magritte, *La Gâcheuse*, 1935. Private collection.

37. Joan Miro, *Tête de femme*, 1938. Pierre Matisse Gallery, New York. Courtesy of A.D.A.G.P., Paris. Copyright © Spadem.

38. Max Ernst, *L'Ange du foyer*, 1937. © ADAGP, Paris/VAGA, New York, 1985.

relief from this fear by immobilizing the woman's sexuality. This is especially evident in Magritte's *L'Invention collective* (Figure 39, 1934). The creature stranded on the shore appears to be the contrary of a mermaid: The upper part of her body is that of a fish; the lower part is human. She just lies on the sand, completely helpless. In that respect she is a surrealist collective invention rendered passive—as well as repulsive—by an incorrect mythological rearrangement. Another example of the painting immobilizing woman's sexuality is Brauner's *La Ville*. A staring woman dressed in black seems to float in the air; light falls on her face, breast, and genitalia, emphasizing her womanhood. But the little snake-spermatozoid in the painting does not dance in front of her; it is attracted instead by another, (h)armless, sleeping female. Here, active female sexuality is acknowledged but remains somehow unenticing because of its dangerous absence of controls; the less threatening female figure, asleep and literally disarmed, is preferred.

According to Gessain, the interest of the *vagina dentata* myth lies in its initiatic strength: Through confronting it, one can dominate this fear and reach a good understanding of woman.[11] But this positive phase does not seem to have been reached within these paintings per se: The female surrealist monster, either dangerous or crippled, is alienated from and by male painters. As in the traditional ideologies whose reactionary attitudes the surrealists ironically reproduce, any productive association with

39. René Magritte, *L'Invention collective*, 1934. © ADAGP, Paris/VAGA, New York, 1985.

this monstrous "other" and its different sexuality remains impossible at the practical level.

NOTES

1. Gerard Durozoi and Bernard Charbonnier, *Le Surréalisme: théories, thèmes, techniques* (Paris: Larousse, 1972), p. 175.

2. R. Short, "Eros and Surrealism," in *The Erotic Arts*, ed. Peter Webb (Boston: New York Graphic Society, 1975), pp. 254–255.

3. Robert Benayoun, *Érotique du Surréalisme* (Paris: Pauvert, 1965), pp. 162–174.

4. Xavière Gauthier, *Surréalisme et Sexualité* (Paris: Gallimard, 1971), pp. 111, 149–151.

5. Ibid., pp. 145–155.

6. Ibid., pp. 331–333.

7. Sigmund Freud, *The Interpretation of Dreams* (New York: Random House, 1950), pp. 207–208.

8. Robert Gessain, "Vagina Dentata dans la clinique et la mythologie," *La Psychoanalyse* 3 (1957): 271.

9. Ibid., pp. 249–250.

10. Ibid., pp. 294, 265.

11. Ibid., p. 293.

7

Subliminal Seduction in Fantasy Illustration

GWENDOLYN LAYNE

Apparently directed at the minds and hearts of adolescents of all genders and ages, fantasy cover art, in reflecting something of the nature of the stories between the covers, suggests that the fantasy genre has ventured into areas of sexuality hitherto unexplored—except, perhaps, in Polaroid home photo sessions. Scantily clad damsels cling, struggle, swoon, or pose alluringly, while grim, improbably muscled heroes fend off equally grim, improbably muscled villains—or such mightily sinewed monsters as only Grendel's dam could love. Of course, there is nothing new in such compositions per se: Early pulps of all genres commonly depict this woman-in-danger/woman-in-bondage motif. But today's cover often is not only astonishingly erotic; it is also sometimes overtly, and once in a while covertly, pornographic.

Magazines such as *Heavy Metal* and *Epic* have helped raise the open expression of sexuality in popular fantasy art to a new plateau. The artwork has redefined "comic" graphics, for throughout it is often only a shade less sophisticated and elegant than the sumptuous cover illustrations. One of the reasons for this may be the concomitant change in story line. The transition from Superman to Conan means more than a shift in setting. The inhumanly chaste and virtuous superhero has become in some cases merely superhuman. He can now be a sexual creature as well as a character of uncertain virtue and slippery ethics. And he is sometimes portrayed in a graphic manner more commonly associated with artwork found in underground "comix." Also, despite Robert E. Howard's persistent vision, many heroines now resist the old stereotype and refuse to cling, swoon, or pose alluringly—unless it is with sword in hand. Yet even the most casual eye will notice that these women are of decidedly hardy stock; they still prefer to be encumbered by as few garments as possible, as do their men, whatever the climate.

The biggest change, of course, is in the handling of sex and sexuality in the narrative. Not only are the hero and heroine now permitted sexual awareness, but they are also sexually alert, and their adventures often include the satisfaction of an awakened libido. Red Sonya is the updated version of the chaste but coy Lois Lane, and characters like Marvel's Eros, a.k.a. Starfox, possess an intrinsic sexuality undreamt of by the original Captain Marvel. In short, even the funnies ain't what they used to be.

But then, nothing is what it used to be, including America's confidence in its perceptions and the trust it formerly invested in the fabricators of consumer goods and in those who sell them. A Frank Frazetta cover for *Conan the Warrior* or a Boris Vallejo cover for *Outlaw of Gor*, the covers for a recent reprint of *Dr. Jekyll and Mr. Hyde* and for a scholarly work on popular narrative forms, a full-page magazine ad for gin or the telephone company, a pack of Camel cigarettes—all have one thing in common: They are advertisements. Beyond that, all may also practice certain subliminal marketing strategies.

Wilson Bryan Key's *Subliminal Seduction* was published in 1973 and was shortly followed by *Media Sexploitation* (1976) and *The Clam-Plate Orgy and Other Subliminal Techniques for Manipulating Your Behavior* (1980). Key's thesis is that ad artists embed in advertisements certain figures, words, and shapes that the audience normally perceives only on a subconscious or subliminal level. According to Key, artists such as Rembrandt, Bosch, Picasso, and even Norman Rockwell employed subliminal techniques, which have also been used on various paper monies, on political posters, and even on Ritz crackers. Key is controversial, and his tone can put off even the most open-minded reader; however, his three books provide numerous examples of subliminal embeds in art and advertising that reexamination reveals are undeniably there. Further, Key is especially persuasive when he writes of the American predilection to believe in anything American:

As long as consumers are uncertain, should they detect subliminal stimuli they will assume they are imagining things and pass the notion off without a second conscious thought. People in North America have been culturally trained to believe in the inherent honesty of their governmental and commercial institutions. They find it very difficult, if not impossible, to believe anyone would do anything as outrageous as these subliminals.[1]

Subliminal perceptions are by definition not consciously perceived phenomena, and most people are quite resistant to the idea that images or messages pertaining to sex and death are embedded in ads for products that have nothing to do with sex or death. Also, it has never been conclusively proven that people are actually affected by subliminals. Yet Key offers a provocative, if essentially circular, argument: "The most persuasive evidence for the effectiveness of subliminals is the billions of dollars annually invested by advertisers and media industries on the assumption that subs are effective merchandising stimuli."[2] In fact, artists have been using subliminal techniques for centuries— although not always to promote sales—and in quite dissimilar cultures and situations.

Sixteenth-century Iranian (Persian) painting is a good example of the artistic use of subliminal images. Fantastic, exquisite Iranian miniatures are richly colored, precisely executed, and often rife with embedded forms. Weird figures lurk in cotton candy rocks and clouds; trees writhe and sway with strange life; rivers boil up curiously nonaquatic beings. But these creatures of fancy were not long-lived, for within the century they were exorcised as being no longer acceptable to a stricter religious orthodoxy.[3]

Yet, in the same century, the development in India of Mughal painting—an amalgam of Indian and Iranian miniatures—briefly provided sanctuary for these spirits from the Persian Twilight Zone. Figure 40, *Mirdukht's Escape from Dangerous Men* (c. 1500–

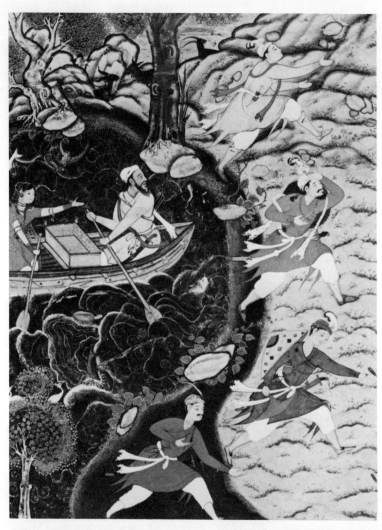

40. Anonymous, *Mirdukht's Escape From Dangerous Men*, c. 1500–1600. Austrian Museum of Applied Art, Vienna. Reproduced in *Hamza Nama*, facsimile edition (Graz, Austria: Akademische Druck, 1974). Courtesy of Akademische Druck.

41. Pablo Picasso, *Woman in an Armchair: The Dream*, 1932. © VAGA, New York/ SPADEM, Paris 1984.

1600), is an exuberant example of this art form. Close scrutiny reveals several of those creatures of the imagination surfing on the river's wild waters: the heads of a lion, a ram, and an ibex, a fish, and several Neanderthal-like faces.[4] In fact, illustrations from this period are known for their subversive plasticity, and the studio artists were encouraged to continue the tradition of embedding. Eventually, when less tolerant emperors came to power, Muslim orthodoxy caught up with these fantasies as well, and they were likewise banished.

Western culture is no stranger to the entwining of things that go bump in the night with the stuff of the daily grind. Also in the sixteenth century, Hieronymus Bosch filled his canvases with the ineffably odd. One of his triptychs, *The Garden of Earthly Delights* (Figure 2), is so imbued with the right fantastic stuff that it illustrates the covers of two recent books on fantasy, Rosemary Jackson's *Fantasy: The Literature of Subversion* and Eric Rabkin's *Fantastic Worlds: Myths, Tales, and Stories*. Others who tinkered with subliminal effects, such as Giuseppe Arcimboldo (c. 1527–1593) and Paul Delvaux, are part of a tradition of fantastic art that is best-known in modern times through the works of two of its foremost practitioners, Salvador Dali and Pablo Picasso.

Dali's playfully Freudian Surrealism defines modern fantastic art—enigmatic, suggestive, unsettling. The eroticism in Dali's work is not so much subliminal as merely obvious to the non-casual observer. Picasso, on the other hand, is not considered a covert seducer; his vision is usually boldly frank and multi-dimensional. Even so, a sophisticated and comically raunchy example of subliminal technique is found in his *Woman in an Armchair: The Dream* (Figure 41, 1932). As Key observes of this seemingly innocent composition, the picture "somehow communicates a subtle feeling of significance." One needs only to look at the top of the woman's face to discover the content of her dream. "If you mask off the lower portion of her face, the left plane appears as a long, cylindrical object. The left eye forms the coronal ridge at the head of an erect penis." Key, of course, avers that there are all sorts of obscene but subliminal goings-on, not only in art, but also—perhaps more insidiously—in ads.[5]

Contemporary ads are easy targets for such *explication de texte*. If Norman Rockwell, consciously or not, put embeds into his homey, warm, all-American paintings, as Key argues,[6] why should an adman refrain? And if advertising artists play such games, so can commercial artists of any kind. Figure 42, a page from a fifty-year-old *Flip the Frog Coloring Book*, is not the only scene in which Flip is involved with some fairly blatant phallic imagery, but it is one of the more obvious. If they are acting with any conscious intent at all, it is likely the artists are simply having some fun with Flip and the characters in Figure 43 by slipping in a subliminal joke here or there. In this *Captain America* panel, Mister Grover seems to be getting more help—and help of a different kind—from the woman behind him than the narrative situation indicates. And with his left hand he seems to be helping himself quite vigorously. Comic book cover, splash, and individual panel art, then and now, contain such visual double entendres as a facet of the relatively harmless fun of the genre.

Fantasy covers have an intent beyond the mere beauty or cleverness of their art, however, for they are meant to sell artists as well as authors. In order to have the latest cover, a collector will often buy a second edition of a text he already has. Thus it is that advertising industry techiques are employed in the creation of fantasy cover art. All the normal tricks of the trade are used, including innuendo and embedded words and shapes suggesting sex, sexuality, and sexism. Are these subliminals only in the mind of the beholder, or are they part of the illustration's subtext, thereby imparting another dimension to the

42. Ub Iwerks, title page from *Flip the Frog Coloring Book* (New York: Saalfield, 1932).

43. Marvel Comics Group, *Captain America* panel. Copyright © 1984 Marvel Comics Group. Used with permission.

narrative? Or perhaps Key's observations apply only to the more blatant areas of the advertising industry?

Frank Kelly Freas, a prolific and popular science fiction and fantasy illustrator, marvels that the face embedded in the wall in Figure 44 (1956 illustration for *Plus—X* by Eric Frank Russell) was so long undetected: "I thought the face coming thru the wall was rather aggressively obvious, but a lot of people—including the editor—didn't even NOTICE it! For years. Some never saw it at all until I pointed it out!"[7] The black-and-white reproduction somewhat enhances the hoary face of the creature pushing its way through the wall, but even in color the embed is by no means difficult to see. Of course, Freas is not "selling" sexuality with this little subliminal trick, which has no erotic content; nor, ostensibly, is he promoting a book or magazine.

Neither is Artzybasheff playing huckster with his subtle and witty craft. Figure 45 (1935), from *The Circus of Dr. Lao*, is captioned "Miss Birdsong in Arcadia." Here, the subliminals not only are amusingly obvious (the "face" in the rock upon which Miss Birdsong and the satyr perch), but also strongly reinforce the scene's implicit sexual motif (the trees, which, upside down, are suggestively intertwined male and female figures, and the cypress in silhouette, which is a phallic symbol). Both subliminally and overtly, Artzybasheff and Freas (see Figure 29) present a healthy vision of sexuality in their fantasy illustrations that complements rather than detracts from the texts they accompany.

To some observers, however, the fantasy artist is more the purveyor of pseudo-cosmic Vargas girls gone kinky. Of course, cover art is part of a marketing strategy, and many subliminals are there to help sell a product as well as to provide the viewer with a sense that he is partaking of a "guilty pleasure." Not surprisingly, fantasy cover and poster art contains the same type of embedded subliminals, as well as more obvious reflections of sexual themes, as art devised to sell cigarettes or beer. Frazetta, for example, has one of the better known fantasy art styles, one which is readily recognizable because of its vitality as well as its sexual innuendo: Men grapple with enormous serpents that appear to be monstrous parts of their own anatomy; women of tremendous proportions are hauled around like so much timber by burly males; faces and creatures lurk in smoky shadows or

44. Frank Kelly Freas, illustration for *Plus—X* by Eric Frank Russell, in *Astounding Science Fiction* (June 1956). From *Frank Kelly Freas: The Art of Science Fiction*, published by The Donning Company/Publishers.

45. Boris Artzybasheff, "Miss Birdsong in Arcadia," 1935. From *The Circus of Dr. Lao* by Charles G. Finney, with drawings by Boris Artzybasheff. Copyright 1935, renewed © 1962 by Charles G. Finney. Reprinted with permission of Viking Penguin Inc.

peer out from dense foliage. That the enjoyment such imagination and skill afford is sometimes tinged with sexist voyeurism is an unfortunate by-product of the new permissiveness.

John Norman is a leading purveyor of sadomasochistic fantasy, and his works are illustrated in a manner that, appropriately enough, might also befit those of the Marquis de Sade. Ten years separate the two editions of his *Outlaw of Gor*, shown in Figure 46. The first cover is by Robert Foster, the second by Boris Vallejo. Truly, the times have changed, and so has the artwork's emphasis. The 1967 cover depicts the hero about to be "chastised" in the Gorean manner. Both he and the lady presiding over his punishment are garbed in casually revealing clothing. The second cover concentrates on flesh: The hero, now stripped down to near-bare essentials, is dressed for work; the "heroine" is dressed for abuse, as is her tormentor. Both illustrations accurately portray scenes from the novel, but the latter more accurately captures the ambiance of Counter-Earth. Also, the 1977 cover is more colorful, the figures alive with movement and the suggestion of dimensionality.

Many artists, such as Frazetta or Boris, produce covers as well as poster illustrations. Others, like the former members of the Studio, have shifted their attention from comic book art and "the strictures of editors, deadlines, and pure conservatism in the field of popular graphics"[8] to explore more thoroughly the art of fantasy illustration. Major names in comic graphics, the four who comprised the Studio made vital contributions to the field: Jeffrey Jones created *Idyl* and *National Lampoon*; Michael William Kaluta developed *The Shadow*; Barry Windsor-Smith gave the world its favorite barbarian couple, *Conan* and *Red Sonya*; and Berni Wrightson produced *Swamp Thing*. Superb artists all, they have worked both sides of the commercial fence; therefore, they have employed and exploited subliminal persuaders of various kinds, either for splash panels or for their lushly romantic paintings.

One example of an especially elegant subliminal is Kaluta's *The Sacrifice* (Figure 47, 1976), which is astonishingly beautiful even in black and white. In color, it glows with rich golden tones, especially the body of the priestess, whose hue is picked up in the ornamental ceiling behind the serpent altar. The snak-

46. Left illustration by Robert Foster, from *Outlaw of Gor* by John Norman, 1967. Published by DelRey Books, used with permission. Right illustration by Boris Vallejo, from *Outlaw of Gor* by John Norman, 1977. Published by DelRey Books, used with permission.

47. Michael William Kaluta, *The Sacrifice*, 1976. From Jeffrey Jones, Michael William Kaluta, Barry Windsor-Smith, Berni Wrightson, *The Studio* (Holland: Dragon's Dream, Ltd., 1979). Courtesy of Michael William Kaluta.

ing chain, ripped from the wall, whips across the girl's figure and frames the illustration's center—fantasy's favorite piece of anatomy. This finely accomplished work of art could easily be a splash panel for a Conan adventure. It was produced after the artist's comic book stint had ended, however, and was created purely for "entertainment." Ostensibly inspired by Beardsley's *Salome with the Head of John the Baptist*, it clearly owes a great deal to Kaluta's contemporary inspirations, Roy G. Krenkel and Frank Frazetta.

The scene is a busy one, its nooks and crannies filled with things familiar to fantasy fans. But the eye always returns to the conjunction of the barbarian and the woman, her body covering his nakedness. It seems to denote a scene of sacrifice, and certainly connotes a typical fantasy adventure. Beyond that? Kaluta's words on the subject might be illuminating: "In titling this work *The Sacrifice*, I've done *two* things. I've deliberately misled the viewer, especially if they are familiar with this brand of fantasy, into assuming the barbarian is the sacrifice. And I've given a clue to the real action being portrayed."[9]

In studying this picture for Kaluta's clue, one looks for the "real action." Why has the artist been so very enigmatic? The chain that dominates the composition forms a big "S." The configuration of the barbarian's left side—arm, body, leg—and a peculiar shadow parallel to his arm (it is his arm's shadow, but lit from where?) makes an "E." As for the "X," it is the line formed by the arm's shadow and part of the ceiling decoration crossed by the line denoting the edge of the altar. However this text is read, it literally spells out "SEX" in big, bold letters. Kaluta's "clue" is right out of an adman's bag of tricks: a gigantic, if collapsed, word boldly embedded in the composition. Also, in sinuously curving around the focal point of the painting as it does, the chain cleverly serves two functions: show and tell.

A critical assessment of fantasy cover art might observe that this art dehumanizes women, abuses the dignity of both sexes, exploits sex and sexuality both openly and subtly, barely skirts the edge of soft-core pornography, and reduces consumers to voyeurs. But the same might also be said of the advertising industry generally, much of commercial television, music videos in particular, and "Monday Night Football." Such manipulations are dangerous only when the audience, left unaware of the game being played, is not invited to join in the laughter at the visual puns. As contemporary admen, as well as artists from the Persians through Picasso, have demonstrated, "guilty pleasures" can infiltrate the most innocuous settings and wear the most innocent guises.

NOTES

1. Wilson Bryan Key, *Subliminal Seduction* (Englewood Cliffs, N.J.: Prentice-Hall, 1973), p. 110.

2. Wilson Bryan Key, *The Clam-Plate Orgy and Other Subliminal Techniques for Manipulating Your Behavior* (Englewood Cliffs, N.J.: Prentice-Hall, 1980), p. 28.

3. Stuart Cary Welch, *Persian Painting: Five Royal Safavid Manuscripts of the Sixteenth Century* (New York: George Braziller, 1976), p. 22.

4. Stuart Cary Welch, *Imperial Mughal Painting* (New York: George Braziller, 1978), p. 43.

5. Key, *The Clam-Plate Orgy*, pp. 57–60.

6. Wilson Bryan Key, *Media Sexploitation* (Englewood Cliffs, N.J.: Prentice-Hall, 1976), p. 10.

7. Frank Kelly Freas, *The Art of Science Fiction* (Norfolk, Va.: The Donning Company, 1977), p. 98.

8. Jeffrey Jones, Michael Kaluta, Barry Windsor-Smith, Berni Wrightson, *The Studio* (Holland: Dragon's Dream, Ltd., 1979), p. 11.

9. Ibid., p. 74.

8

And Now, This Brief Commercial Message: Sex Sells Fantasy!

SARAH CLEMENS

The August 1984 cover of *Twilight Zone Magazine* features a voluptuous female extraterrestrial and the banner slogan, *"Star Trek III*: More Aliens, More Action, More Sex!"* Within, the logic behind this cover is explained:

> Why, you ask, has a tradition-minded, somewhat prim magazine like *Twilight Zone* devoted its cover to a busty Klingon spy from the latest Star Trek movie?
>
>   Well, kids it is time you learned the truth: it has not exactly been lost upon our publisher that the bestselling issue of *Sports Illustrated* is traditionally its annual bathing suit issue. . . . We at *Twilight Zone* decided, therefore, that it was high time we tested the old adage, Sex Sells.

No doubt about it: "Sex Sells." By necessity, fantastic art and film are commercial enterprises governed by the supreme law of economic survival: The product must make money. It is crass to speak of such a thing, but this is the only essay in this book to dwell on profit as a motive behind the overt sexuality of fantastic art and film. Classic paintings and movies, science fiction cover art and the most recent celluloid remakes, and a lot that falls in between, are discussed in these pages. Any film or artwork with sexual content evokes response, and both the con-

tent of the work itself and the reactions it evokes are within the
scholar's domain. But why do filmmakers and artists produce
the visions they create? And what do their audiences make of
these visions? The depiction of sexuality in fantastic art and film
provides not only a vehicle for gaining insight into the artist and
his culture, but also the opportunity to take a new look at ourselves as well.

On one level, motivation seems reasonably clear: If a sexual
hype will make one more person buy a ticket to a movie or pluck
a book from a rack, it is worthwhile. This philosophy is dispas-
sionate and, in itself, generally devoid of sexism. The publisher
of a magazine is not necessarily a lecher, nor is the marketing
division at Paramount composed entirely of people with One
Thing On Their Minds. Certain formulas are tried and true; not
only should people refrain from fixing what isn't broken and
not mess with something that has worked so well so far, but
they should also use it whenever possible. Sex Sells.

There are two ways the appeal of sexuality can be utilized to
merchandise a work of art or a film. First, sexuality can be an
inherent element of the work, in which case the product can,
through emphasis on this attribute, be permitted to sell itself.
Barbarella (1968), a film based on the adventures of the French
comic book heroine, contains many scenes with sexual content;
indeed, the sexuality of the major character—as well as that of
nearly all the other characters—is an element of crucial importance to the film's plot. Barbarella comes from a universe in
which there are no weapons, in which the customary word of
greeting is "love." In the course of her adventures she discovers
and comes to appreciate the primitive, physical sexuality that
her society has abandoned and forgotten. At one point she even
overwhelms the villain's chosen instrument for her destruction,
the orgasmatron, with her boundless capacity to endure sensual
stimulation. Jane Fonda, wide-eyed and nubile in the title role,
was featured prominently in both the original movie poster and
the recent Boris Vallejo rerelease; and the film's campy, 1960s
sexuality is stressed in all its promotional advertising. The very
name "Barbarella" is synonymous with fantasy and sexuality.

Much of the fantastic art created in the twentieth century has
been commercial. In addition to poster art, there is packaging:

the covers of pulps, magazines, books, and record albums. Therefore, an artist can develop a reputation based on the treatment of sexuality in his or her work that can become the selling point in merchandising both the artist and those products the artwork promotes. Reference to Frank Frazetta inevitably brings to mind "The Frazetta Girl." Distressed maid or savage warrior, she is voluptuous, busty, and under-clad. Her face is round, her eyes dark and inviting. Perhaps she doesn't appear on every canvas Frazetta has ever painted, but she is on every other one; when she is absent, she is replaced by a fantasy male who is every bit as hard-muscled and virile as she is soft and compliant. Frazetta's men and women are fantastic figures who in themselves exhibit impossible beauty, stature, and sensuality, regardless of their contexts.

The second way sexuality can be used to market an artistic or cinematic product is through stressing sex in the product's promotion even when there is little or no eroticism in the product itself. The poster for the 1956 film classic *Forbidden Planet* depicts Robby the Robot carrying a limp and skimpily clad Anne Francis. Many promotional approaches could have been taken: The poster could have shown the heroes firing at the Id monster, thus stressing the action; or emphasis could have been placed on the Krell's underground machinery, or the spaceship landing on the alien planet, thus highlighting the film's science fiction elements and the sense of wonder a viewer could anticipate. Instead, the prospective viewer was lured into the theater by an attractive woman helplessly prostrate in the arms of an apparent menace; ironically, such a scene never occurs in the film.

Yet this scene is repeated *ad nauseam* in other movie posters and publicity stills—most of which have just as little to do with the film's actual content. A 1955 publicity still for *The Day the World Ended* places a limp Lori Nelson in the arms of a mutant monster. In the same year, *Fire Maidens of Outer Space* spawned a poster so marvelously tacky it seems to be a caricature of the whole maiden-molested-by-menace school of film promotion: A woman struggles in the inevitable clutches of the monster; her dress is so precariously loose it is certain her breasts are going to fall out (ker-plop!) at any moment. Yvette Mimieux is about to suffer the same fate in a 1960 publicity still from *The Time*

Machine. This visual image is recycled again and again in the posters for such 1950s films as *The Day the Earth Stood Still* (1951), *Tobor the Great* (1954), *Revenge of the Creature* (1954), *Beginning of the End* (1957), and so on. And it is not simply some cultural oddity from a less sophisticated decade; the same pose occurs in promotional materials for *Day of the Triffids* (1962), *When Dinosaurs Ruled the Earth* (1970), and *Q* (1982).

This type of marketing was nothing new to anyone who had ever looked at the covers of such old pulp magazines as *Weird Tales* or *Amazing Stories,* however. Margaret Brundage, who drew pastel illustrations for the covers of *Weird Tales* in the 1930s, often depicted women in bondage. Earle K. Bergey, who illustrated for several pulps and is credited with having invented the "brass brassiere," drew beautiful women who wore almost nothing and were usually menaced by a B. E. M. (Bug Eyed Monster). Of course, these covers usually had nothing to do with the pulps' content either; mothers made their youngsters tear the covers off the magazines before they could read them. Women were being threatened on the covers of pulps even in the first decade of this century; and Frank R. Paul, the father of science fiction illustration, used this maiden-molested-by-menace formula repeatedly on his *Amazing Stories* covers soon after Hugo Gernsbach founded the magazine in 1926. In fact, examples of hapless maidens swooning before some fantastic, quasi-erotic threat predate the present and its intense commercialism by hundreds of years. In the 1780s Swiss painter Henry Fuseli, something of an *enfant terrible* in English society, scandalized and fascinated his contemporaries with several renditions of *The Nightmare,* paintings in which a woman sleeps in a filmy garment, her head and shoulders dangling limply over the side of the bed, while a hot-eyed incubus perches heavily on her chest. The lurking implication of sex and menace attracted an audience then, and still does today. Perhaps in the 1980s the audience is more jaded, more accustomed to the use of sexual imagery in art as well as in advertising, but the formula still works. And yet fantastic book and magazine illustration really is relatively "tradition minded and somewhat prim," for it is found in and on publications that are directed at an audience of all ages. As commercial art for a mass audience, it seems to have reached the current acceptable frontier of contemporary mass sensibility; it can push the boundaries of marketable sexual imagery only so far. A sword and sorcery book cover has become nearly as stereotypical as a cover for a gothic novel. Though science fiction and fantasy literature is still exploring new sexual terrain, the covers in which such works are bound retread the same comparatively conservative path. Except for the comic book and animated children's cartoon, cover art is the most sexually conservative visual fantasy medium. A science fiction book cover is as likely to display an astronomical phenomenon, or an action scene from the story, or even an abstract painting, as it is to display visual erotica. Michael Whelan's vivid cover for the best-selling *The White Dragon* is completely nonsexual, yet it is also one of the best-selling prints available at science fiction convention art shows. Sometimes, Dragons Sell.

Perhaps readers are expected to be less swayed by erotic images than moviegoers. But, of course, there is not so much at stake if a book loses money. The losses can total thousands when a literary project fails, but a film can lose millions. When more money is at stake, formulas are adhered to all the more rigidly because they are safe; they are proven ways of bringing in the customer. In the 1976 Hildebrandt *Star Wars* poster, Princess Leia's gown is hiked up to show a good length of thigh as she assumes what could be taken as a submissive posture beneath Luke's upraised light saber. Not even Carrie Fisher's feet are seen in *Star Wars*, much less her thighs, although she does show more skin in the last film of the trilogy. In the foreground of the 1978 poster for *Warlords of Atlantis*, among all the other people fighting a giant octopus, a scantily clad female throttles the thrashing tip of the monster tentacle thrust between her legs.

A magnificent example of pure sexploitation is the incomparable Sybil Danning's appearance in 1980's *Battle Beyond the Stars*. In this forgettable science fiction remake of *The Seven Samurai*, Danning fills a brass brassiere that would have sent Earle Bergey back to the drawing board. She also delivers the immortal line, "You've never seen a Valkyrian go down before." Her only purpose is to provide sexual hype for the film. *Galaxina*, on the other hand, while released the same year, is more honest in its use of 1980's Playmate of the Year Dorothy Stratton. Galaxina

matures from aloof robot to warm lover in this science fiction
spoof. Stratton's name and face were featured prominently in
the film's advertising campaign, but her character's sexuality is
integral to the plot. Incidently, pornography is quite arguably a
fantasy genre, and is unarguably the most obvious of the visual
products sex sells. It is no wonder, then, that pornography has
invaded the domain of the explicitly fantastic, in such films as
Deep Ghost or *Through the Looking Glass*, just as, conversely, science fiction and fantasy have maintained their long flirtation
with sexuality.

Sexuality is a proven seller of products, including films, literature, and art; and few products would ever reach an audience
if their producers did not think they would make money. Particularly in the twentieth century, and especially in such tech-
nologically intensive (and, therefore, expensive) endeavors as
film production, artistic efforts coexist with commercialism. Take
a look at the covers of science fiction novels displayed in the
bookstore. Try to find more than one movie poster from a current
crop of fantasy films that doesn't have a pretty girl on it. Sexuality embroiders the thin layer of marketing vestments that
accompanies such products. These vestments have wrought their
own place in the genres of fantastic film and art. Who cannot
visualize an image of some scantily clad female, or of the B. E.
M., "remembered" from an amalgam of individually forgotten
pulp covers? How many are completely unaware of Frazetta
calendars, or of promotional photographs of nearly all the rest
of Princess Leia's body, finally on display in *Return of the Jedi*?
Sex sells, and probably always will, whether it merely clothes a
fantastic artifact or is woven into the texture of the work as an
integral part of the whole.

9

The Beast Within: Sexuality and Metamorphosis in Horror Films

LEONARD G. HELDRETH

From *Werewolf of London* (1935) to *Teen Wolf* (1985), films in which people change into beasts have been consistently popular, especially among young audiences. The appeal of fantasy films in general has been attributed to a variety of factors. For example, Apter attributes their popularity to an ability to provide awareness of those gaps in an individual's knowledge that "impede self-realization"; he argues that "the impediments to self-realization become humiliations. The self feels responsible for its ignorance and confusion, indeed for its very irresponsibility."[1] Tolkien writes that part of fantasy's value derives from its "setting free needs and desires, confirming the validity of their pursuit and fulfillment, presenting the recovery of fragmented or lost desires, and thus also offering consolation."[2] The violence that often occurs in fantasy, and especially in horror fantasy, may even serve some purpose: Stanley Solomon writes that "recognition of that impulse in the uncertainty of a horror film may be one way of restraining it in the reality of civilization."[3] Another function of fantasy may be to examine the worst possible situation: Apter sees such a fantasy as being "predominately 'negative' in that it does not resolve problems but rather magnifies them."[4] And Solomon hypothesizes that the ultimate stage of such a "moment of horror in the nightmare film represents our own subsconscious desire to confront our inevitable dread: to meet death before we really die."[5]

Walter Evans points out that the adolescent film viewer's "experiences with irrational desires, fears, urges which are incomprehensible yet clearly stronger than the barriers erected by reason or by society, are deeper and more painful than adults are likely to remember," and that the most pervasive subject and desire that manifests itself in horror fantasy is sexuality: "Monster movies unconsciously exploit the fact that most adolescents already know the 'secret of life,' which is, indeed, the 'forbidden knowledge' of sex. The driving need [is] to master the 'forbidden knowledge' of 'the secret of life.' " Fantasy provides both a way of exploring uncomfortable situations and, more important, an objective correlative upon which adolescents can project their turbulent emotions. Evans has demonstrated that adolescents identify with the Frankenstein monster and the vampire. But the werewolf film, more centrally concerned with unwanted physical metamorphoses, is especially appropriate to adolescence, for

Adolescents find themselves trapped in an unwilled change from a comparatively comprehensible and secure childhood to some mysterious new state which they do not understand, cannot control, and have some reason to fear. Mysterious feelings and desires begin to develop and they find themselves strangely fascinated with disturbing new physical characteristics—emerging hair, budding breasts, and others—which, given the forbidding texture of the X-rated American mentality, they associate with mystery, darkness, secrecy, and evil.[6]

In the werewolf films the adolescent confronts the fear, as Prawer describes it, that his "own animal nature or 'lower' instincts may suddenly and disastrously break out—a threat which is felt in proportion to the degree of repression to which such instincts are subjected in a civilized society."[7] Unlike Frankenstein's monster and Dracula, the other great stars of the horror film, the werewolf has no worthy literary antecedent; therefore, much of its mythology comes from Hollywood and reflects Hollywood's marketable obsessions with sex and violence. Moreover, many of the characteristics Hollywood associates with werewolves parallel sexual changes that occur in early adolescence.

Just as children are propelled into adolescence by time and their genes, people subject to lycanthropy have little control over their transfigurations into beasts. They change because of ancestry and circumstances of birth or because they were bitten by another werewolf. Each of these origins parallels human sexuality. The most obvious parallel is the hereditary affliction, which first manifests itself in adoldescent physical changes. The werewolf's bite, like that of the vampire, transmits the affliction as if it were some contagious venereal disease. Contracted through intimate physical contact, the resulting infection, like herpes, may wax and wane and sometimes be controlled, but it can be cured only by death. The werewolf's bite also suggests a symbolic loss of virginity: It involves penetration, a loss of blood, carnal satisfaction for the werewolf, and a nonreversible change in the victim; it awakens appetites the victim can satisfy only by taking up a different lifestyle. Moreover, no one is immune: Just as anyone, regardless of social conditioning, can succumb to sexual temptation, "Even a man who is pure at heart . . . can become a wolf when the wolfbane blooms."

The physical changes the werewolf undergoes parallel those of adolescence. As the werewolf finds his body changing against his will, so teenagers contend with unwanted erections, expanding bosoms, and menstrual periods that frighten and embarrass them. The werewolf's most obvious physical change is the growth of hair on the face and body; the growth of facial hair in men and body hair in both sexes is a secondary sexual characteristic that signals puberty. In some stories the werewolf grows hair in the palm of the hand, a characteristic associated with masturbation. Teenage boys in every generation warn each other of the physical signs of self-abuse, among which is "hair on your hands."[8] The werewolf loses rational control during his transformation and is compelled to kill; hormone imbalances in teenagers lead to wild emotional swings, destructive actions, and homicidal desires they often turn back upon themselves. The werewolf's transformation occurs once a month, at the time of the full moon, and lasts for two or three days, during which he or she must indulge in bloodletting; the most obvious manifestation of sexual maturity in adolescent women is the commencement of monthly menstrual periods. And in some werewolf films drugs, such as wolfbane, either cause or relieve lycanthropy. Wolfbane has parallels in drugs such as Spanish fly or saltpeter, which allegedly exaggerate or inhibit sexual behavior.

The afflicted human in most werewolf films seeks to kill the person of the opposite sex he or she loves most. This situation dramatizes a conflict common to adolescent males: A young man is lustfully attracted to the same individual for whom he feels an idealistic, "pure" love. The sense that these physical and romantic attractions are contrary and incompatible often leads to trauma: The youth runs away from the conflict rather than face it, just as the werewolf warns his beloved to stay away. Further, the sex act has been called a "little death," and the werewolf's desire to kill the one he loves may simply be an extension of this metaphor. It is no coincidence that the hero or heroine of virtually every werewolf film, and of most horror films, is a young man or woman who has recently fallen in love or become engaged; consider the heroes and heroines of *Frankenstein, Bride of Frankenstein, Dracula,* and even *The Rocky Horror Picture Show,* as well as those of *Werewolf of London, The Wolfman, Curse of the Werewolf, An American Werewolf in London,* and both versions of *Cat People.*

Finally, the people tainted with lycanthropy are totally alienated. Society hates and tries to destroy them, and their loved ones are frightened or disgusted by them. Even the animal kingdom rejects them: Dogs howl in *The Wolfman*; cats hiss in *Cat People.* Like the stereotypical adolescent, the werewolf feels totally rejected and unloved. Only death, it seems, will free either from this impossible state of isolation. The ever-increasing suicide rate among adolescents is a well-known phenomenon, and every werebeast film, except for a very few quite recent examples, ends with the death of the afflicted individual, at which time he is released from his bestial nature and his body reverts to human form. This transformation suggests that the beast within can be destroyed only through the destruction of the body. Symbolically, perhaps only the "little death" of sexual intercourse will subdue the adolescent's animalistic nature enough to permit a return to a normal state. Evans presents another possibility:

"Only upon the death of adolescence, the mysterious madness which has possessed them, can they enter into a mature state where sexuality is tamed and sanctified by marriage."[9] In either interpretation, only death—literal or symbolic—can end the werewolf's conflict with his animal nature.

Over the years the depiction of the sexual content of the werewolf myth in films has become steadily more explicit. *The Wolfman* (1941), which stars Lon Chaney, Jr., as Lawrence Talbot, and *An American Werewolf of London* (1981), directed by John Landis, are basically similar films that exhibit revealing differences. In *The Wolfman* Talbot, the youngest son of a British aristocrat, returns to England as heir to the family estate after many years in America. His absence has distanced him from his family and local society; and he tries to establish a new relationship with his father, played by Claude Rains, but has little success with either his father or the townspeople, who remain suspicious. Chaney's Talbot is very physical; he towers over his father and says he likes to work with his hands, but he seems awkward and not completely in control of his body. He is also, like many adolescents, a voyeur, and trains his father's telescope on the bedroom window of the heroine, played by Evelyn Ankers.

When he later attempts to meet the heroine, whose father owns a shop, Talbot buys from her a cane that has a large silver handle shaped like the head of a wolf. He had not previously exhibited any need for such a conveniently phallic symbol, and as he buys the cane he runs his hand up and down the shaft. In his first transformation the camera focuses on Talbot's feet: They sprout hair, become rigid, curve upward, and make walking difficult. Carl Jung thought that feet were "frequently phallic,"[10] and Talbot's feet here represent the adoldescent's erection. The morning after the transformation, Talbot finds muddy tracks (associating the feet with dirt and animalism) leading from a window to his bed. Other references are made to the bare feet of Bela, the gypsy, and later to Talbot's bare foot when it is caught in a steel trap. After he is infected by the bite of a werewolf, Talbot desires to kill the woman he loves. At the end of the film, in a reversal of the Oedipal conflict's usual resolution, he gives the cane to his father, who beats him to death with it.

While the sexual symbols in *The Wolfman* remain veiled and

often oblique, they are neither in *An American Werewolf in London*, a movie that, while clumsy and awkward, is also full of wit. The hip tone of the film, which indulges in numerous double entendres, is established during the opening credits: The production company is identified as "Lycanthrope Films, Ltd.," as the sound track provides a romantic rendition of "Blue Moon" (reprised in a rock version at the film's conclusion). The link between animalism and sex is established almost immediately: The hero and his friend are first seen sitting in the back of a truck loaded with sheep, a vignette suggestive of the legendary sexual contact between sheep and farm boys. Jack reinforces this association by calling, "Bye, girls," as the truck drives away; and when David then fantasizes aloud about all the girls they are going to meet on their European travels, Jack observes, "Well, we're off to a great start." The conversation shortly turns to Jack's sexual frustration—the fruit of "years of foreplay" with Debbie Kline, a woman with a great body but no brains—and the distinction between romantic love and animalistic sex is established when, after Jack refers to Debbie as the girl he loves, David corrects him by identifying her as "a girl you want to fuck." The two friends are again associated with sheep when the werewolf rips Jack apart like a piece of mutton and infects David with lycanthropy immediately after they leave a tavern called The Slaughtered Lamb.

This film repeats some of the themes of the *The Wolfman*, drops some, and modifies others. Just as the gamekeeper's dog barks at Talbot in *The Wolfman*, so too does a fat dog walked by two little girls sense the infected David's growing strangeness and begin to bark in *American Werewolf*. Then, when David tries to crawl in a window after locking himself out, a cat hisses at him; this sound alludes to similar sequences in Val Lewton's *Cat People*, another 1941 film with many of the same werebeast themes. Like the Americanized Talbot, Jack and David are culturally and personally isolated in England: They do not know the country, the villagers do not like them, the embassy staff treats them badly, the doctor initially ignores David's story, and David and his new girlfriend are eyed suspiciously on the bus by freaky teenagers with green and orange hair. In The Slaughtered Lamb the boys listen to the joke about the Texan who, crying "Remember the Alamo," shoves a Mexican out of a plane; ironically, they are about to be pushed out into the night to be attacked by the werewolf. Other references to the American West also highlight the cultural differences. Even the book the nurse reads to David in the hospital, *A Connecticut Yankee in King Arthur's Court*, suggests the boys' cultural isolation. And the scene in the hospital room reinstates the sexual motifs while further underlining the theme of alienation. Just before David wakes up, one nurse says to the other, "He's a Jew. . . . I had a look." Nurse Pride, with whom David later has intercourse, notes that "It's a common practice."

As the disease of lycanthropy progresses through David's system, he dreams of running naked through the woods and attacking a doe. Other dreams associate nudity, violence, and sexuality. The most interesting of these is a three-part sequence in which the dreamer wakes to other dreams instead of reality, an allusion to the fantasy structure of Louis Buñuel's *The Discreet Charm of the Bourgeoisie* (1972). The sequence features a bloody, walking corpse, as does Buñuel's film, and storm troopers with animal heads who mow down innocent people with machine guns. David first dreams of his family in America. When his father answers the door, storm troopers burst in, kill the family, and cut David's throat. He wakes, screaming, to see the nurse by his bed. When she opens the window, an animal-headed storm trooper leaps in and stabs her repeatedly with a long knife. David screams again and wakes to find an orderly about to serve him breakfast. Then Jack appears, a reanimated corpse covered with wounds and gore, to tell David about the drawbacks of lycanthropy.

Each dream functions symbolically in the film. The first shows the mindless ferocity of the werewolf and demonstrates the threat David's lycanthropy poses to his family—as werewolves kill those they love most—and ultimately to himself; it anticipates the phone call David makes, near the end of the film, to say farewell to his family and thereby protect them from the effects of his disease. The second dream extends this danger to his new love, the nurse; that she is killed on the bed with a long knife rather than machine-gunned is a symbolic representation of the dangerous sexual attraction David feels toward her. The last sequence introduces the new element added by this film to the werewolf legend. Although Jack was killed on the moor and buried in New York, he tells David, "I walk the Earth in limbo until the curse is lifted." According to Jack, each werewolf's victim must linger as one of the living dead until that werewolf and all those it has infected are destroyed. This concept, although illogical, adds an interesting, macabre twist to the film: For the victims shortly begin to band together and urge David to kill himself. The three-dream sequence ends with Jack's departure and the nurse's return to the room. David kisses her and says, "I'm a werewolf."

After leaving the hospital, David moves in with the nurse and they immediately go to bed. Sexuality is associated with biting in the soft-core seduction scene featuring simulated cunnilingus that follows. Late the next day David looks in a mirror, growling at himself and checking for fangs like an adolescent looking for the first signs of beard growth. His metamorphosis to werewolf is no soft-focus, stop-motion animation sequence, as in the older films, but a bone-crunching, tendon-snapping transformation in which fingers lengthen, muscles bulge, the skeleton reshapes itself, and David howls in anguish. Like the physical and emotional changes of adolescence, it is a painful process during which David tears off his clothes, falls to the floor, and writhes in agony. When he wakes up the next morning, after having killed six people, David finds himself in the wolf cage at the zoo. The foot references from *The Wolfman* are humorously echoed here as the camera pans along a row of legs wearing various styles of shoes to stop at David's bare feet.

The most direct cinematic association of lycanthropy and sexuality, however, occurs near the end of the film in the pornographic movie theatre. David's blood-covered victims sit in the dark with Jack, who is now thoroughly decayed, and urge David to kill himself before he changes again. As the actors on the screen hop in and out of bed, the porno film's dialogue echoes the comments of David's victims: "What are you doing here? You promised never to do this sort of thing again." When David's second transformation occurs in the same theatre, his thrashings and moans are intercut with those of the copulators on the screen, suggesting the essentially sexual nature of the werewolf's metamorphosis.

In many ways, *An American Werewolf in London* is a remake of Chaney's *The Wolfman* updated to reflect the sexual frankness and new cinematic techniques of the 1980s. Both illustrate that the werewolf legend, as Hollywood has fashioned it, is essentially a metaphor for adolescent sexual development. Losing control of the body, turning into an animal, letting the impulse towards violence take control, being rejected by society—these fears, especially prevalent in adolescence, suggest that the animal side of human nature, the beast within, can overcome the human side. Horror fantasy films provide one way of symbolically approaching these fears and conflicts.

NOTES

1. T. E. Apter, *Fantasy Literature: An Approach to Reality* (Bloomington: Indiana University Press, 1982), p. 7.

2. J.R.R. Tolkien, "On Fairy Tales," cited by Apter, p. 6.

3. Stanley J. Solomon, *Beyond Formula: American Film Genres* (New York: Harcourt Brace Jovanovich, 1976), p. 122.

4. Apter, p. 6.

5. Solomon, p. 114.

6. Walter Evans, "Monster Movies: A Sexual Theory," in *Sexuality in the Movies*, ed. Thomas R. Atkins (Bloomington: Indiana University Press, 1975), pp. 149, 152, 146.

7. S. S. Prawer, *Caligari's Children: The Film as Tale of Terror* (New York: Oxford University Press, 1980), p. 53.

8. George V. Higgins, *The Digger's Game* (1973), cited by Norman Kiell, *Varieties of Sexual Experience: Psychosexuality in Literature* (New York: International Universities Press, 1976), p. 361.

9. Evans, p. 152.

10. J. E. Cirlot, *A Dictionary of Symbols* (New York: Philosophical Library, 1962), p. 106.

10

Fay Wray: Horror Films' First Sex Symbol

ANTHONY AMBROGIO

At their most elemental level, horror films are often sexual psychodramas wherein the heroine is menaced by a monstrous Fate Worse Than Death from which the hero must save her in the Nick of Time. This heroine-monster-hero trio is an eternal triangle, an isosceles triangle with hero and monster at the base; they are opposite numbers on the same plane converging equally toward the same point. The hero must overcome the monster—his ignoble double, the manifestation of a darker nature that lusts blindly after the heroine—by exerting his nobler, civilized side to defeat his personal demon, the beast within, and thus legally possess the woman in a socially acceptable context. The horror genre is littered with such variations on this theme as *The Most Dangerous Game* (1932), whose two big game hunter antagonists provide a perfect representation of this doppelgänger motif. When horror films merge these two warring aspects of the hero's personality into one character—as in *Dr. Jekyll and Mr. Hyde* (1932; 1941), *The Wolfman* (1941), and even, in its own peculiar way, *King Kong* (1933)—they overstep the bounds of melodrama and approach tragedy.

The typical horror film scenario may not seem much different from the formula for nonfantastic melodrama: The mustachioed villain (his pubic hair displaced upward, his leer as shocking as frontal nudity) binds the heroine to the tracks after she refuses to marry him, thus inviting the phallic locomotive to accomplish the symbolic rape he is apparently incapable (by Victorian convention) of performing in "reality"—which coitus the hero interruptus. One might wonder, then, why horror films did not flourish in the silent era, the heyday of this other type of picture. It may be because horror films were too blatant an assault on still-Victorian sensibilities; their fantastic iconography is more sexually explicit than the more oblique representations found in "realistic" pictures. In addition, that iconography requires for its completeness the defining attribute silent films lacked: sound.[1]

The scream—particularly the female scream—is essential to horror films, and its absence stunted the development of a silent horror film genre. The ear-piercing shriek—the literal expression of agony or alarm that actually signifies unbidden ecstasy during the genre's usually symbolic sexual act—is an important component of the horror film's metaphorical rape or near-rape. (Madeline Kahn's melodious "scream" at the conclusion of *Young Frankenstein*, a parody, literalizes symbol and metaphor for comic effect.) Monsters just get excited when women scream, and this is where Fay Wray came in. Nobody did it better than Wray, who thus stimulated those beasts to perform (or try to perform) acts even more unspeakable upon her person. Steve Vertlieb reports that RKO, which produced *King Kong*, "used that contract scream in the voices of countless other actresses whose tonsils were not as healthily endowed. When Helen Mack opened her fragile lips to cry out in *Son of Kong*, it was not her voice audiences heard but that of Fay Wray. As late as 1945 her scream could be heard for Audrey Long in Robert Wise's *Game of Death*, a remake of *The Most Dangerous Game*."[2] But, her uncanny vocal ability aside, Wray was an undistinguished actress; a pretty woman with a nice face and figure but little acting talent, she merely decorated scores of pictures between 1925 and 1941, when she went into semiretirement. Except for her horror films, these movies and her appearances in them are mostly forgotten.

It is moot whether Wray's horror films made her immortal or vice versa. In this genre, her limitations as an actress worked to her advantage because they effectively highlighted by contrast her one big asset, her lungs, which made her a monster's perfect victim. In all her horror films Wray spoke affectedly or stiltedly, but screamed uninhibitedly, with total abandon. Since she could only "let go" in direst jeopardy, Wray became the horror film equivalent of the woman who is reserved in public but passionately unrestrained in private—the lady in the drawing room who is a whore in the bedroom. Wray's physical appearance complemented and reinforced this stereotype. Her fresh, young face always projected an innocence, a naivete that highlighted by contrast her shapely, mature figure, making her seem a wide-eyed ingenue unaware of the carnal lusts she nonetheless inspired in men and monsters. As such, she was a pervert's delight—purity in an alluring package just asking to be penetrated and soiled. Given the sexual undercurrent of most horror films, and the aberrant nature of most monsters' sexual appetites, Wray's particular sex appeal was that most suited to the horror genre.

Fay Wray made six other horror films besides *King Kong*, four of them before *Kong* was even released. But for most people Wray's career begins and ends with *Kong*, no doubt because of that film's great appeal to the imagination and impact on the public (and because Wray screams longer and louder in it than in all the rest of her horror films combined). Certainly, *Kong* was the (ahem) apex of her career. And she worked in other horror films due to her performance in *Kong*; she made the first four during breaks in *Kong*'s production, while live-action shooting was halted so Willis O'Brien could painstakingly prepare the film's celebrated special effects, and her role in each was patterned after her work in *Kong*: She screamed in all of them.

During *Kong*'s early shooting, *The Most Dangerous Game* was also filmed at RKO, used much of *Kong*'s production and acting talent, and provided a trial run for some of *Kong*'s sets (most notably the giant log) and ideas. In *Game* Wray is the sex-object-cum-love-interest, a role she refines and repeats in *Kong*. Word of her facility with this type of character quickly spread beyond RKO; during other *Kong* hiatuses, she secured similar roles in Warner's *Dr. X* (1932) and *Mystery of the Wax Museum* (1933), and Majestic's *Vampire Bat* (1932). In each film Wray played the passive, helpless heroine. When *Kong* premiered in March 1933, audiences were well prepared to accept her as a giant ape's plaything, having already seen her manhandled by a quartet of madmen and monsters during the previous eight months.

Dr. X was the first Wray genre film to be released. A mystery in which a reporter, Lee Taylor, discovers which of five prominent scientists is the "Moon Killer," and not a bad picture, it can be almost summarily dismissed as a Wray vehicle. As Joan Xavier, Dr. X's daughter and Lee's hate-turned-to-love interest, Wray is largely superfluous and delivers her lines even more affectedly than usual, as if she has something extremely unpleasant in her mouth and must talk around it. Her best lines are her screams, some of which have no dramatic justification: e.g., her first shriek, upon the sudden appearance of her father, is a red herring—an attempt to make the viewer think kindly Dr. X is really sinister. As Wray's first utterance of any kind in a horror film, however, this scream both introduces audiences to her uncanny lung power and effectively defines her screen persona.

She screams again, this time while nearly undressed, at film's end, when she is almost murdered by the Killer. (Lee saves her in the Nick of Time.) But Joan is just an arbitrary victim: The monster commits his crimes in the name of science, without regard to his victims' sex or age, to obtain the materials he needs to create "synthetic flesh." No personal relationship between Joan and the Killer—even in his human guise—is established. So *Dr. X* lacks the appropriate psychosexual geometry, the essential horror film triangle, and substitutes for it simple cheesecake, hoping a scantily clad girl in distress will do.

There is no horror film triangle in the low-budget *Vampire Bat*, either. Hero, heroine, and villain are not related thematically, and Wray's role is again superfluous. Accidentally discovering her employer, the villain, engaged in his nefarious enterprise, Wray falls into his clutches until she is rescued by the hero in the Nick of Time. *Bat* doesn't even contrive to display an underclad Wray, although at one point, perhaps in compensation, she is bound, gagged, and strapped to a chair.

The Most Dangerous Game features Wray's first portrayal of the horror film sex object *par excellence*. Her Eve Trowbridge is the "prize" in the "manly" contest between villainous Count Zaroff and heroic Bob Rainsford. The film follows the basic plot of the

Richard Connell story on which it is based. Zaroff, a deranged former big game hunter, has established his own hunting preserve on a remote island to which he lures and wrecks ships, forcing the survivors to become his prey. The most dangerous "game" is man, and Zaroff gives his prey a "sporting chance" to elude him for a specified time and supposedly gain their freedom. So far, no one has. Big game hunter Rainsford survives one of Zaroff's shipwrecks and then manages to beat the madman at his own game. To this story of elemental conflict, scenarist James Creelman adds several new characters—most notably a female shipwreck survivor, Eve, and her dissipated brother, Martin.

In both story and film, Zaroff has ostensibly turned to hunting humans because he no longer derives any satisfaction from picking off lions, tigers, and elephants; since hunting is his *raison d'être*, he hopes to recapture the thrill by stalking man—the only creature, he feels, who may challenge his skill. But the film provides a deeper rationale for Zaroff's obsession: When Eve asks if losing interest in hunting is so bad, the Count replies, with feeling, "It is, dear lady, when hunting has been the whip for all other passions. When I lost my love for hunting, I lost my love for living, for loving." In other words, the jaded nobleman needs the stimulation only the hunt can give him to get it up. He looks significantly at Eve. She understands and drops her eyes, abashed.

Shortly after this confession, Zaroff ridicules Eve's alcoholic brother to fellow hunter Rainsford, whom he considers a kindred soul:

He [Martin] talks of wine and women as a prelude to the hunt. We barbarians know that it is after the chase, and then only, that man revels. You know the saying of the Ogandi chieftains: "Hunt first the enemy, then the woman." It is the natural instinct. The blood is quickened by the kill. One passion builds upon another. Kill, then love! Then you will know ecstasy.

The film's Zaroff equates violence with sex (an all-too-common pathology) and must kill to get "in the mood." But slaughtering animals is no longer adequate foreplay. He must now swell his manhood by killing men (through simulated sex, the phallic bow-and-arrow being his weapon of choice) before figuratively "slaying" women with his now-potent penis-weapon. For such a desirable prize as Eve, Zaroff needs extra stimulation; so first he hunts down her brother—easy prey, but the idea of taking the brother and then the sister gives him an almost incestuous thrill—and then goes after Rainsford, whom he feels will provide him with real sport.

Game is essentially an antihunting tract that details big game hunter Rainsford's acquisition of an ecological consciousness. Before the shipwreck, his friends question him about hunting's fairness, ask what chance animals have against man with his weapons, and wonder how the hunted feel. Rainsford (in a shot framing him with his trophies) insists that the pleasure for hunter and hunted is the same. But when Rainsford gets to experience what the hunted feel, he doesn't like it. Though he makes no overt admission of a change of heart, by film's end it is clear that Rainsford will never consider hunting a "sport" again. Only after conquering his darker nature—represented externally by Zaroff, another hunter, and internally by his own love of hunting—is he able to possess the heroine.

Throughout, Eve remains the decorative trophy, the spoils. His arrows proving ineffectual against Rainsford, Zaroff shoots him with a gun; Rainsford grapples with a dog and topples over a waterfall to his apparent death. Zaroff then claims Eve as his prize. Swooning, she is brought face to face with the Count— and once again knows what he is thinking: Now, after the kill, he has regained his love for living, and for "loving." But Zaroff never satisfies his lust. A still-alive, angry Rainsford bursts in upon him, grapples with him, stabs him with one of his own arrows, and takes Eve away before Zaroff can touch her. The wounded Count attempts to stop the fleeing couple, but—now rendered forever impotent through having been vanquished in a hunt—he can hardly fit an arrow to his bow, let alone get it up to loose it, and (paralleling Rainsford's earlier fall) topples to his death among the dogs. His fortunes fall as Rainsford's rise: The prize goes to the now-civilized hunter, his counterpart, who has earned her.

In Wray's last horror film released before *Kong*, *Mystery of the*

Wax Museum, a deranged sculptor, Ivan Igor, is trapped inside his melting waxworks when his partner burns down their museum for the insurance money. Igor escapes, but with a horribly melted visage he hides under a wax mask and with hands too damaged to be used for shaping and modeling. Unable to sculpt, the seemingly wheelchair-bound Igor resorts to illegal means to recreate his destroyed waxworks; reduced to body-snatching and murder, he now preserves in wax corpses that resemble his former sculptures.

As Wray's Charlotte Duncan has the dubious honor of being a flesh-and-blood replica of Igor's most beloved creation, Marie Antoinette, she occupies an exalted position in Igor's mind, and in the plot. Unlike Wray's characters' accidental, incidental victimizations in *X* and *Bat*, Charlotte's victimization is essential to *Wax*'s story, as are Wray's characters' predicaments in *Game* and *Kong*, for she is a victim in a peculiar sexual sense, the object of a strange passion. Since Charlotte appears to him to be only his wax figure made flesh, Igor—who feels he gave her "life" in the first place—feels also that he has the right to take life away from or to do what he wants with her; her transformation to wax (again) is merely his way of bestowing immortality upon one of his subjects. Thus, at the film's climax, he offers his version of paradise to an unwilling Charlotte—the promise of "eternal life" through preservation in wax.

Kingsley Canham calls Igor's obsession "necrophiliac," though it seems likely, especially after Igor's ordeal through fire, that it is a displacement, a compensation for his artistic—and probably physical—impotence. Canham himself suggests as much when he writes, "The dramatic confusion in [Igor's] mind between flesh and wax enables director Michael Curtiz to put across a number of sly, cynical, visual jokes about the sexual satisfaction which he obtains from making these life-like simulacra." The finale provides a graphic visual metaphor for Igor's passion as he attempts to convert Charlotte into one of his waxworks. Strapped to an operating table and filmed in bare-shouldered close-ups so she appears to be nude, Charlotte is very much at the mercy of Igor's sexual frenzy. Elated to have his Marie Antoinette again, Igor is about to let the wax—his surrogate semen, swelling in its vat, bubbling over with his passion—spew forth and inundate her. Of course, like Count Zaroff and other screen villains, Igor never achieves coitus. Interrupted by the police, he is shot and plummets into his hot wax vat himself—victim (like Zaroff) of his own roiling passions.[3]

Though Charlotte is largely the object of all this pseudosex, *Wax* is the only horror film (perhaps the only film) in which a Fay Wray character even seems to get any sexual satisfaction of her own. *Wax* introduces Charlotte lying flat on her back on her bedroom floor, wearing an abbreviated gym suit and weaving one leg in the air—supposedly doing calisthenics. Just then she receives a phone call from her fiancé. "Oh, Ralph," she says, "I was just thinking about you." This is Wray's best line in *Wax*; director Curtiz indulges in this sly visual joke concerning the sexual pleasure a young lady obtains from masturbating while fantasizing about her lover to foreshadow ironically Charlotte's equally supine position as Igor's prisoner at the film's climax, when she is no longer free to gratify herself.

Save for this introductory moment, Charlotte follows in *Wax* the pattern established for the heroines in *X* and *Bat*: Her function is to be captured, then rescued in the Nick of Time. However, this last-minute rescue is effected, not by her fiancé, but by a fast-talking, wise-cracking newswoman. Obviously, this reporter-heroine does not form the third side of the horror film triangle, and neither does Charlotte's simpy fiancé: One of Igor's assistants, Ralph is constantly berated by the master for his lack of sculpting talent. He too is unable to use his hands, which may explain why Charlotte is reduced, it seems, to using her own. Thus, the film offers no strong counterpoint to Igor, and the anticipated triangle collapses.

King Kong, Wray's next film, more than corrects this problem by presenting the audience with an almost four-sided triangle. *Kong*'s chief components seem to be a helpless white woman and the ideas of miscegenation and rape, but—like its giant beasts, which are really tiny models—things aren't what they seem. *Kong* is full of ethnic stereotypes: The "dago" fruit peddler from whom Carl Denham rescues Ann Darrow (Fay Wray); the ship's cook, Charley, an excitable Chinaman; and Skull Island's black inhabitants, all ignorant savages who, Denham claims, have "slipped back, forgotten the higher [i.e., probably white, somehow] civilization" that built the great wall separating them from the island's jungle. (When the native chief offers six black females for "golden woman" Ann, Denham mutters, "Yeah, blondes are scarce around here.")

And Kong is the biggest black of all. Merian C. Cooper stressed Kong's blackness when he described Wray's part to her: "Of course you'd have to be a blonde. We've got to have that contrast. We thought about Jean Harlow, then we decided you could wear a blonde wig."[4] Kong's blackness, although some literalists may deny it, blunts the rest of the film's racism. Kong is the misunderstood, wronged individual who stands up for his rights. Captured and sold into slavery, he breaks his chains and wreaks havoc on his enslavers. And he fights and dies all for love, proving to be quite chivalrous. This black is not out to rape the white woman; on the contrary, his intentions are honorable.

Kong marks a turning point in fictional portrayals of simian-human sexual relations. Before *Kong*, all gorillas were popularly thought to be single-minded about women; the idea of the ape as an "aggressive carnivore with a lustful passion for white girls"[5] has a long tradition. For example, in 1859 Charles Baudelaire referred to it to explain a sculpture called "Orang-outang Carrying Off a Woman Deep into the Woods":

Why not a crocodile, a tiger, or any other beast that might eat a woman? Because it's not a question of mastication but of violation. For the ape alone, the gigantic ape—at the same time more and less than a man— has sometimes demonstrated a human appetite for women. And in this the artist finds the means to astonish his viewer. "*He* abducts her; will *she* be able to resist?"—this is the question that the female public will ask itself.[6]

In several Tarzan books (e.g., *Tarzan of the Apes, Tarzan and the Jewels of Opar*) Jane is the unhealthy object of a gorilla's passion. Gerald Peary notes that the primary appeal of *Ingagi* (1930), a phony "documentary," was that it depicted "a tribe of completely naked 'ape women' (though modestly obstructed from full view by thickets) sacrificing a black woman to a gorilla. *Ingagi* publicity . . . blatantly emphasizes the sexual aspects of the sacrifice, the perverse union of woman and jungle animal.'"[7] And in 1932 deMille's *Sign of the Cross* featured a very white, very naked, bound woman endangered by a very black ape, while *Murders in the Rue Morgue* chronicled Dr. Mirakle's attempts to prove the theory of evolution by comingling ape and human blood in experiments that go awry when a concupiscent ape tries to mingle more than his blood with the virginal heroine.

Kong recycles these clichés—the tribal sacrifice of a woman to an ape, an ape abducting a woman—to contradict the stereotype that blacks/apes are bestial rapists by depicting its black ape as a chivalrous, noble savage. Thus, despite his savagery, Kong elicits sympathy. A victim of circumstances, like Frankenstein's monster, he lashes out only at those who wrong him while pathetically searching for love. Ann's (and the audience's) first view of Kong is deceptive. Though he seems to leer down at her with a lustful black-ape face, he is really exhibiting love at first sight. The menace is in the eye of his beholder—in the subjective shot from Ann's understandably frightened point of view.

Unfortunately, Ann never overcomes her first impression. She can never realize he means her no harm, and he can never realize she cannot love him. Yet Kong behaves impeccably (almost) toward Ann. He treats her gently, protects and saves her from dinosaurs, and takes no liberties with her virtue—though he does take some with her garments. However, Kong peels Ann, like a human banana, not out of lust, but out of innocent curiosity.

Kong's tag line, " 'Twas beauty killed the beast," upsets some who feel Ann is merely the pawn of every male in the cast. But beauty is responsible for the beast's death both literally and figuratively. Not only does Kong's love for Ann make him vulnerable and eventually doom him, but love also kills the beast in his breast, civilizing and ennobling him. Ann similarly alters the destinies of the other men in her life. Innocent and ingenuous, she also profoundly affects the film's other male principals, Denham and Driscoll—childish misogynists who pretend to be macho but are actually arrested at the "ugh—girls!" stage of social development. She affects them like a sharp attack of puberty, shattering their "confirmed" bachelors' convictions, raising their consciousnesses, causing them to revise drastically their negative opinions about women, and even prompting them to contemplate marriage. Catalyst Ann is the only character who remains unchanged; she influences those who supposedly manipulate her.

Before meeting Ann, adventure filmmaker Denham gets his thrills through sublimation, by figuratively—with camera in hand—shooting big game. Women have no place in Denham's world, and he complains because the public forces him to include one (for "love interest") in his newest film. He doesn't understand why his audiences cannot get as excited as he can over a charging rhinoceros, until he gets a look at Ann through his viewfinder. The adventure he shares with her makes Denham appreciate women. He introduces her at Carnegie Hall as "Miss Ann Darrow, bravest girl I have ever known," and his change of heart makes it possible for him to fall in love in the sequel, *Son of Kong* (1933).

Jack Driscoll, the *Venture*'s first mate, has an even more negative attitude toward women than Denham; he claims that women aboard a ship (in a man's world)—and women generally—are a nuisance. But Jack is captivated by Ann almost at once, and his gruff attitude merely camouflages his chivalrous, bashful concern. Before the voyage is over, in *Kong*'s most embarrassing scene, Jack confesses his love for Ann. She has overcome his little-boy mentality even more completely than she does Denham's, for Jack—like Kong—is a beast destined to be tamed by beauty.

The parallel between Jack and Kong is clear. When Ann foreshadows her winning way with anthropoids by fondling a small monkey, Denham remarks, "Beauty and the beast, eh?" Jack takes mock offense, inferring that "beast" refers to him. This identification with Kong is strengthened when Denham compares Jack's love for Ann to the love felt by the beast in his picture: "You're a pretty tough guy. . . . The beast was a tough guy, too. He could lick the world. But when he saw beauty, she got him. He went soft. He forgot his wisdom, and the little fellows licked him. Think it over, Jack."

In the fairy tale, beauty "kills" the beast with a kiss and makes him human. After Ann kisses Jack, he becomes progressively more human and tender under her influence. Ann affects Kong similarly, although she never kisses him. Thus does *Kong* fit the archetypal monster movie pattern; Jack and Kong are two sides of the same coin, and both desire the heroine. But Jack doesn't have to defeat his "darker" side, for Ann defeats the beast in both of them. Yet the real beast must still die (sacrifice himself) because innocent Ann cannot have two lovers. And even in his ennobled state, Kong still represents for Ann every virgin's worst fears for her wedding night—that her husband is going to reveal himself as some monster whose monstrous sexuality will kill her. So Kong must take Ann to the tip of "the most elaborate phallic symbol in the world"[8] and leave her there, unmolested, until Jack can replace him, remove her from the pedestal Kong has put her on, and establish their married life on a more equal footing.

A subtle but significant shift occurs in Wray's horror film persona after *Kong*. She becomes one side of the triangle instead of its point. In both *Black Moon* (1934) and *The Clairvoyant* (1935) she plays one of two women between whom the central male must choose. In each film she represents the loyal, normal female who is pitted against, respectively, the abnormal wife and mother who prefers voodoo to family and the "other woman" who awakens her husband's latent extrasensory perceptions. And in each, the hero forsakes Wray's darker side (the other woman) to embrace Wray by picture's end.

Had Wray not forsaken films for family life, she could have played a major role in the second horror cycle. She, rather than Evelyn Ankers, might have starred opposite Lon Chaney, Jr., in *The Wolfman* (1941). Once again, she would have been at the triangle's apex, caught between two more beasts—this time a literal and figurative wolf. When the science fiction film boom peaked in the 1950s, a still attractive Wray was again active in movies, but in matronly roles. So she never had the chance to play the title role in *Attack of the 50-Foot Woman* (1958), which features another eternal triangle as well as an enlarged, enraged female who gets even with her cheating spouse and his paramour. This would have been a more fitting end to the career of horror films' first sex symbol than *Summer Love* or *Dragstrip Riot* (both also 1958), but neat parallels like that only occur in the movies.

NOTES

1. William K. Everson points out that horror films could not become a major genre until the sound era because—like musicals and newspaper pictures—they need an aural dimension to be complete. From the obligatory jarring sounds that accompany startling "bus effects," to the subtler off-screen noises of unseen things in the dark, to the traditional, often clichéd creaking doors, crashing thunderclaps, and crackling rheostats—sound is as important to and inseparable from horror films as orchestrated production numbers and fast-talking reporters are to musicals and newspaper pictures. *Classics of the Horror Film* (Secaucus, N.J.: Citadel Press, 1974), pp. 3–4.

2. Steve Vertlieb, "The Man Who Saved King Kong," *The Monster Times* 1, no. 1 (January 1972); rev. and rpt. in *The Girl in the Hairy Paw: King Kong as Myth, Movie, and Monster*, eds. Ronald Gottesman and Harry Geduld (New York: Avon Books, 1976), p. 35.

3. Kingsley Canham, *The Hollywood Professionals*, vol. 1, *Michael Curtiz, Raoul Walsh, Henry Hathaway* (New York: A. S. Barnes & Co., 1973), p. 13.

4. "How Wray Met Kong, or the Scream That Shook the World," *The New York Times*, September 21, 1969, p. 17.

5. Gottesman and Geduld, *The Girl in the Hairy Paw*, pp. 21–22.

6. Charles Baudelaire, *Oeuvres Complètes* (Paris: Editions Gallimard, 1961), pp. 1091–1092, translated by the author.

7. Gerald Peary, "Missing Links: The Jungle Origins of *King Kong*," in *The Girl in the Hairy Paw*, p. 42.

8. Bosley Crowther, *The Great Films* (New York: G. P. Putnam's Sons, 1967), p. 97.

11

Sexual References in James Whale's *Bride of Frankenstein*

MARTIN F. NORDEN

The few critical evaluations of the cult favorite *Bride of Franken-stein* (1935), directed by James Whale, have largely been limited to explorations of the film's horrific and humorous qualities. Critics have commonly observed that *Bride*, an early example of the American horror film, is a worthy successor to the original *Frankenstein* (1931), also directed by Whale. *New York Times* film critic Frank Nugent, one of the earliest to recognize the impor-tance of the film to the genre, termed it "a first-rate horror film" in a 1935 review.[1] *Bride*'s reputation as a masterpiece of horror remains undiminished, as is indicated by Michael G. Fitzgerald's late–1970s classification of it as "one of the best films of the genre."[2] The alternative perspective is to examine the film as a parody that satirized the horror genre. As James Curtis notes of *Bride* in his biography of Whale, "Those looking for an exciting, well-paced monster movie are not disappointed. But adults and the more sophisticated can enjoy *Bride* as not so much a horror show as a whimsical fantasy and an exciting piece of cinema. *Bride* is frequently hilariously funny. What distinguishes it from a lot of other such films is that the humor is entirely intentional."[3]

A third, relatively unexplored quality is the film's presentation of sexual issues. This lack of attention is surprising, since *Bride*'s status as a cult classic depends in no small way on the sexual themes and motifs that run rampant through it. In addition to offering a depiction of "normal" heterosexual love, the film is replete with veiled references to bisexuality, homosexuality, necrophilia, incest, the Oedipus complex, and the Virgin Birth, and also features a prominent sperm-egg metaphor.

The genesis of *Bride of Frankenstein* is itself a strange story. The original *Frankenstein*, featuring Boris Karloff as the Monster, proved so successful at the box office that Carl Laemmle, Jr., the film's producer, immediately made plans for a sequel. Whale, however, initially wanted nothing to do with the new project, tentatively titled *The Return of Frankenstein*. Said he of Laemmle and producers in general:

They're always like that. If they score a hit with a picture they always want to do it again. They've got a perfectly sound commercial reason. *Frankenstein* was a gold-mine at the box office, and a sequel is bound to win, however rotten it is. They've had a script made for a sequel, and it stinks to heaven. In any case, I squeezed the idea dry on the original picture, and I never want to work on it again.

Nevertheless, Whale eventually relented and agreed to direct the film. He decided to treat the project as a "hoot," however, and had "no intention of making a straight sequel to *Frankenstein*."[4]

One of the first tasks facing Whale and scenarists William Hurlbut and John L. Balderston was to build a new story from the literal ashes of *Frankenstein*'s conclusion: the Monster's fiery end in an old windmill. Despite the seeming definitiveness of this scene, the filmmakers managed to continue the story in the now-retitled *Bride of Frankenstein* by showing that the Monster (again played by Karloff) had avoided a barbecued fate by falling into the mill's conveniently flooded cellar. The filmmakers gave this explanation more credibility by framing the new film with a short prologue that features *Frankenstein* author Mary Shelley (Elsa Lanchester) weaving a sequel to her famous novel for an enraptured Lord Byron and Percy Bysshe Shelley. The story she spins is indeed bizarre.

As the Monster lays waste to the countryside once again, the loving Elizabeth nurses her fiancé, Baron Henry Frankenstein,

back to health from the ravages of his frightening ordeal. Their
tender moments are shattered in short order by the arrival of
Dr. Pretorius, an eccentric old scientist who, like Frankenstein,
engages in grave-robbing to meet an obsessive end: the artificial
creation of life. He proposes to Frankenstein that they work
together to create a woman, but the younger scientist, still shaken
from the heinous results of his previous experiment, will have
none of it. Undaunted, Pretorius enlists the aid of the Monster
to convince Frankenstein of his proposed project's worthiness.
The Monster obliges by abducting Elizabeth and holding her
captive until Frankenstein and Pretorius make a woman for him.
The scientists eventually create a Monstress (Elsa Lanchester, in
a dual role) stitched together from corpse bits and animated by
lightning bolts, but the Monstress rejects the Monster and develops an attraction to Dr. Frankenstein. In response to this
unanticipated turn of events, a deeply wounded Monster blows
the laboratory, himself, the Monstress, and Pretorius to smith-
ereens after allowing Frankenstein and Elizabeth to escape.

With aberrant procreation and "love among the dead" as its
main foci, *Bride* cannot help but raise questions concerning sexuality. The answers do not coalesce into any single, neat, un-
ambiguous interpretation, however; though they overlap, they
often conflict. Since *Bride*'s sexual themes and motifs are con-
siderably varied, they are best discussed in terms of a series of
love triangles that structure the film.

Elizabeth, Pretorius, and Henry, who respectively exemplify
heterosexuality, homosexuality, and bisexuality, constitute the
first love triangle. Without question, the premiere heterosexual
in the film is Elizabeth, technically the "Bride" of the title (though
there are a number of other contenders for this titular honor).
She is engaged to Henry, and her love for him seems genuine
if not downright obsessive. Indeed, neither her dogged devotion
to the troubled Henry nor her love for him ever wavers. If anything, they grow even stronger when it appears as if the Monster
has permanently deferred their wedding by nearly killing Henry
on the day it was to have occurred. The filmmakers not only
endow Elizabeth with the "mainstream" sexual orientation, but
also made her the sanest and least "hung up" of all the characters. Hers is the only voice of reason, of common sense, in

the entire film. Indeed, next to such unquestionably fey characters as Henry, Pretorius, their squirrelly grave-robbing assistant Karl, and Henry's paroxysmal housekeeper Minnie, Elizabeth is a bedrock of normalcy. The filmmakers do allow her one flight of fancy, however; on the night of their would-be wedding, she tells Henry with mounting hysteria that she has seen a strange apparition: "It comes, a figure like Death, and each time he comes more clearly...nearer. It seems to be reaching out for you, as if it would take you away from me."[5]

Her words are prescient, for within moments her rival for Henry appears at the door. Dr. Pretorius, described by critic Carlos Clarens as exuding a "waspish effeminacy,"[6] represents the homosexual in the love triangle formed by the three principal characters. He is a threat to Elizabeth and Henry's relationship; his attempts to convince Henry to work with him to create artificial life constitute nothing less than a seduction, and threaten to pull the couple apart. Arriving at the Frankenstein manor late at night "on a secret matter of grave importance" (tongue securely in cheek, no doubt), Pretorius tells Henry his business with him is private and insists on their being alone. The first thing Pretorius says to Henry after Elizabeth has withdrawn is, "We must work together" to create new life, but Henry vehemently rejects this proposal. In discussing their past experiments, Pretorius claims he and Henry "have gone too far to stop, nor can it be stopped so easily." After Pretorius tells Henry that he too has created life, Henry suddenly drops his opposition and becomes very interested. That very evening, when Henry and Elizabeth would otherwise have shared their first honeymoon night, Henry and Pretorius run off to the latter's laboratory and leave Elizabeth behind. In a sense, Pretorius is as much a claimant to the title "Bride of Frankenstein" as Elizabeth.

Pretorius needs Henry's assistance to create a new race. He is so desperate to create life—but without female participation—that he has already grown miniature human beings from seed, beings he eagerly shows to Henry as proof of his "fertility." Pretorius observes to his would-be consort, "My experiments did not turn out quite like yours, Henry, but science, like love, has her little surprises." He invokes the first chapter of Genesis in describing his plan:

Pretorius: Leave the charnel house and follow the lead of Nature, or of God if you like your Bible stories. "Male *and* female created he them. Be fruitful and multiply." Create a race, a manmade race, upon the face of the earth. Why not?

Henry: I daren't. I daren't even think of such a thing.

Pretorius: Our mad dream is only half realized. Alone you have created a man. Now, together, we will create his mate.

Henry: (leaning forward): You mean . . . ?

Pretorius: Yes. A woman. That should be *really* interesting.

Representing the bisexual caught between the advances of Elizabeth and Pretorius, Henry is easily the most troubled of all the characters. He desires a normal relationship with a woman, yet is quite amenable to Pretorius's seductive powers. His resultant behavior—frequent and agonized vacillations between Elizabeth and Pretorius—borders on the schizophrenic. He is secretly relieved that he must work with Pretorius to create a mate for the Monster to save Elizabeth; he is thus able to serve both "brides" simultaneously—while, ironically, creating a third.

A number of critics, most notably Roy Huss,[7] have paid special attention to the pyrotechnics that suffuse the creation scene in *Bride of Frankenstein*. With its rapid editing, dramatic high-contrast lighting, flashing lights, flying sparks, smoke, fire, pulsing buzz of electrical equipment, frequent explosions, and throbbing musical score, the scene unmistakably resembles an extended orgasm. Its climax—lightning striking the inert female body raised on a platform high above the laboratory floor—thus takes on a new meaning; the body, consisting of corpse bits that Henry and Pretorius have stitched together, may be likened to an egg, while the lightning may symbolize the sperm that penetrates it. A line of Karl's dialogue early in the creation scene—"The storm is rising!"—reinforces this association with its suggestion that nature is experiencing a tumescence. Metaphorically, then, the doctors are linked with the female principle, the ovum, while nature, in the form of the lightning, is associated with the male principle, the sperm. Natural and unnatural forces, in the respective forms of lightning and the sutured body, thus combine to create life. It is as if Henry and Pretorius, knowing they cannot between them bring a child into being through sexual union, create instead the female contribution to the embryo-to-be; having thus "ovulated," the doctors then arrange for their egg to be fertilized.

Critics have discovered a number of Christian allegories in *Bride*, most notably in the scene in which the Monster is shackled to a crosslike structure by angry villagers.[8] Conspicuously absent from this discussion is any consideration of the creation of the Monstress, which is a Virgin Birth. By equating Nature with God, Pretorius invites the film's audience to find in *Bride of Frankenstein* references to the nativity; just as Jesus was born of Mary and God in the form of the Holy Ghost, the Monstress is conceived (and thoroughly maculated) by two human "mothers" and Nature in the form of the lightning. The strange triangle formed by Henry, Pretorius, and Elizabeth is superseded by an even stranger *ménage à trois* consisting of Henry, Pretorius, and a decidedly potent Nature.

A third love triangle, formed by Elizabeth, Henry, and the Monster, resembles nothing so much as a manifestation of the Oedipal complex. Tania Modleski has echoed a number of modern critics in opining that "all traditional narratives re-enact the male Oedipal crisis."[9] While this assertion is no doubt moot, the Oedipal complex does act as a major structuring element in *Bride of Frankenstein*. The Monster's awkward movements and halting speech (he actually learns a few words in this film) reinforce the natural inclination to accept him as Henry's metaphorical child, and his smoldering hatred for Henry suggests he has entered the phallic stage of development. The Monster's feelings toward Henry, his clear father figure, contrast sharply with his feelings toward many others in the film. Despite the townspeople's xenophobia, the Monster craves friendship and eagerly seeks it in almost every individual he meets: a blind hermit, Pretorius, the Monstress. "Alone—bad. Friend—good!" he rumbles at one point. In a most pathetic scene, he ironically queries "Friend?" of a beautiful female corpse he has stumbled upon inside a crypt. Yet he immediately grows sullen when his newfound friend Pretorius asks him if he knows Henry. Bitterly, he responds, "Yes, I know. Made me, from dead. I love dead. Hate living." The Monster has his gentle moments in this film, but virtually all his scenes with Henry are marked by expressions of enmity that range from glowering at the mere thought of his "father," to ordering the poor scientist about, to threatening him with violence. In a distinctly Oedipal act of hostility, the Monster abducts Elizabeth and holds her captive in a cave while Henry and Pretorius work together to create his mate. The Monster's demand for a wife represents a possible resolution of his Oedipal crisis. He definitively resolves it at the end of the film in telling Henry to go back to Elizabeth before obliterating himself, Pretorius, and the Monstress.

The Monster, the Monstress, and Henry form a tenuous love triangle that hinges on one of the movie's ambiguities: the real identity of the "Bride of Frankenstein." The official title of the film, *Bride of Frankenstein* (not *The Bride of Frankenstein*, as some sources list it), underscores this uncertainty. The absence of the definite article suggests the possibility of more than one bride: Elizabeth, Pretorius, even the Monstress. The Monstress would not normally be listed among Henry's potential mates were it not for a conspicuous deletion from the screenplay and a troublesome line of dialogue that is retained. The script originally called for Karl to murder Elizabeth and bring her body back to the laboratory after the doctors summon him to find a fresh female corpse. Had this scene been included in the final film, two contenders for the title role would have been combined into one.

The troublesome line of dialogue occurs immediately after the Monstress is brought to life and unveiled; Pretorius delightedly proclaims her "the Bride of Frankenstein" as a wedding-bell motif plays in the background. Over the years, audiences have associated the name "Frankenstein" with the Monster, but it actually refers only to Henry Frankenstein, the hapless young doctor played in the movies by Colin Clive. Throughout both *Frankenstein* and *Bride of Frankenstein*, the filmmakers scrupulously adhered to the correct usage, with this one possible exception. If it is not a mistake, then Pretorius may view the new creature as Henry's bride, not the Monster's, and thus suggest a symbolically incestuous relationship, as Henry is a parental figure for her just as he is for the original Monster. This potential relationship is suggested further by the fact that the Monstress, after registering her disgust for the Monster with an ear-splitting shriek, is unmistakably drawn to her creator. Protective of her new "mate," she even shields Henry with her body from the others in the room. The movie in any case suggests an incestuous relationship between the Monstress and the Monster, Henry's other metaphorical offspring whose "sister"—or, perhaps, "half sister," considering Pretorius' involvement—humiliatingly rebuffs his romantic advances.

Incest is only one of several dark aspects of human sexuality suggested by the Monster/Monstress/Henry triangle; necrophilia is another. If this term refers not only to an erotic attraction to corpses but also to an abnormal fascination with the dead in general, then *Bride of Frankenstein* is a veritable necrophilic love-in. The Monster's utterance, "I love dead," is only the most overt of the many references to a necrophilic fascination lurking at the heart of this film, which is based on the bizarre premise that two entities constructed from pieces of previously dead bodies are about to be united in holy matrimony. Universal was quick to exploit this grotesque "love story" angle—and at the same time to satirize the conventional Hollywood love story— in its promotion of the film, which featured images of the Karloff and Lanchester characters gazing tenderly into each other's eyes. The interests of the scientists and their body-snatching helpers, particularly as revealed in the grave-robbing scene, further illustrate the film's flirtation with necrophilia. When Pretorius and his assistants come across the remains of a young woman in a crypt, Karl remarks, "Pretty little thing in her way, wasn't she?" Pretorius responds, "I hope her bones are firm." Later, Pretorius is enjoying a candlelight dinner in the crypt, his only "companion" the skeletal detritus of a woman, when the Monster interrupts him (or them, perhaps). Hinting at a fifth love triangle (Pretorius/Monstress-to-be/Monster), the scene concludes with a reiteration of the movie's aberrant love theme; after Pretorius promises that a woman will be made for him, the Monster gently examines the disconnected skull of his "betrothed" and slowly intones, "Woman, friend, wife."

In summation, the many sexual references in *Bride of Franken-stein* may be seen as elaborations of several love triangles: Pretorius/Henry/Elizabeth, who represent hetero-, homo-, and bisexuality; Pretorius/Henry/Nature, through which the mystery of conception takes on a preternatural, mock-religious quality; Henry/Elizabeth/Monster, which embodies the Oedipal triangle; and Henry/Monstress/Monster and Pretorius/Monstress-to-be/ Monster, which reverberate with the unsavory suggestions of incest and necrophilia. With Henry a conspicuous component of each *ménage à trois* save the last, the film might well have been subtitled "The Many Loves of Henry Frankenstein." More importantly, *Bride* has taken such archetypal subject matter as the mysteries of birth, death, sexuality, love, marriage, and religion, turned them upside down, turned them inside out, and intermingled them in such unexpected ways as to subvert or defile them all.

The most disturbing aspect of *Bride of Frankenstein* is its understated degradation of women and indictment of their role in reproduction. Ordinarily, of course, men cannot give birth, yet they manage to do so (albeit with disastrous results) in this film. Moreover, the scientists seem shockingly unconcerned when they sense that Karl, whom they have commissioned to retrieve the body of a recently deceased young female, plans to commit murder; when Henry feebly notes that "There are always accidental deaths occurring," Pretorius replies laconically, "Always." Mesmerized by the promises of a huge reward, Karl does murder an anonymous young woman, an act only one step removed from the filmmakers' original plan to have him kill Elizabeth. There is also the bondage imagery associated with the Monstress, whom the doctors initially immobilize with metal bonds and the bandages that cover her, mummylike, from head to foot. Even after she is free of these restraints, she remains figuratively (and sometimes literally) in the grip of the scientists. And while Elizabeth is the most sympathetically treated of the female characters, she too is victimized by men; most notably, she is abducted and held hostage by the Monster. On a more subtle level, she lacks any "personhood" apart from her relationship to Henry; her identity is presented solely in terms of the man to whom she is engaged. Her background, her interests apart from Henry, even her prenuptial surname remain enigmatic.

Since Whale was a known homosexual,[10] one might assume

that his sexual preference contributed to some extent to the aura
of misogyny that lurks beneath the humor and horror of the
film, although no particularly dark or bitter tone tinges its superficial depiction of women. The film's many sexual references,
quirky humor, and overall kinkiness may have been responsible
for its initially limited appeal to the moviegoing public. As Curtis
has suggested, "The problem with the film was that it was a
little too much toward Whale's own peculiar tastes to relate fully
to the mass audiences of the period."[11] These same qualities,
however, enabled Whale to give birth to something significantly
his own: one of the film world's first camp classics.

NOTES

1. Frank S. Nugent, review of *Bride of Frankenstein*, *New York Times*,
May 11, 1939, p. 21.

2. Michael G. Fitzgerald, *Universal Pictures: A Panoramic History in
Words, Pictures, and Filmographies* (New Rochelle, N.Y.: Arlington House,
1977), p. 105. John Brosnan offers a dissenting view in stating that he
has never found either *Frankenstein* or *Bride of Frankenstein* to be hor-
rifying, only beautiful. See John Brosnan, *The Horror People* (New York:
St. Martins Press, 1976), p. 4.

3. James Curtis, *James Whale* (Metuchen, N.J.: Scarecrow Press, 1982),
p. x.

4. Curtis, pp. 102–103, xii, 118.

5. All dialogue appearing in this article is taken directly from the
film's soundtrack.

6. Carlos Clarens, *An Illustrated History of the Horror Film* (New York:
Capricorn Books, 1976), p. 67.

7. Roy Huss, "Almost Eve: The Creation Scene in *The Bride of Frankenstein*," in *Focus on the Horror Film*, eds. Roy Huss and T. J. Ross
(Englewood Cliffs, N.J.: Prentice-Hall, 1972), pp. 74–82.

8. Clarens, p. 69; Harvey R. Greenberg, *The Movies on Your Mind*
(New York: Saturday Review Press, 1975), pp. 215–216; Marge Baumgarten, "*Bride of Frankenstein*," *CinemaTexas Film Notes* 13 (September 7,
1977): 23–24.

9. Tania Modleski, "Never to Be Thirty-Six Years Old: *Rebecca* as
Female Oedipal Drama," *Wide Angle* 5 (1982): 34.

10. Brosnan, p. 72; Curtis, p. xix.

11. Curtis, p. 127.

12

Sexuality and Identity in *The Rocky Horror Picture Show*

JOHN KILGORE

In the decade since its virtually unnoticed release in 1974, *The Rocky Horror Picture Show* has risen to a position of unique preeminence among America's "cult films." Attended in steadily increasing numbers by largely teenaged, extraordinarily devoted audiences, the low-budget rock musical has spawned an elaborate viewer-participation ritual that gives new literalness to the term "cult," and that is by now more notorious than anything that happens on the screen itself. Among the faithful, this point is never in dispute: It is the audience as much as the film that makes *Rocky Horror* worth seeing.

At the right sort of theater, the film is shown regularly at midnight on Fridays or Saturdays. Serious devotees arrive costumed as their favorite screen characters and equipped with such props as flashlights, squirt guns, and bags of rice. Most of them will already have seen the film often enough to have memorized not only the dialogue but virtually every gesture and camera angle. As the lights dim, the audience affirms its basic loyalties by chanting, "Sex! Drugs! Rock 'n' roll! Rocky Horror Picture Show!" This litany gives way to a rhythmic cry of "Lips! Lips! Lips!"—whereupon a gargantuan red mouth appears on the screen. And so it goes, without letup, for the next two hours. The crowd dances through "The Time Warp" and shines flashlights during "There's a Light." It tosses rice during the wedding scene and simulates a thunderstorm with squirt guns. And it fills up anticipated pauses in the dialogue with droll, smutty, ingenious commentary of its own, most of its established and traditional but some of it ad-lib. For example, the audience invariably shouts "What do you think of oral sex?" just before Frank N. Furter, on-screen and responding to another question entirely, smacks his lips and exclaims, "Excellent!"[1]

The plot of the film—it does have one—is a scrapbook of Hollywood clichés approached in a manner that varies from parody to camp nostalgia to serious reinterpretation. One dark and stormy night, Brad and Janet—two absurdly clean-cut young lovers—have car trouble. Seeking help at a lonely castle somewhere in Ohio, they meet Riff Raff, the hunchbacked assistant. He ushers them into the main ballroom and the "Annual Transylvanian Convention," an assemblage whose wardrobe might have been codesigned by Fellini and Walt Disney. Then, in a moment the audience greets with the warmest applause, Frank N. Furter, the film's hero and resident mad scientist, appears. An unforgettably androgynous composite of Dracula, white-faced minstrel, cabaret chanteuse, muscleman, stripper, and Phantom of the Opera, he flings off his cape to reveal his infamous fantasy-in-black drag outfit—sequined corset, fishnet stockings, and all—and sings a wonderfully lewd number that identifies him as a "Sweet transvestite from Transsexual Transylvania."

The goggling Brad and Janet are then stripped to their skivvies and whisked upstairs to the Master's lab to witness the animation of Rocky, the artificial man Frank N. Furter has been constructing. In contrast to literary and cinematic tradition, Rocky emerges from his mummy-wraps no monster but a gleaming vision of thickly muscled, blue-eyed, blond perfection—a creature ideally suited to the "playmate" role his cad of a creator intends for him. Frank swoons in Pygmalionesque ecstasy at the first sight of his creation. But the animation scene sours with the arrival of Frank's ex-lover, Eddie, a beefy punk-figure recycled from 1950s biker films whom Frank murders with a pickaxe.

In the night that follows, Frank presides over Brad and Janet's passages from phony sexual innocence to an equally ridiculous sexual awakening: The good doctor seduces Janet by impersonating Brad, then Brad by impersonating Janet. Meanwhile, Rocky breaks his chains, escapes, and eventually winds up in the arms of Janet, who proves comically eager to exchange postcoital repentance for renewed arousal. The shenanigans cease temporarily with the arrival of Dr. Scott, an all-purpose authority figure. (He is Eddie's uncle, Brad and Janet's former teacher, and a government investigator.) And the whole group next sits down to dinner only to rise in indignation when Frank reveals that the main course is Eddie. Frank is compelled to subdue his mutinous guests by freezing them to the floor with a "sonic transducer" and turning them to stone with a "Medusa Ray."

Yet Frank N. Furter's ultimate intentions seem gentle enough. He dresses all his ossified guests in drag costumes identical to his own, reanimates them with his "de-Medusa Ray," and leads them into a swimming pool for some heavy communal fondling. But the frolic is terminated by the electrifying reentrance of Riff Raff, now humpless and splendidly recostumed as an extraterrestrial. Riff Raff reveals that he, Frank, and a few of the others comprise an expedition from "the planet of Transsexual in the galaxy of Transylvania." Apparently acting on orders from home, Riff Raff declares Frank's "lifestyle too extreme" and his mission, therefore, a failure. Assuming command, he kills both Frank and Rocky with his ray-gun, then teleports the whole mansion back to Transylvania.

One may feel that the relation of "cult" to "culture" is, in this case, strictly etymological. Yet, for all its gleeful camp absurdity, *Rocky Horror* also has surprising subtlety and depth. Modulating from farce to melodrama, using media clichés as a symbolic shorthand, incorporating visual and verbal allusions to everything from *The Wizard of Oz* to Michelangelo's *Creation of Adam*, the film sustains a witty and sometimes moving commentary on several fundamental themes: sexuality, identity, and the old tugof-war between Eros and repression.

Most simply, of course, *Rocky Horror* is a manifesto for sexand-whatever-else-feels-good. The crowd roots for Pleasure as if it were the home team, cheering on Frank N. Furter's transgressions while it hurls abuse at superego types like Brad and Dr. Scott. "Give yourself over to absolute pleasure," advises

Frank; and the "movie-novel" picture book issued by the *Rocky Horror* fan club confides, in fact, that "a feeling of love pervades this cult as they give themselves over to pleasure."[2]

It is surprising how deftly the film manages to enlist the conventions of the Hollywood horror and science fiction film in the service of this unlikely cause. Start with Frank N. Furter himself. In the myth that descends to Hollywood from Mary Shelley,[3] the mad scientist is a nervous, overachieving hyperintellectual, a slave to the controlling forces in his psyche. Frank, of course, is the direct opposite: In his flamboyant bisexuality, reminiscent of Alice Cooper, David Bowie, and Mick Jagger, he personifies sensuous release and the union of the sexes. The fact that *his* work produces Rocky rather than some patchwork monstrosity implies that Dionysian values, sexuality and excess, are incomparably more "creative" than Apollonian ones, self-discipline and willpower. The point is underscored later, in the swimming scene, by a fresco on the pool's bottom that duplicates Michelangelo's *Creation of Adam*.

Likewise, in converting Transylvania into an alien galaxy devoid of sexual taboos, the film offers a pithy comment on B-movie tradition: The real native land of monsters and aliens is the id. When the creatures slither out of the dark to kidnap cheerleaders, terrorize the town council, and suffer eventual defeat by whatever incarnation of Justice is most handy, they are enacting our own essentially ambivalent desires and fears. In the old films, the suspicion that the monster embodies some "outlaw" portion of ourselves is ubiquitous but obstinately murky; *Rocky Horror* provides considerable clarification. The voice singing the overture, for instance, admits to being enthralled by the latent erotic possibilities of *Day of the Triffids*: "And I really got hot / When I saw Jeanette Scott / Fight a Triffid that spits poison and kills."

Familiar, too, is the presumption that "society"—or at any rate some external force—is to blame for the monstrification of monsters, the twisting of healthy desires into shapes of horror and vindictiveness. Even in Shelley's original *Frankenstein*, the Monster's rage is explicitly the result of frustrated affection, and Hollywood has rarely forgotten the lesson. Within Quasimodo, King Kong, and Chaney's Wolfman beat innocently romantic hearts, and even such uncanny nemeses as the shark in *Jaws* and the Alien in *Alien* have their moments with the ladies, as if they could have been decent enough fellows given the right upbringing.

Rocky Horror parodies these themes and conventions, but with an affectionate touch, striving less for ridicule than for illumination. It prefers to make the sexual subtext explicit. Scraping off pounds of makeup and layers of evasion from Boris Karloff, the film discovers that the true essence of monsterdom is Rocky, the irresistible love child, the libido personified. When Janet meets the "creature," her sweet soprano response offers the last word on the relationship of princesses to toads, beasts, blobs, outlaws, giant apes, and all the other unlikely forms love can assume:

> Toucha toucha toucha touch me.
> I wanna be dirty!
> Thrill me chill me fulfill me,
> Creature of the night!

Other gothic and science fiction conventions receive much the same treatment. The film takes a comically Freudian approach to tradition, interpreting the old thrillers and space operas as overly sublimated fantasies best understood in terms of the sexual themes they so meticulously evade. The sinister scientist's ominously sibilant summons to his laboratory becomes a Mae West takeoff: "Come up to the lab, and see what's on the slab." "The Time Warp" is converted from a hazy pseudoscientific phenomenon to a sexy dance; its lyrics interpret "timelessness" as a type of erotic dizziness. Even the "scientific" hardware is recast to make previously more subtle sexual metaphors more evident. Frank N. Further writhes with pleasure as he activates an electromagnet; during the creation of Rocky, he squeals with delight while fiddling with a contraption that resembles a cow's udder.

This process of raising sexual subtexts to the surface extends to the central motif of the film. The weird proposition at the core of *Rocky Horror*—that building Rocky is the quintessential sexual act—proves finally convincing. Frank vis-à-vis Rocky is the father-mother of his husband-wife; theirs is an omnisexual relationship. More important, Frank's role as the creator of his own lover evokes the most romantic aspects of sexual love; like Pygmalion, Narcissus, and Percy Shelley rolled into one, he is determined to achieve union with an idealized second self. The element of naive idealism in his work is suggested by a priceless refrain, borrowed from the old Charles Atlas bodybuilding ads, that he sings in triumph during the creation scene: "In just seven days / I can make you a man!" Bodybuilding, with its wholesome overtones of conventional American self-improvement, is revealed as one more surrogate for the real thing: creature-making, or the full recreation of the self in sexual love.

Frank and Rocky, then, are alter egos, as creators and their creatures usually are.[4] But the key difference here is that Frank takes the onus of sexuality on himself, rather than project it onto his offspring; it is he rather than Rocky who is the monster. Hence, his role has messianic overtones, as the *Last Supper* tableau worked into the film's banquet scene suggests. Frank assumes the burden of monsterdom, of the "sins of the flesh." The final scene spoofs *King Kong* by casting Rocky as the giant ape and Frank as Fay Wray; unlike the heartless "Beauty that killed the Beast" in the older film, however, Frank shares his lover's demise.

Yet a Saturnalia's ritual loosing of inhibitions must take place within strict limits, and what is finally best about *Rocky Horror* is its sense of balance. The film only seems to preach the gospel of absolute pleasure; in reality it acknowledges the existence of sensible limitations. Frank's misadventures precipitate a traditional, retributive climax; long before this, his ill-mannered killing and eating of Eddie provides an adequate hint that his philosophy may be less than perfect. But the most essential note of caution, which is more subtle and continuous, is implicit throughout in Frank's bizarre polymorphism. Hedonism has transformed him into an endearingly ridiculous freak, a sexual Charlie Chaplin more likely to attract sympathy than emulation. If giving oneself over to pleasure means becoming what Frank is, the price seems rather high.

And apparently it does mean just that. When the film reaches its apogee of sensuousness in the swimming scene, the other characters do all look and behave like Frank-clones, or like zombies fresh from a shopping trip to Frederick's of Transylvania. Their change into drag outfits identical to Frank's clarifies the point that his transvestism has little to do with homosexuality as such: On the contrary, it suggests the potential vertigo of heterosexual union. As the cast descends into "the warm waters/ Of sins of the flesh," they chant a lyric a less perspicacious screenplay (or a Honda commercial) would have rendered, "Don't dream it, do it." However, the line is "Don't dream it, *be* it," and that makes all the difference. The real danger in sexuality is its transformative (or, as the film puts it, "transsexual") power. The passionate melting of bodies and egos carries a threat of metamorphosis; its price is a loss of identity, or at least of dignity and autonomy. Thus, Frank falls helplessly at the feet of Rocky, the love child. But Rocky himself is hardly any better off; his first angst-ridden words lament the helpless dependency that can accompany love: "The sword of Damocles is hanging over my head, / And I've got a feeling someone's going to be cutting the thread." This presentation of the ego as a frail fortress besieged by Eros probably is responsible for the film's special appeal to teenagers, and impresses them more deeply than could any cruder cautionary tactic.

In any case, it is clear all along that Frank's Reign of Pleasure must eventually give way to traditional authority. The symbolism of the death scene fulfills expectations of Nemesis with a kind of Wildean flippancy: Riff Raff's ray-gun is shaped like a pitchfork, evoking associations with both the aroused peasantry who pursue the monster in James Whale's *Frankenstein* and the *American Gothic* patriarch whom Riff Raff impersonates in a brief tableau early in *Rocky Horror*. In effect, community standards and "American decency" prove to be Frank's undoing.

It is a little strange, though, that Riff Raff should play the triggerman in this final scene. His action fulfills the cliché of the tortured assistant who at last takes vengeance on his brutal master. Yet the cliché is artfully dislocated. Frank's brutality vis-à-vis Riff Raff is little more than nominal, and for most of the night Riff Raff—with his demented leer and incestuous ogling of Magenta—seems to epitomize the spirit of Saturnalia nearly as much as Frank himself. Then, when he makes his nimble switch from fellow "creature of the night" to the Party of Decency, he actually takes command. Looking at the film as a whole, however, one sees that Riff Raff's strong point is versatility. His is the voice behind the giant lips synching the overture, his the farmer's face in the *American Gothic* shot, his the fey smirk that flicks across the screen before most of the scenes at the castle, so that he appears to be secretly guiding much of the action. The first lines he sings on-camera show him already thinking ahead, looking past the *Walpurgisnacht* of Frank's rule to the return of daylight and sanity:

> Darkness must go
> Down the river of night's dreaming;
> Flow morphia slow,
> Let the sunlight come streaming
> Into my life

A little later, he and Magenta tell Brad and Janet,

> Madness takes its toll.
> But listen closely
> Not for very much longer.
> I've got to keep control.

The fact that Riff Raff is played by Richard O'Brien, the screen-writer, lyricist, and composer, brings all this into focus: He stands for control, but for the enlightened, almost reluctant control of art and imagination. Though the *Last Supper* tableau briefly fore-casts him as Judas to Frank's Christ, Riff Raff finally emerges, not as a traitor, but as an attractive realist and middleman. If Frank represents what the audience in its wildest fantasies might wish for, Riff Raff represents what it will settle for.

Thus the boisterous crowd at *Rocky Horror* accepts from Riff Raff what it would accept from no one else, the restoration of order. There are no jeers as he guns down Frank and Rocky; and he displays his own ambivalence. As soon as the victims quit thrasing, Dr. Scott, despicable toady that he is, bleats, "You did right." In response Riff Raff stalks over and, for a moment, waves the ray-gun longingly under Scott's nose. Here is what he would *really* like to kill: the loathsome Janus-face of social respectability, half lackey and half martinent. But it is in the nature of things that Scott must survive while Frank dies. Riff Raff lets him go.

Nobody will claim that the audience leaves the theater in a Miltonic "calm of mind, all passion spent." Yet the noise level does decline appreciably during the last ten minutes or so of the film, and it is clear that *Rocky Horror* does not end where it began. The film moves from a raucous celebration of sexuality, through a lament for its dangers and confusions, to a final, sporting admission of the need to control it. Far from promoting rebellious sensuality, its ultimate "balance and reconciliation of opposites" leads in just the opposite direction—toward psychic detachment and an amiable acceptance of the need for compromise.

NOTES

1. For a fully detailed account of the origins and rituals of the *Rocky Horror* cult, see J. Hoberman and Jonathan Rosenbaum, *Midnight Movies* (New York: Harper and Row, 1983), chs. 1 and 7; pp. 321–327 offer a useful bibliography.

2. Richard Anobile, Richard O'Brien, and Jim Sharman, *The Official Rocky Horror Picture Show Movie Novel* (New York: A & W Publishers, 1980), unpaginated.

3. For a useful survey of film adaptations, see Albert J. Lavalley, "The Stage and Film Children of *Frankenstein*: A Survey," in *The Endurance of Frankenstein*, eds. George Levine and U. C. Knoepflamacher (Berkeley: University of California Press, 1979), pp. 243–289.

4. On the popularity of the doppelgänger interpretation of *Frankenstein*, see George Levine, "The Ambiguous Heritage of *Frankenstein*," in *The Endurance of Frankenstein*, pp. 14–16, and Kenneth Von Gunden, "The RH Factor," *Film Comment* 15 (September 1979), p. 55.

13

Dr. Freud Meets Dr. Frank N. Furter

RAYMOND RUBLE

Twentieth-century philosophers such as Paul Tillich and Susanne Langer have called attention to the important role symbols have played in depicting our visions of reality. While philosophers have had much to say about symbols, they have said little about their new vehicles, motion pictures and television, leaving these media to the film critic and the popular culture analyst. Motion pictures can fulfill the same functions in the symbolic recreation of existence as music or literature, but they have not yet been recognized as having this potential, undoubtedly in part because most of them are relatively inartistic. But most literature and music is also second-rate, or worse. The motion picture has been around for less than a century, however, and television is newer still. Perhaps the intellectual establishment has not noticed them yet.

Investigation of 20th Century Fox's *Rocky Horror Picture Show* may be a step towards bringing philosophy a bit more up-to-date. This film is unique in that it not only illustrates the age-old human conflict between reason and desire, but also succeeds in getting the audience itself to reenact this conflict. Richard O'Brien (who also plays Riff Raff) seems to have written the film with tongue in cheek and a copy of the collected works of Freud in hand. Thus, some understanding of Freud is necessary to a proper appreciation of this film.

Sigmund Freud's psychoanalytic theory of the human mind revolutionized our self-understanding. Following Descartes' lead, previous philosopher-psychologists had viewed human nature as essentially static and conscious. Freud decisively changed this picture by exhuming a metaphor of Plato's and presenting the mind as a committee. He argued that the mind is essentially dynamic, that each individual undergoes an evolutionary development that parallels the social development of the human species, and that consciousness (or ego) is a product of the preexistent unconscious (or id, the dynamic force of which is called the libido). In agreement with Descartes, Freud thought humans had an essential nature, which he called the id. The id consists of unconscious, instinctual desires—chiefly for pleasure (the pleasure principle) but also for death (the death wish). These instincts exist prior to consciousness. To Freudians a newborn is chiefly a mass of instincts seeking gratification, a libido. The id is naturally polymorphously perverse, but the maximization of gratification leads quickly to the development of the ego, which is constructed out of the id to serve the id. It becomes fixed upon the mother figures that surround it, those who supply it with nourishment and love. The satisfaction of the id's instinctual desires, experienced by the id as pleasure, causes the id to fixate upon the mother figure. In short, the id falls in love with whatever gratifies it, and experiences this gratification as sexually pleasing.

Growth is facilitated by the development of the ego, which is confronted quickly by cold, cruel reality. The individual id has rivals, each seeking its own self-gratification. To make matters worse, the gratification of one person's id frequently conflicts with that of another's. Thus, competition will direct the ego's development. With this Hobbesian recognition of natural conflict between humans, the philosophical basis of Freud's theory is complete. The war between the egos can only be settled by compromise. The ego is forced to recognize a reality greater than the puny power of the child, the ego of the father figure or social super ego. The forces of the father/society figure quickly become internalized, and by the time the child is three years old he has

become a full-fledged member of the species with his own committee of the unconscious, composed of the id, the ego, and the
superego.

Peace with other egos carries a heavy price. In exchange for
survival, the child is forced to capitulate to the demands of the
superego. This means the id will have to learn to delay and
defuse its incessant demands for instant gratification. The ego
must mediate between the conflicting demands of the id and
the superego, a heavy burden; failure to meet it causes neurotic
and psychotic behavior.

The Rocky Horror Picture Show does a superb job of unveiling
the hidden dynamics of the committee of the unconscious mind.
Representing the id are Dr. Frank N. Furter and the audience
of the movie; the ego is represented by Rocky Horror and Riff
Raff; the superego is represented by Dr. Scott and the Inspector.
Brad and Janet, the "normal" couple caught up in the action,
are two humans caught between the conflicting aims of the committee members. They represent the conscious mind.

Freud describes the id as polymorphously perverse—i.e., interested only in gratifying its every whim—and this surely describes Dr. Frank N. Furter, one of film history's most bizzarre
characters. From his grand entrance in drag to his death with
his creation, Rocky Horror, after a swimming-pool orgy, Frank
N. Furter relentlessly pursues the sexual conquest of all the other
members of the cast. Frank's theme is "give yourself over to
absolute pleasure; don't dream it, be it." He creates Rocky Horror "with blond hair and a tan" in order to "relieve his dynamic
tension." True to his philosophy, the good doctor seduces Little
Nell, Eddie, Brad, Janet, and Rocky. Had he survived long
enough, he undoubtedly would have seduced even the crippled
Dr. Scott.

But surely Frank N. Furter's greatest conquest is the film's
audience. The genius of *The Rocky Horror Picture Show* is its ability
to get the audience to identify with, to become, the id. Conventional movie decorum goes right out the window with each
performance. The *Rocky Horror* virgin is at first absolutely shocked
at how outrageously the audience behaves. Audience members
shout obscene, hilarious remarks throughout the movie; one
must see the film a number of times simply to hear most of

dialogue. But no one remains a virgin for long. And the audience, with its ad-lib dialogue, makes each showing a new and exciting experience, a fresh seduction. Fertility symbols like rice, water, and bread are thrown around the theater. The audience dances the wild "Time Warp" along with the film's characters. Libidos flower, like Frank N. Furter, only to die. By the end of the film the audience is completely exhausted from the effort.

The unconscious ego is represented by Rocky and Riff Raff. Frank N. Furter creates Rocky to satisfy his endless desires. But Rocky is not destined to live long enough to satisfy fully his Freudian role. "Reality" in the form of a laser gun puts an end to his brief career before he can fully mature.

Riff Raff, Frank's hunchbacked retainer, is a much more successful, fully integrated ego figure. He labors with diligence to satisfy Frank N. Furter's every whim until Frank's wildness becomes too much for him. Then, bowing to the will of the superego at the conclusion of the film, he kills Frank, assumes command of the Transylvanians, and leads them back to their home galaxy. Like the ego, Riff Raff is caught in an impossible position. He cannot serve that "wild and untamed thing" without precipitating his own destruction. "Frank N. Furter," he sings, "it's all over. Your mission is a failure. Your lifestyle's too extreme."

Reality in the form of social consciousness subjugates Frank's plans. The superego is clearly represented by Dr. Scott and the Inspector. Dr. Scott arrives on the scene as a governmental investigator of UFO phenomena. Confined to a wheelchair, he has no power (libido) of his own; yet he is all too familiar with Frank N. Furter, whom he believes must be prevented from completing the seduction of humankind. He is confident that Frank N. Furter's excessive lifestyle fully warrants his death, and assures Riff Raff, "You did the right thing; he had to die."

The Inspector shows up periodically to condemn the activities of Frank N. Furter's followers. His negative tone of voice, his raised eyebrows, the way he shakes his head constantly at the Transylvanians' shenanigans—all express society's obvious disapproval of Frank N. Furter's design. As would be expected, the id/audience hates the Inspector; it greets his every appearance with a constant rain of vile abuse. In the end the Inspector too washes his hands of moral responsibility for Frank N. Furter's murder.

Brad and Janet are the two earthlings around whom the plot turns. They represent two psyches undergoing a maturation process. At the beginning of the film they are both virgins who have just become engaged to one another and who are about to embark on an unwitting quest to discover their own sexuality. Brad represents the failure of this process to reach a healthy conclusion. He is no match for Frank N. Furter's wiles and is easily seduced. But he rejects his newfound sexuality: "Help me, mommy. Take this dream away from me," he laments. Freud calls this refusal to recognize one's own sexual desires repression. Brad refuses to recognize that he has dynamic sexual desires, and at the film's conclusion is a ruined person obviously in need of psychoanalytic therapy. The id/audience, as might be expected, treats him with absolute scorn, heaping on him some of its vilest epithets.

While Brad's fiancé, Janet, is initially as innocent as Brad and likewise falls victim to Frank N. Furter's power, she represents a healthy adjustment to her newfound sexuality. "Toucha toucha toucha touch me. I wanna be dirty," she cries after her seduction. While the audience at first treats her to the same abuse they heap on Brad, by the end of the movie she is no longer an object of ridicule. Unlike Brad, she is capable of growing into a complete, healthy personality following the liberating experiences provided by Frank. As Freud maintains, psychic health calls for us to recognize and accept our own basic sexual nature, not to reject it.

An audience unfamiliar with Freud will miss much of the richness of the film. But the allusive and symbolic richness of *Rocky Horror* aside, what is the relationship between its symbols and truth? Symbols and their first cousins, metaphors, are the vehicles through which films attempt to portray their conceptions of values and reality to us. There are two Western schools of thought that attempt to explain how this is possible. The first is Platonic, which is best articulated in Plato's *Republic*, Descartes' *Discourse on Method*, and Kant's *Critique of Pure Reason*. Broadly speaking, a Platonic view has the following characteristics: It assumes that truth and reality exist independently of the conscious mind; that truth and reality are constant and unchanging, and therefore knowable; that an absolutely objective methodology (logos) may be discovered, the application of which will assure the discovery of truth; and that art and its products are not and cannot be the means for discovering truth and reality.

The Platonist sees the world as an intrinsically organized collection of "brute facts" lying there to be discovered. It is the function of philosophy/science to discover truth. To do so the philosopher/scientist must discover some methodology, such as the scientific method, the proper application of which will reveal reality. From this viewpoint art is, if anything, an antimethod. The conceptions of the artist are creations of the imagination that are either intrinsically wrong because they are imaginary or, at best, may represent aids for picturing what the truth that has yet to be discovered may be like, aids that will be abandoned with the actual uncovering of the truth. Thus, in the Platonic worldview, symbols and metaphors would either serve to keep the truth from us (by distracting our attention and energies from the proper application of logical methods of discovery) or, at best, serve as models that may help us to devise proper ways of uncovering the truth. In no case could truth itself be presented by symbols or metaphors. From this perspective *Rocky Horror* represents an impediment to attaining truth.

Opposed to the Platonic view of symbols is one articulated best by Nietzsche. From Nietzsche's perspective, truth, beauty, and reality do not exist independently of the knowing mind because knowledge is not a discovery but a creation. In some ways truth and reality are fabrications of the psyche. Nietzsche argues,

What, then is truth? A mobile army of metaphors, metanyms, and anthropomorphisms—in short, a sum of relations, which have been enhanced, transposed, and embellished poetically and rhetorically, and which after long use seem firm, canonical, and obligatory to a people. Truths are illusions which we have forgotten are illusions; they are metaphors that have become worn out and have been drained of sensuous force.

To be truthful, according to Nietzsche, "means using the customary metaphors . . . the obligation to lie according to fixed conventions." Nietzsche calls these dead metaphors lies because they abstract from all the possible uses and interpretations of data to construct a "great columbarium of concepts, the graveyard of perceptions."[1]

Contrary to the Platonist, as might be expected, Nietzsche places a great emphasis on art and the products of the artistic imagination in representing—in fact, in creating—"truth, beauty, and reality." Only the philosopher-artist is a truly creative person. All of us remain alive by doing what the philosopher-artist does supremely well, by inventing symbols and metaphors, by interpreting the world, interacting with it, creating it. But all interpretations are necessarily incomplete, one-sided abstractions—lies. "Life needs illusions, that is, untruths which are taken for truths," Nietzsche asserts; "We have art in order not to die from the truth."[2]

Freud was a philosopher/artist. Nietzsche would have said of Freud, "He invents no new evidence; rather, he invents a new way of looking at the 'evidence.' It is only after Freud that these 'facts' become facts." The Freudian system of psychoanalysis was once a new group of metaphors, the function of which is to control and organize life. Prior to Freud, for example, there was no unconscious. The unconscious only came into existence when Freud imagined it to explain (i.e., control) certain phenomena. And now the Freudian system has in turn become for many the customary metaphor. Richard O'Brien uses it to say, "Look at the actions of Frank N. Furter, Rocky, etc., and you will see the unconscious forces of your own libido at work."

In the early part of this century Freud had to fight against well-entrenched metaphors (chiefly Cartesian) in order to establish his system. Those who find *Rocky Honor* dirty and disgusting still see the world largely through these Cartesian metaphors. But the Freudian revolution was successful; it has now become the status quo for many, the new set of lies that govern thinking. Now, when an audience sees *Rocky Horror*, it too will be under the spell of this metaphor, this bewitchment of the imagination. But this metaphor too is a lie, a one-sided abstraction, a graveyard of other possible perceptions. Each individual in the audience should exploit the range of his or her own imagination to become a philosopher-artist, and to avoid becoming mired in Truth.

NOTES

1. Friedrich Nietzsche, "On Truth and Lies in a Nonmoral Sense," in *Philosophy and Truth*, trans. Daniel Breazeale (Atlantic Highlands, N.J.: Humanities Press, 1979), pp. 84, 88.

2. Ibid., p. 16.

14

Alien: In Space, No One Can Hear Your Primal Scream

ANTHONY AMBROGIO

Alien has sometimes been criticized for its apparent lack of solid characterization and its plot holes. Steve Vertlieb maintains that *"Alien's* plot and script are its weakest elements."[1] Mark Carducci argues that *"Alien* is out of balance, as long on forward momentum and shock as it is short on logic, depth of characterization or at times even clarity."[2] And even *Alien's* associate producer, Ivor Powell, describes the film as "a hardcore adult cartoon" (*CFQ*, p. 32). If this criticism is justified, why is *Alien* an effective movie? Its director, Ridley Scott, claims that the film "works on a very visceral level and its only point is terror, and more terror" (*CFQ*, p. 12). But what is the impetus for that terror? It is not simply *Alien's* superficial tale of an isolated, trapped group of people struggling alone against some evil, inhuman, murderous menace. After all, that formula is ubiquitous in horror films, from haunted-house tales of the 1920s to such more recent *Alien* analogues as *The Thing* (1951; 1982) and the *Thing*-inspired *It! The Terror from Beyond Space* (1958). Nor is it *Alien's* stylish sets and cinematography, though these add to the film's effectiveness.

Alien's structure is similar to *Psycho's* (1960). Both films were criticized for excessive gore and violence, but both actually contain little on-screen carnage; they leave the worst of it to the

viewer's imagination, but startle viewers with an early, unexpected outburst of violence (the shower murder, the chest-burster) that so unsettles the audience by catching it off guard that
it remains on guard and apprehensive thereafter. Moreover,
voyeurism, perverse parent-child relations, and sexually motivated murders are similar motifs suffusing both films, although
in different ways. Manipulation of these motifs, as it does in
Psycho, creates the "terror" in *Alien*, and hence the film's impact.

Alien's images and events touch a nerve in us all by resonating
with some mythic archetype, as do most fantasy films that strive
to be popular successes. But *Alien* contains no myth of the dying
god, found in such films as *The Day the Earth Stood Still* (1951)
and *E. T.: The Extraterrestrial* (1982), nor the related quest for the
celestial that infuses *Close Encounters of the Third Kind* (1977).
Instead, *Alien* is a double-edged nightmare: Embodying every
child's worst fear, it subtextually suggests the problems of siblings, supposedly secure in their mother's bosom (here, the space
ship as womb), who are suddenly abandoned by their mother
and threatened by a sexually aggressive, child-molesting mon-
ster/"father" (the Alien). This phallic intruder first displaces them
in their mother's affections and then seeks to exploit them by
forcing on them the most horrendous aspect of adult sex—violent penetration. The W. H. Auden epigraph appended to the
finished screenplay—"Science fiction plucks from within us our
deepest fears and hopes, then shows them to us in rough disguise: the monster and the rocket" (*CFQ*, p. 13)—indicates that
the scenarists know which mythic nerve they are plucking.

Alien also suggests the first, terrible journey all must take
through the birth canal; only through this journey can the protagonists escape the "mother" who has betrayed them and
(though ill-equipped to do so) thus prevent their violation by
the phallic intruder. In this scheme, the *Nostromo*'s crew members enact dual symbolic roles, as children and as homunculi—
unborn fetuses scurrying about the womb, waiting to be born,
while some rough beast slouches after them. Caught between
Scylla and Charybdis—penis and vagina in the violent throes of
copulation—they become unwilling, uncomprehending performers in a primal scene. Others have advanced various facets
of the psychosexual interpretation of *Alien*[3]; however, no critic

has demonstrated the skillful coordination in the film of all these elements, and it is this failure to perceive the artistic integration of the film's motifs on this primal level that causes some to dismiss *Alien* as grossly imperfect or ill-constructed.

That the *Nostromo*'s crew members interact like children is evident. They are a close-knit, familial group and mimic the interplay among siblings. During their meals, for example, Yaphet Kotto's Parker delights in annoying the others (his "elder siblings," as they occupy positions of authority over him) with constant complaints; he is usually seconded in his childish grievances by his "twin" in the ship's hierarchy, his otherwise taciturn buddy, Brett. The crew members' nominally explicit relationship to the computer, aptly named Mother, that controls the ship and their lives is one of children to parent. And, like good children, they do not indulge in sex but exhibit a childlike naivete concerning it that is mirrored in their naive, inept responses to the Alien, who represents intrusive sexuality.

The ship, an extension of Mother, the computer, is the first "character" introduced in *Alien*. Panning across compartments and dollying down corridors, the camera implies that the ship is a presence—a rather ominous one, as the shadowy spaces and ponderous background music combine to suggest. Mother, the mind that is one with the body of the *Nostromo*, suddenly "awakens" and reveals herself by flashing her rapid thought processes on a telescreen. An empty space helmet's glass visor reflects the text that demonstrates her sentience, graphically anthropomorphizing this maternal intelligence that controls the ship.

Then Mother awakens her children, who are innocently sleeping together in their nursery. The crew members' coeducational dormitory and unconcern for each other's undress upon arising underscore their childlike disinterest in sexual matters. The imagery Vertlieb employs in describing this sequence is telling:

Her systems activated by a distress signal emanating from an uncharted planet, Mother releases the slumbering technicians from their womblike bedchambers prematurely so that they may . . . investigate the source of the emission. The sleeping quarters . . . are white and sterile. . . . The crew members arise wearing only white sheets or bikini briefs. It is as

though they are children awakening for the first time. Here in the simple
shelter of this hospital environment, these children in space awake from
. . . primal innocence . . . into a strange new world that they are entirely
unprepared for. (p.24)

"Primal innocence," "womblike bedchamber," "released prematurely," "white and sterile hospital environment": These and
other phrases, which quite accurately capture the scene's ambience, suggest a significance beyond the metaphorical that Vertlieb leaves quite unexplored. The crew sleeps (in one of the film's
many wombs) in a cryogenic state, and thus must be warmed
to be roused; the "womblike" beds are incubators, and as such
associate the awakening with the idea of hatching, being born.
The crew is awakened, or born, prematurely because it is nowhere near the end of its journey, its gestation. Moreover, its
members are literally not yet ready to deal with the matters that
now confront them. Their premature (in several senses) reani-
mation here is the first example of *Alien*'s several false/unnatural
births.

Sigourney Weaver, who plays Ripley, notes that the actors
"did a lot of improvising because the script was absolutely bare
bones."[4] The largely impromptu dialogue that results resembles
the babbling of a bunch of kids. Like kids, the characters often
react to hitherto unexperienced events; and the film's dialogue,
when it is not merely a vehicle for conveying information, is
often inconsequential and banal. While this may be seen as a
flaw, *Alien*'s unsophisticated dialogue and characterizations
reinforce the idea that its characters are not complete, that they
are going through a birthing and maturation process they only
partly comprehend and about which they are able to say nothing
particularly intelligent or insightful.

In the original screenplay, the *Nostromo*'s crew members were
all male (*CFQ*, p. 16). Making Ripley and Lambert female was
a fortuitous afterthought. While some critics still insist that Ripley and Lambert act like stereotypically helpless science fiction
females,[5] their sex is never an issue for their fellow crew members. They are as scruffy-looking as their coworkers, are never
thought of as members of a "weaker" sex, and share equally in
all shipboard duties. Lambert's frightened passivity when the

Alien is about to kill her is due to her innate character, not to her "femininity." Throughout the film, she is the reluctant, whining astronaut; when told to quit griping, she snaps, "I like to gripe." Never eager to go on a dangerous assignment, she is a foil to the gung-ho Kane, who is the first out of hypersleep, the first to volunteer for the expedition to the derelict ship, and the first to find and be attacked by the Alien. Lambert, in contrast, is the first to suggest abandoning ship.

Their unglamorous appearance and equal participation in the crew's activities demonstrate that the women are not aboard as sex objects, to service the males. They do not engage in sexual intercourse because they are professionals doing a job in a situation in which the close proximity of male and female does not automatically imply a physical relationship. But, on a mythic level, none of the characters engages in sexual intercourse because they are all children. And, like prepubescent tomboys, the women are treated as equals by the equally prepubescent men.

In contrast to the *Nostromo*'s crew (and especially its human members), the one markedly sexual, thoroughly noninnocent character in the film is the Alien. Its only purposes are self-preservation and reproduction, and it accomplishes both through penetration and violation, symbolic rape. In all its sentient incarnations it is almost pure phallus. Although it makes its first appearance in "female" form, the ovum, even here it bursts from the Alien egg's labial folds to penetrate virgin explorer Kane's faceplate (a hymen) and force itself down Kane's throat to deposit its seed. Here the film suddenly reverses what at first seems to be Kane and company's metaphorical penetration of the "female" derelict ship. The party enters the ship through an orifice, and Kane descends into a uterine chamber where he accidentally breaks the layer of light (another hymen) above the Alien's eggs. Since the Alien has previously penetrated the ship and raped its crew, it is natural to see the derelict ship as a ravaged womb, especially as it has become the depository for the Alien's eggs.

In its first ex-utero appearance, the Alien is a grotesque claw tenaciously gripping Kane's face; it also has one appendage wrapped around his neck as well as another thrust down his gullet. In the act of implanting its seed it is the quintessence of the grasping, groping, rapacious male. After a brief gestation period, Kane gives birth to the Alien's next form, the chest-burster. "Kane's son," mutters Ash later, after the Alien murders Brett. Its symbolic masculinity never in question, even the Alien's infant form effectively expresses its essential sexual nature: the ravenous, aggressive penis-as-weapon—ironically, a *penis dentata*. "I wanted it to be like an obscene phallic thing that was all mouth," says Scott.[6] It skitters away to mature in the *Nostromo*'s airshafts, those yonic corridors providing a natural habitat for the penis-creature.

The mature Alien's appearance likewise suggests its symbolic function as monster rapist. Its protruding steel tongue, dripping with lubricant, its tail, and especially its priapean head indicate its phallic nature. Its form was inspired by two drawings in H.R. Giger's *Necronomicon*, "Necronom II" and "Necronom IV," a fact variously reported and instantly confirmed by one glance at the paintings. As Palumbo points out, "The Alien's head in 'Necronom IV' is even more pronouncedly phallic than is the head of the film's Alien, and 'Necronom II' has what are unmistakably erect penises instead of tongues protruding from its death's head jaws."[7]

After the Alien matures, the audience almost always sees it tumefying—expanding, unfolding, and otherwise erecting itself as it prepares to strike. The Alien's own sense of arousal is vicerally conveyed to the audience through the excruciating suspense created during these scenes, and perhaps once through the audience's own experience of sexual arousal. At film's end, after Ripley escapes in the shuttle, she innocently begins to strip, leaving herself more symbolically open to attack and clearly revealing for the first time her woman's body underneath her unisex work clothes. Henry Golemba suggests that here, as Ripley's disrobing and half-nakedness are the only elements in *Alien* that could induce normal sexual excitement, "the movie invites the audience to be vicariously as monstrous for a moment as the alien." To prove his point, he describes the scene's eroticism:

Ripley sheds her sexless fatigues and strips down to her . . . bikini pants. . . . The camera lingers in a level frontal shot on Ripley's masked Venus mound, completely covered by a pure white triangle. . . . Her undershirt clings to her work shirt, lifts, and almost—maddeningly almost—exposes her left breast.

Ripley pulls her shirt down innocently, unaware of the audience's voyeurism, and . . . bends over the [control] panel's right side, thus exposing half her anal cleavage, and stands there bent over for a long, long time.[8]

Ripley's strip is shot from a subjective point of view, the Alien's, which literally does place the audience in the Alien's position— even though audiences are at this point overwhelmed, not by lust, but with empathic concern for Ripley's vulnerability. When the attack finally comes, the again tumescent Alien's protracted struggle to get free of the ducts and tubes in which it has nestled gives Ripley time to protect herself.

Throughout her crew's ordeal, however, Mother never seems to protect or help them. In fact, she is responsible for that ordeal; apparently acting on orders from "the Company," she has sent her children to procure the Alien—the invading penis for which she betrays them—for her. The trip to the storm planet on which they find the Alien is another of the film's false births: When the shuttle detaches itself from the *Nostromo*, Ripley, who remains behind, announces, "Umbilicus clear." Later she does not want to admit the Alien into the ship; she insists on following established quarantine procedure—probably obeying every mother's standing order not to open the door to strangers—until her will is subverted by Ash, who is acting in Mother's (and the Company's) behalf. The human crew later cannot understand why Mother and the science officer, Ash, are unable to help them against the intruder.

But the last survivors discover that Ash is a robot—and that he and Mother, both machines, have conspired to sacrifice the *Nostromo*'s human crew in order to protect the machinelike Alien. While viewers would probably have no trouble believing that a human Ash, who seems all along to be an "ordinary company stooge,"[9] would behave as the robot Ash does, it is more appropriate that Ash should be different from the humans on the *Nostromo* and more akin to both Mother and the Alien, his real allies. Mythically, Ash is not a real kid, like the rest of the crew; he is instead a midget, sexually aware, more sexually advanced than his brothers and sisters, in league with Mother, and envious/emulous of the Alien he protects. Ash is never really threatened by the Alien, and doesn't meet his end at its hands, because they are two of a kind. Like the Alien and Mother, he is defeated by the humans.

He is both revealed for what he is and then dispatched as he emulates the sexual rapacity of the Alien in attempting to murder Ripley through symbolic forced fellatio. This sequence begins with a suggestion of sibling rivalry. After Ash again feigns ignorance regarding the Alien, Ripley—who has inherited command of the ship through the deaths of the more senior crew—tells him, "I've got access to Mother now, and I'll get my own answers, thank you." She enters the ship's inner sanctum—the womb of wombs, the privileged place where, previously, only eldest child Dallas had been permitted—and finally gets Mother to admit her dark secret, that she is programmed to "Insure return of organism . . . All other considerations secondary. Crew expendable."

At this point thoroughly dejected because she now knows she has been supplanted in Mother's affections by the Alien, Ripley is confronted by Ash, whose seemingly effortless penetration of this area mocks the elaborate ritual she and Dallas had had to perform to gain admittance. In no mood to listen to Ash's unctuous reasoning, she lashes out at him. In reply, Ash foreshadows the Alien's final attack—symbolic attempted rape in the confines of the shuttle—by assaulting her and brutally attempting to shove a rolled-up magazine down her throat. The pin-up pictures on the wall behind them suggest that Ash's weapon is, appropriately enough, a men's magazine. The rolled-up magazine is Ash's surrogate penis, and Ash is in this scene a surrogate Alien. His sterile violation of Ripley, which can only result in her death, echoes the Alien's oral rape of Kane. Parker and Lambert come to Ripley's aid and, in bashing Ash into submission, discover he is a robot—a machine with organic innards that is physically an inverse double of the Alien, an organism with machinelike innards. Ash is decapitated, symbolically castrated in the struggle.

Ash's spectacular death was planned for Mother in the original script. Armed with her own surrogate phallus, a screwdriver, Ripley was to crawl inside Mother's most private parts to perform a symbolic hysterectomy, a parallel to the symbolic lobotomy sole survivor Bowman performs on Hal in *2001: A Space Odyssey* (1968). Ripley was to smash delicate glass crystals (Mother's ovaries) as Mother was alternately to scream at and plead with her child, whom she was to call a "bitch" and a "little cocksucker," to refrain. At the same time, Mother was to remove all the air from the compartment (denying the needed oxygen the placenta provides the fetus via the umbilical cord), forcing Ripley to struggle in a vacuum—the void created by the withdrawal of parental love.[10]

Though this confrontation within Mother's electrical circuitry would have demonstrated Ripley's Electra complex, the finished film's resolution of that complex is not so simple. Ripley doesn't destroy Mother until nearly the end, when she programs the ship to self-destruct. Even after initiating the self-destruct sequence, Ripley has difficulty abandoning Mother, especially after the Alien blocks her passage to the escape shuttle. To save herself, Ripley must override the self-destruct sequence; she seems to succeed just in the nick of time, but Mother ignores her child's efforts to save them both and dispassionately continues her countdown, the only time in the film when Mother speaks. Again reacting like a child betrayed, punished even though she has behaved herself and performed all her chores, Ripley first pleads—"Mother! I've turned the cooling unit back on. Mother!"—and then, ignored and unanswered, lashes out physically and verbally. But there is no alternative except for Ripley to try to make it to the shuttle and get away on her own.

Certainly Mother seems heartless and unfeeling in her final rejection of Ripley, but this is judging events from the child's perspective. Ripley cannot understand that Mother must force her to cut the apron strings, the umbilicus—to achieve finally a true, timely birth, the only one in the film. The screaming klaxons, strobing lights, and streaming gases represent the anguish of labor for Mother and child alike and cannot be stopped once set in motion. The split-screen explosion marking the *Nostromo*'s destruction is "feminine": labia opening to expel a child.

But there remains one last thing Ripley must do to prove she can survive on her own, especially since her birth/escape from Mother is not entirely an act of her own volition. Now in her own shuttle, her own womb, herself, she must once again meet and this time defeat the Alien by herself. Ripley uses "feminine" means to overcome the Alien, resorting only briefly (and with near-disastrous results) to anything phallic. After clothing herself in her own egg, a spacesuit, she straps herself in her chair and depressurizes the cabin, forcing the Alien almost out the shuttle door. To eject it completely, however, she fires the grappling hook; ironically, her use of this phallic instrument allows the Alien to hang on, to climb back up the outside of the rocket and attempt one last penetration through the shuttle's exhaust. Ripley steps on the gas, finally employing Newtonian physics in the form of a stellar douche to rid herself of the creature for good. Scott reports, "We used water for the exhaust effect . . . I wanted that whiteness" (*CFQ*, p.14).

With this victory, Ripley is inviolate, whole, and can now curl up in a womb of her own and sleep the sleep of the innocent. The film's last image, perhaps *Alien's* only unequivocally comforting shot, is a slow zoom in on Ripley in her cryogenic case, a sleeping beauty ready to be awakened by a kiss; *Alien* co-producer (and uncredited co-writer) David Giler admits the filmmakers "wanted a *Sleeping Beauty* ending" (*CFQ*, p.20). In its return-to-the-womb conclusion, *Alien* is again reminiscent of *2001*, which ends with the star-child's return to Earth not yet free of its amniotic membrane. But, although the birth metaphor is very much a part of *2001*,[11] it is more appropriate here because the birth is earned through a stark, life-or-death confrontation the audience can comprehend, because the heroine has matured through her experience, not beyond humanity, but into a self-sufficient human being.

NOTES

1. Steve Vertlieb, "In Search of *Alien*," *Cinemacabre* 1, no. 2 (Fall 1979): 26. Further references to this article appear parenthetically in the text.

2. Mark Carducci, "Making *Alien*: Behind the Scenes," *Cinefantas-

tique 9, no. 1 (Fall 1979): 13. Further references to this article are cited in the notes and, parenthetically, in the text as *CFQ*.

3. See, for example, Vertlieb, who discusses the crew-as-children metaphor; Alex Eisenstein, "*Alien* Dissected," *Fantastic Films*, no. 13 (January 1980): 51–63, who makes valid points about the sibling-Mother relationship and the rape motif but ultimately misinterprets their significance; Henry Golemba, "Not Quite So Alien," a paper presented at the First International Conference on the Fantastic in the Arts, March 1980, who also articulates several important observations on the crew as siblings, Mother as mother, rape, and the explicit eroticism of the film's climax but often stops short of making necessary connections; and Donald Palumbo, "Loving That Machine; or, the Mechanical Egg: Sexual Mechanisms and Metaphors in Science Fiction Films," in *The Mechanical God: Machines in Science Fiction*, eds. Thomas P. Dunn and Richard D. Erlich (Westport, Conn.: Greenwood Press, 1982), pp. 117–128, who succinctly, insightfully enumerates several of *Alien*'s significant motifs but, in this discussion of a dozen science fiction films, fails to elaborate.

4. "An Interview with Sigourney Weaver," *Fantastic Films*, no. 12 (November 1979): 36.

5. See, for example, Vertlieb, p. 26, and Eisenstein, p. 58. For a discussion of Ripley as hero and the male critics' inability to accept the image of a strong woman *Alien* presents, see Rebecca Bell-Metereau's "Woman: The Other Alien in *Alien*," a paper presented at "Women Worldwalkers: New Dimensions of Science Fiction and Fantasy," the Sixteenth Annual Comparative Literature Symposium, Texas Tech University, Lubbock, TX, January 28, 1983.

6. "*Alien* from the Inside Out, Part I," *Fantastic Films*, no. 11 (October 1979): 34.

7. Palumbo, p. 122; see also *CFQ*, p. 23, and "*Alien* Pre-Production: The Artists," *Fantastic Films*, no. 11, (October 1979): 17.

8. Golemba, pp. 7–8.

9. Eisenstein, p. 58.

10. See co-producer and uncredited scenarist Walter Hill's draft of this scene, cited in *CFQ*, p. 17.

11. See Palumbo, pp. 122–123.

15

Pilgrims in Space: Puritan Ideology and the American Science Fiction Film

JIM HOLTE

In the vastness of space and the amplitude of time available to science fiction, anything conceivable is possible, and countless variations of our world have been created. Yet always there is something recognizable. We create our imaginary worlds from the raw stuff of the world we know. Japanese science fiction reflects a culture shattered by two atomic bombs; Soviet science fiction draws upon over a half century of collectivism; and American science fiction, especially in film, draws upon still older American myths and attitudes.

Forbidden Planet is a puritanical rewrite of *The Tempest. 2001: A Space Odyssey* is Stanley Kubrick's version of *Pilgrim's Progress*. *Star Wars* is a space opera replay of the American Revolution, complete with divine mandate. And *Outland* is an archetypal frontier showdown, *High Noon* in space. Each of these films draws on the popular concept of America's Puritan heritage—one of the first and most powerful of America's indigenous cultural myths—in numerous ways. An essential element of this myth, evident in each film, is the repression of sexuality and concomitant understatement or denial of the importance of women. The tendency for mass culture in general, and the science fiction film in particular, to exploit popular mythology and replicate its elements explains why American science fiction has often—even characteristically—been a macho genre that ignores women and represses or sublimates sexuality.

Writing about film and society in *Film Theory and Criticism*, Gerald Mast and Marshall Cohen echo the French film theorists of *Cahiers du Cinéma*, who believe that "every film is part of the ideological superstructure which reflects a society's economic base. Inevitably, therefore, a Hollywood film will reflect the ideology of American capitalism. This ideological undertaking will, among other things, require the repression of politics and eroticism." Yet cultural attitudes may not be conscious constructs. Parker Tyler argues that

the true field of the movies is not art but myth, between which—in the sense "myth" is invariably used here—there is a perhaps unsuspected wide difference. Assuredly a myth is a fiction, and this is its bare link with art, but a myth is specifically a free, unharnessed fiction, a basic, prototypic pattern capable of many variations and distortions, many betrayals and disguises, even though it remains *imaginative* truth.

Whether as conscious reflections of ideology or disguised myth, basic cultural assumptions embedded in our national mythology often appear in our popular forms of entertainment.[1]

In *Regeneration Through Violence: The Mythology of the American Frontier 1600–1860*, Richard Slotkin defines the mythology of a nation as

the intelligible mask of that enigma called the "national character." Through myths the psychology and the world view of our cultural ancestors are transmitted to modern descendants, in such a way and with such power that our perception of contemporary reality and our ability to function in the world are directly, and often tragically, affected.[2]

To a greater degree than we are usually willing to admit, our contemporary wishes and dreams, narratives and dramas, are those of our fathers. Beneath the surface of many American science fiction films lies the pattern of one of the oldest mythological archetypes in our culture, the American Puritan.

During the past half century the simplistic image of the Puritan as grim bluestocking has been replaced by a more realistic picture. Vernon Parrington, Perry Miller, Sacvan Bercovitch, Richard Slotkin, and others have provided details that fill in the rough outline. Yet the myth of the Puritan lives on; perhaps it is nowhere better illustrated than by Hawthorne's steeple-crowned progenitor who, convinced he is one of the elect and viewing his life in the New World as a pilgrimage full of moral and spiritual significance, shuns sexuality and embraces work, spending his days building a city on a hill and his nights examining his conscience. This stereotype, while not the entire truth, has some validity. As Slotkin observes,

The Puritans' attitude toward the way in which myths express man's passional nature is a good index to their sexual attitudes. Sexual expression was synonymous with the sin of lust, save where such expression was placed under the patriarchial authority of marriage and where the passional element was repressed in favor of more reasoned and social behaviors.[3]

In America, the very word "Puritan" has become synonymous with sexual repression, but there are other essential elements in the Puritan character. In establishing the New Jerusalem, the Puritans drew upon a number of sources; the most influential were the *Old Testament* and the writings of John Calvin. Both sources suggested to the Puritan that the way to succeed on the heroic quest, the errand into the wilderness, was to establish a closed society committed to the great mission. Both in theory and practice, Puritan theocracy was moralistic and paternalistic. Dedication to the greater cause had precedence over any private desires.

This ideology can be seen clearly in the confrontation between the Puritans and Thomas Morton, founder of the free community at Merrymount. Hawthorne's "The Maypole of Merrymount," which depicts the Puritans' horror at the discovery of open sensuality and rigidity of their response, is the most famous fictionalization of this encounter. Puritan ideology stated that sexuality was an outward and visible sign of a corruption that would destroy any covenanted community beset with such real and immediate external dangers as the wilderness, the Indians, and a seemingly endless number of heresies. To confront the terrors of the unknown and continue his mission, the Puritan needed all the discipline and resolve he could muster. No distractions were permitted. It was enough to make anyone grim.

While the character type has endured, the external shape of the Puritan has changed over the years; it has been at different times that of the cowboy, the soldier, or the policeman. Recent science fiction films depict the Puritan as well, but transformed again to meet the demands and conventions of the genre. The Puritan may have traded in his steeple hat and black coat for a space helmet and thruster pack, but he is still dedicated to continuing the heroic quest and to avoiding or sublimating all serious sexual expression in the process. No single science fiction film completely captures the Puritan, but many draw on the values, ideologies, past narrative depictions, or popular images of the type. The Puritan and his attitude toward sexuality is alive and well, and can be found on our movie screens and in the popular imagination.

Director George Pal's *Forbidden Planet* (1956) retains the major elements of William Shakespeare's *The Tempest* while remaking it into a psychological space drama. An abandoned genius and his young daughter isolated for a number of years from the rest of mankind, magical servants, and a confused party of visitors provide a dramatization of the temptations of power. But, as a product of American culture, *Forbidden Planet* is ultimately more Puritan than Shakespearean. The plot is simple. In the year 2200 a space cruiser visits Altair Four to determine the fate of the previous mission to the planet. Upon landing, the crew members discover a scientist, Morbius (Prospero), his young daughter (Miranda), and their servant, Robby the Robot (Ariel). Altair Four, like Prospero's island, is a place of both terror and delight. Some unknown force on the planet kills the crewmen one by one, and yet the ruins left by the long-gone Altaireans suggest the possibility of dramatically enhancing human intelligence. Eventually the rescuers discover that the same abandoned underground structures that boost mental ability have released enormous forces from Morbius's id (Caliban), which are responsible for the deaths. Morbius dies, and the ship's captain finally rescues the young girl shortly before the planet itself explodes.

The nature of the film's deviations from its Elizabethan source

reveals the extent to which American and Puritan elements suffuse *Forbidden Planet*. *The Tempest* is a romantic comedy. Prospero, the island's ruler and master wizard, is in total control of
all the action; what dangers do appear are lessons meant to test
and instruct his daughter and the shipwrecked visitors. The
dangers are more illusory than actual; and Prospero's servants
are spirits, forces totally outside the world of man. In *Forbidden
Planet* the dangers are real; Morbius only mistakenly believes he
is in control of his environment; and his servant is a machine.
Other changes are even more significant.

The most obvious change is in the nature of the place itself.
Prospero's island, while seemingly hostile, is a garden, un-
spoiled nature under the watchful eye of a benign caretaker.
Altair Four is a curious combination of garden and desert, a
place of both potential perfection and potential destruction.
Everyone, eventually even Morbius, becomes aware of the contradiction, and no one can resolve it. Altair Four is, in fact, an
extrapolation of the Puritans' perception of the New World. The
Puritans saw and described the New World alternately as a wilderness, home of the Devil and full of evil, and as a garden, a
land of potential to be husbanded by the Saints. In numerous
Puritan sermons, narratives, and histories these two views stand
side by side. Facing a strange new land, the Puritans did not
know what to make of it. Neither do the pilgrims on Altair Four.

An equally important change occurs in the romantic subplot.
The Tempest both develops the sensual and sexual nature of the
love between Ferdinand and Miranda and suggests the darker
side of desire, the possibility of rape by Caliban. Miranda and
Ferdinand are attracted to each other physically as well as psych-
ically. Their sexuality develops, and they mature as characters
through the treatment given their maturing sexual awareness.
Morbius's daughter and the heroic cruiser captain, on the other
hand, are lovers only by convention. There is never any intimacy
between them; it is clear that they are supposed to be feeling
something, but one is too innocent and the other too dedicated
to duty for either to do more than gaze fondly at the other. All
the sexual energy of *The Tempest* has been sublimated in *Forbidden
Planet*.

Sublimation is, in fact, the central theme of the film. The force that threatens to destroy all the characters is the "monster" from the id. The id, according to Freud, is the source of instinctive energy seeking gratification according to the dictates of the pleasure principle. For the makers of *Forbidden Planet*, like their cultural ancestors, any manifestation of the id is literally a monster, and something to be fought. It is powerful: The brilliant civilization whose machines still hum below the surface of Altair Four was destroyed by it, and no mere man can withstand it. It wells up from those depths to which the Elizabethan treatment of sexuality has been expelled. Behind the enhanced intelligence of Morbius, the heroism of the captain, and the cheerful bleeps and whizzes of Robby the Robot lurks desire—a repressed sexuality that is presented as something monstrous, indomitable, and forbidden.

Stanley Kubrick's *2001: A Space Odyssey* (1968) is about many things: the origins of man, wise guardians from beyond the solar system, perhaps the meaning of life itself. Yet it is also curiously one-sided. There are almost no women in the film, and those few who do appear have insignificant roles. In *2001* the great quest belongs to men.

Amidst the sights and sounds of *2001*, and within its four-part narrative structure, the viewer has difficulty discerning the central theme. From a panorama of the Earth, moon, and sun in space, the film moves on to the first use of tools by prehistoric man, a voyage to the moon, an expedition towards Jupiter, death in an eighteenth-century drawing room, and an impending rebirth in the void above the Earth. The film moves full circle, visually ending where it began. But to what purpose?

The purpose is the rebirth, and the path is a pilgrimage. Kubrick's morality play is a futuristic *Pilgrim's Progress* in which mankind is literally born again. Kubrick employs two traditional Puritan conventions in his film. The first is his metaphoric use of the journey. The Puritans saw their passage through life as part of a larger design: The passage out of Egypt by the Children of Israel prefigured Christ's leading all men out of the bondage of sin; this in turn foreshadowed the Puritans leaving the Old World for the New, which was a microcosmic parallel to the microcosmic movement of the individual soul from damnation to salvation. Also parts of a larger design, the separate episodes of *2001* take on meaning in relation to each other. Each is a step on the path of conversion from ape to angel, but each is also part of the movement from ignorance to understanding. The physical journey is a real journey, but it is also an outward sign of an even greater, inward transformation.

The second Puritan convention informing *2001* is the focus on the individual. For the Puritan, the ultimate conflict was that between good and evil for the individual soul. While family and national considerations were important, personal salvation was primary. The entire movement of *2001* is from the communal to the personal. Each section narrows the scope of the action. The first episode focuses on the tribe. The second moves from Earth, family, and hostile nations to the moon and an elite scientific community. The third section involves two astronauts and a computer—until finally only one man survives to undergo alone the transformation experienced in section four. The protagonist symbolically leaves all earthly attachments behind before he is reborn. And rebirth is more than a metaphor in *2001*. The final image is that of a human embryo turning through space toward Earth, approaching the one moment of cosmic renewal to which all the film's recapitulation of human history has been leading.

What are we to make of the curious metamorphosis? The answer again lies in our cultural myths. *2001* is a refashioned version of the myth of America. The reports circulating in Europe during the sixteenth century emphasized the Edenic nature of the New World; and the extreme hope was to create a new man in the newly discovered paradise, an American Adam. Led by God, the Puritans and other settlers set out boldly into the unknown. In Kubrick's retelling of the tale, black slabs have replaced the word of God, and space, the ocean, but the quest for transformation remains the same.

The most curious part of the film is its almost total expurgation of women. But if the film is a disguised version of the American Quest, the absence of sexuality is not surprising. The film portrays in all of its sections patriarchal situations. Since each episode presents a significant moment in mankind's pilgrimage, it is fitting, following the dictates of Puritan ideology, that men should be the primary actors in the cosmic drama. Women are shown only as helpmates, until Kubrick introduces Hal. Then the computer with a problem becomes the helpmate, and the need for women is almost eliminated. But Kubrick's final image of rebirth, a sphere of light rising from the aged, dying astronaut's breast, is asexual. Now women are no longer needed at all; man has evolved beyond biology. The modern Puritans have, it seems, finally solved the problem of sexuality. *Forbidden Planet* demonstrates the sublimation of sexuality; *2001* suggests its elimination. With all women off the screen and out of the way, men can at last concentrate on important things.

George Lucas' *Star Wars* (1977) is an intergalactic fairy tale. In *An Introduction to American Movies* Steven Early acknowledges the film's innocence:

Audiences cheer the direct story line of *Star Wars*. Like the old-fashioned films of Douglas Fairbanks and Errol Flynn, the good guys are out to defeat the bad guys in a story of fast pursuit, unexpected encounters, and breathless escapes before sweeping to a happy ending. Lucas offers a tale of suspense and adventure with no message, no sex, and only a superficial sight of blood.[4]

Yet, while it may be innocent, *Star Wars* does suggest a message, and sexuality is present in a very traditional way. Luke Skywalker, Han Solo, and Princess Leia save the universe from Darth Vader and Grand Moff Tarkin while under the semidivine guidance of Obi-Wan Kenobi and the Force. At the end of the film evil is thwarted and crippled, if not completely eliminated, and there is a promise of a new beginning for the galaxy's freedom-loving inhabitants. But, as do all fairy tales, *Star Wars* draws on several cultural myths that play themselves out not so far beneath the surface.

Sacvan Bercovitch points out in "The Rites of Assent: Rhetoric, Ritual, and the Ideology of American Consensus" that the ideology of the Puritans' errand into the wilderness has become the shaping myth of American culture, the myth that defines how we look at ourselves and our history. In this view of history, migration becomes prophecy, and wars are more than mere struggles between nations; they become battles between good and evil. References to the apocalyptic nature of the conflict abound in *Star Wars*. Darth Vader is a Satanic figure, a servant of evil dressed in black who, like Lucifer, has fallen from grace. Obi-Wan Kenobi is like an Old Testament prophet, an outcast in the wilderness who is still wise and powerful. And the struggle, the "Rebellion," can be seen as a variation on the American Revolution.

The American Revolution confirmed the sacredness of the Puritan errand. Patriotic spokesmen considered that struggle "indissolubly linked with the Redeemer's mission . . . the wonder and the blessing of the world."[5] The victory of the rebel alliance over the Galactic Empire is presented in the same light. It too is guided by a divine hand. With the Force in one's corner—and its mediating spirit, Obi-Wan, calling the crucial shots—the victory belongs to the pure of heart.

And seldom in recent films have viewers seen two characters more pure of heart than Luke Skywalker and Princess Leia. Even Han Solo, the most "worldly" of the central trinity of heroes, exhibits adolescent coquettishness in place of mature sexuality. The heroes of *Star Wars* are essentially sexless. Leia's kiss is (with ironic propriety) more familial than erotic. All three act like shy twelve-year-olds, except that they seem to be even more unaware of their sexuality and its potential.

Again, this absurd innocence of character—while an aspect of the film's comic book charm—can also be seen as an outgrowth of Puritan ideology. First, sexual expression, either in action or awareness, is an obvious outward sign of sin or unworthiness. Thus, as the chosen agents of the Force, the heroes must be sexless. Second, the heroes are engaged in a heroic quest, the salvation of the universe. Leia is priggishly aware of the sacredness of her mission, and of her concomitant need for purity, from the film's beginning. As *Star Wars* progresses, first Luke and then Solo also become aware of this sacredness, and dedicate themselves to it. The quest is too important to risk letting sexuality interfere.

The surface innocence of *Star Wars* does not expunge the threat of sexuality altogether, however. Much of the film deals with Princess Leia's captivity, and the potential for sexuality is inherent in captivity narratives. Significantly, the captivity narrative was the dominant, most popular subgenre of frontier story published in America from 1680 to 1716, and it constitutes the first coherent myth-narrative developed in America for American audiences.[6] Captivity narratives, usually about women, stressed the values of perseverance, virtue, and faith in the face of threatened loss of identity and rape. Readers could, while finding edification in the virtue of the captive heroine, enjoy the vicarious erotic excitement of observing, and sharing, her perils. Such narratives were primarily optimistic and stressed the goodness of God. The captives usually returned with their virtue intact. Of all the forms of Puritan literature, the captivity narrative alone emphasized sexuality. *Star Wars* follows this pattern. Leia is pure and faithful, but her virtue must be tested at the hands of a dark and sinister man. A Puritan might be confused by the setting of *Star Wars*, but he would recognize the story.

Peter Hyam's *Outland* (1980) is another version of the frontier narrative, perhaps America's favorite tale. The earliest American literature—letters, reports, diaries, and histories of the Atlantic colonists—established the genre, and as the frontier moved westward the genre moved with it. On the frontier, the cutting edge of civilization, good and evil are thrown into sharp contrast; and a man, usually alone, must demonstrate his culture's moral and physical superiority over the chaos and evil he faces. The frontiersman, or cowboy, or policeman (in recent, urban-frontier adaptations) embodies the masculine ideals of the culture: He is strong, silent, unemotional, and both willing and able to resort to violence to solve problems. Other cultural ideals—learning, mercy, nurturing, taste—are embodied in the frontiersman's wife or lover, and she is usually shipped home or safely circled by the wagons prior to the major confrontation. Women, according to this pattern, only get in the way when the time comes for making the frontier safe for law and order.

In *Outland*, space stations, rockets, and pressure suits have replaced Tombstone, horses, and cowboy hats, but the story is the same. The frontier has moved into space. Io, one of the moons of Jupiter, has become a mining colony, and the space miners are much like their western counterparts. They work hard, play hard, and patronize the local prostitutes. The colony's marshall attempts alone to uphold law and order; but the mining company manager, to get more productivity from his workers, supplies them with illegal, ultimately deadly amphetamines. The moon soon isn't big enough for both of them; the lawman's wife returns to civilization; the company's hired guns arrive on the next shuttle; and the obligatory gunfight ensues. As usual on the frontier, law and order finally triumph over evil.

Outland illustrates the displacement of sexuality in a straightforward manner. The major action involves men, and those women who do appear are stereotyped. The marshall's wife, who represents both the family and committed sexuality, is shipped back to Earth at the beginning of the film, allowing the marshall the freedom to confront evil without the confining influence of culture or conscience. The company prostitutes are openly sexual, but they are either abstract objects of desire or convenient victims of violence, never individuals. The only woman who has a major part in the film fills a man's role, that of company doctor. As such, she plays the wise but cynical advisor to the marshall, performing the services of a mentor. Past fifty, and apparently long past caring about her own sexuality or anyone else's, she treats the marshall like a son.

Outland in particular demonstrates that the old, simple stories do not die. The essential images and narrative patterns are adapted to suit contemporary audiences, but the message remains the same—in this case, on the frontier real men don't need women. Science fiction portrays possibilities, but possibilities are fashioned on the past. When we look to science fiction to imagine our future, we often end up looking over our shoulders into the past. While there are many, and some far different, types of science fiction film, a Puritanical avoidance of sexuality—and even of women—characterizes the large number of them represented by these four examples.

NOTES

1. Gerald Mast and Marshall Cohen, *Film Theory and Criticism* (New York: Oxford University Press, 1979), pp. 742, 748.

2. Richard Slotkin, *Regeneration Through Violence: The Mythology of the American Frontier 1600–1860* (Middletown, Conn.: Wesleyan University Press, 1973), p. 3.

3. Slotkin, p. 47.

4. Steven Early, *An Introduction to American Movies* (New York: New American Library, 1978), p. 187.

5. Sacvan Bercovitch, *The American Self: Myth, Ideology, and Popular Culture* (Albuquerque: University of New Mexico Press, 1981), p. 14.

6. Slotkin, p. 95.

16

The Power of the Force: Sex in the *Star Wars* Trilogy

ANDREW GORDON

Sex in the *Star Wars* saga? But, one is tempted to say, these are only kiddie shows: In the entire trilogy, a quick kiss or two between Leia and Han Solo, or Leia's harem costume in *Return of the Jedi*, is about as sexy as it gets. In fact, by today's standards, the *Star Wars* series is remarkably chaste, even old-fashioned in its sexual restraint. Other recent science fiction films, such as *Saturn 3* or *Blade Runner*, base their appeal to a great extent on more graphic eroticism as well as more graphic violence.

But the bloodless violence and absence of overt sexuality is deliberate on the part of *Star Wars'* creator George Lucas. He designed the series to appeal to the prepubescent in us all, and wrote it for the twelve-year-old in himself. Twelve years old in 1956, and busy watching reruns of old "Flash Gordon" series on TV and *Forbidden Planet* at the movies, Lucas later crafted his space opera, for all its novelty, as a comforting blend of old and new that hearkens back to the relative sexual innocence of pre–1956 cinema. As Lucas's biographer Dale Pollock reports,

Lucas did all he could to quash [Carrie] Fisher's femininity. A long white dress covered her from throat to ankle. . . . Lucas went so far as to order Fisher's breasts taped to her chest with thick gaffer's electrical

tape. "No breasts bounce in space, there's no jiggling in the Empire,"
Fisher jokes. . . . Lucas simply didn't want sexuality in his fairy tale.

Yet the appeal of the *Star Wars* saga is in large part sensual, or
rather sensory. The films have the kinesthetic pleasure of a roller-
coaster ride. Lucas subjects the audience to sensory overload by
cramming visual information—numerous bizzare characters and
strange, new backgrounds—into each frame and bombarding
the viewer with loud sound effects and constant, pounding
music.[1]

In particular, Lucas eroticizes breakneck speed—in the frequent chase sequences, the pace of the action, the rapidity of
the cutting, and the movement across the frame. Audiences
burst into applause as the *Millennium Falcon* first makes the jump
into hyperspace. This is something many science fiction fans
had been reading about for years, but never before had they
seen it. "Let's all jump into hyperspace!" the movie seems to
say to the audience. The moment is a rush, a release of tension
parallel to a sexual experience. Lucas himself was an ardent car
racer as a teenager, as his *American Graffiti* (1973) suggests, and
has always been a lover of speed. By shifting from car chases
to spaceship chases, he has given that love of speed the widest
possible scope. It is not surprising, then, that an Ewok takes a
joyride on a stolen speeder bike in *Jedi*, for all three films can
be considered elaborate joyrides.

However, one critic of the first *Star Wars* films accuses Lucas
of de-eroticizing sex only in order to eroticize death. According
to Jonathan Rosenbaum,

the cursory treatment of romantic interest . . . leaves the way open for
a different sort of titillation. In the exhilarating space battles, with their
odourless ecstasies of annihilation, and the various space-gun skir-
mishes, with their fancy dismemberings and eliminations, this essentially becomes an occasion for sexual release devoid of any partner.[2]

Surely Rosenbaum exaggerates. Although the films romanticize
combat, they also dramatize pain and death. And the theatrical
experience of the films is communal, not "solitary, narcissistic,"
or masturbatory, as Rosenbaum implies. For sheer eroticism of

death, a filmgoer might try instead a movie directed by Sam Peckinpah.

Apart from the openly kinesthetic appeal of these films, the fundamental eroticism of the *Star Wars* trilogy lies in its plot structure, which is deliberately mythic and Oedipal, a true "family romance," as Freud would put it.[3] But in order to understand the hidden sexual struggle in the series, it is helpful to backtrack for a moment to the Lucas movie that preceded *Star Wars*, *American Graffiti*, for here the sexuality is more overt. If *American Graffiti* is an adolescent rites-of-passage film, then so are all of Lucas's films thus far, and it is in the adolescent and prepubescent struggle for sexual identity that their erotic interest lies. This is not so narrow a territory as it might seem, for every human being who reaches adulthood is permanently shaped by such struggles—and for many adults, the combat never ends.

The setting in *Graffiti* is the mythical American adolescent proving ground, "The Strip." The Strip at night is a locale reserved for teenage rites of passage, an arena of ritual display and courtship, cruising and baiting, between the sexes. Here adolescent males prove their potency by displays of speed and daring, and the pecking order is determined by the acceleration capabilities of one's car. *Graffiti's* four adolescent heroes, Steve, Curt, John, and Terry, pursue a nighttime quest for masculine identity and power, peer status, and sexual conquest. The Strip provides a milieu apart from adult society and the daytime routine of school, a temporary world in which teenagers can struggle toward identity through experimentation with masculine display, defiant lawlessness, and automotive combat. The ritualization of this experimentation contains and channels sex and violence, but the danger of the Strip is that cruising may become a neverending way of life rather than a way station on the road toward a stable, heterosexual adult identity. Endless cruising is, in a sense, allied to homosexual "cruising." In the tight buddy system of the juvenile gang, the Pharaohs, and in the lone gunslinger mentality of dragstrip veteran John Milner, masculine display becomes a ritual performed solely to impress other males or an end in itself. Such characters are aging fast while stuck in fundamentally adolescent, homoerotic roles.

Star Wars is an interstellar version of cruising the Strip. Mil-

ner's "hot rod" (with all that term's phallic implications) is replaced by Han Solo's souped-up spaceship, the *Millennium Falcon*.[4] Harrison Ford, who plays Solo, also played Milner's
dragstrip rival in *Graffiti*, Bob Falfa. One reviewer observes that
Star Wars' "world of romantic combat is structured around male
relationships and male-oriented viewpoints. Women exist primarily to provide motivations for male activity."[5] This comment
applies as well to *Graffiti*, whose four adolescent protagonists
are condensed into the two young heroes of *Star Wars*. Luke is
clean-cut and corn-fed, like Steve, but also shrimpy and, at first,
whiny, like Terry the Toad. But most of all he resembles the
romantic quester, Curt.[6] Han Solo is like the hotshot loner, Milner, of course, but as Luke evolves through the three films into
a free and independent figure still more like Curt, Han changes
also and begins to resemble Steve the Square, trapped by respectability and marriage.

The four women of *Graffiti*, all female stereotypes, are com-
pressed into the single archetypal figure of Princess Leia. Leia
is both the evanescent blonde in the white T-Bird (the unattain-
able Mother Goddess, clad in a white tunic)[7] and Laurie, the
Square Who is Saving It for Marriage. At the same time, she
eventually reveals a bit of Debbie, the Goodtime Girl (when Jabba
turns her temporarily into a harem slave), and continuously
exhibits more than a bit of Carol, the Spunky Tomboy and Pesky
Little Sister who so embarrasses Milner with her aggressiveness.
As composite woman, Leia is Goddess, Whore, Lover, Mother,
Sister, and Castrating Bitch all at once: tempting but taboo.[8]

Considered as adolescent rites-of-passage films, the *Star Wars*
movies are as far from being chaste beneath the surface as they
appear to be on the surface. Luke must remain sexually unaware
throughout the epic precisely because the films deal subtextually
with such explosive, primal material. The repressed sexuality
often emerges as violence: all those flashing lightsabers! all those
rocketships penetrating deep into the Death Star! all those orgasmic explosions! The climax of *Star Wars* is reminiscent of the
climax of *American Graffiti*. *Graffiti's* Steve and Laurie are reunited
at dawn after Laurie had fled from Steve and miraculously survived a car crash; as the couple embrace by the fiery wreck of
Bob Falfa's Chevy, the exploding car seems a substitute for the

physical climax they could not achieve all night long, just as *Star Wars'* climactic detonation of the Death Star is a substitute for the orgasm Luke and Leia can never experience.[9]

Lucas's epic is structured as a family romance. While the parents are deliberately absent in *Graffiti*, in the *Star Wars* series they are omnipresent (in one form or another—Luke's aunt and uncle, Ben Kenobi, Yoda, Leia, Darth Vader, even the Emperor), and all of the conflict is really intrafamilial. Freud sees the family romance as a primal fantasy present in many, and theorizes that those who have failed or left incomplete at the end of childhood the necessary but painful task of liberation from the parents are particularly susceptible to this fantasy: "For a small child his parents are at first the only authority and the source of all belief." Later, when the child discovers that his parents are not all-powerful and feels that he is not receiving all their love or has to share it with siblings, he retaliates by creating fantasy parents: "The child's imagination becomes engaged in the task of getting free from the parents of whom he now has a low opinion and of replacing them by others, who, as a rule, are of higher social standing." In other words, he imagines himself the orphaned child of royalty, forced by circumstance to live with lowly, adoptive parents.[10]

Paradoxically, the fantasy is not so much retaliation against the real parents as it is an effort to exalt them: "The whole effort at replacing the real father by a superior one is only an expression of the child's longing for the happy, vanished days when his father seemed to him the noblest and strongest of men and his mother the dearest and loveliest of women."[11] According to Phyllis Greenacre, the split in the image of the parents in the family romance fantasy is reinforced by "the ambivalence of the anal period in which good and bad, applied to the self and to the parents, appear like black and white twins in so many relationships."[12] This may help to account for the Manichean pattern of the *Star Wars* trilogy, the black-and-white morality of a constant battle between absolute good and absolute evil, the Rebellion and the Empire, the positive side of the Force and "the Dark Side." There is a corresponding split in the image of the father: "The good" Annakin Skywalker and "the evil" Darth Vader are one man.

The second phase of the family romance occurs when the child learns about sexuality. Freud argues that the child then "tends to picture to himself erotic situations and relations, the motive force behind this being his desire to bring his mother . . . into situations of secret infidelity and into secret love-affairs."[13] Thus, Leia is tortured (significantly, with a giant hypodermic needle!) by Vader, and later turned into a harem girl by Jabba.

In *The Myth of the Birth of the Hero*, Otto Rank argues that myth is based on the family romance, is "created by adults, by means of retrograde childhood fantasies." He sees myth as springing from "two opposite motives, both of which are subordinate to the motive of vindication of the individual through the hero: on the one hand the motive of affection and gratitude toward the parents; and on the other hand, the motive of revolt against the father." The myth that is the *Star Wars* trilogy becomes more comprehensible if it is seen to spring from such opposing motives. It justifies rebellion against the parents even though it concludes with an exaltation of the father and sentimental reconciliation with him. The final scene of this family romance, in *Return of the Jedi*, is a joyous family reunion.[14]

The *Star Wars* trilogy, like the family romance, also serves as "the fulfillment of wishes and as a correction of actual life" for the audience.[15] As Oedipal fantasy and power fantasy, it allows the viewer temporarily to fulfill both erotic and ambitious wishes. The action is comfortably distanced—"long ago in a galaxy far away"—and the characters are archetypal.[16] These fairy-tale devices permit an unconscious indulgence that realistic art prevents. The films hook their audience on the surface level—as adventure narrative and as popular entertainment that is visceral, kinesthetic, bright, loud, and fast—at the same time that the underlying myth works on each viewer unconsciously. The mythic pattern of *Star Wars* simultaneously fulfills erotic and ambitious wishes, balances opposing motives to exalt and debase the parents, and always leaves the hero guilt-free.

In the beginning, Luke wishes to restore the early, exalted image of the father and mother. But as he matures and learns, symbolically, about sexuality—"the Force will be with you always," Ben tells him—the Oedipal phase complicates his feelings about the parents. Now he wishes to debase them. He wants to rebel against and slay the father, so he is supplied with a suitable evil father in Darth Vader ("Death Father" or "Dark Invader"), who justifies this revolt. The pure mother figure is likewise degraded—tortured by Vader and captured by Jabba—so that Luke can rescue her. And Luke is also supplied with a rival or older brother figure, Han, who can woo and win her in his place. In the end, Luke is saved not only from the possibility of incestuously mating with his mother/sister, Leia, but also from the terrible burden of having to kill his father: The Emperor, yet another displacement of the tyrant father, does the job for him. Vader dies blessing Luke and is given a hero's funeral; once the Emperor assumes the role of evil father, Vader can be un-masked—his evil facade stripped away—and restored at the end to his exalted role. In the last scene, Luke is reunited with the smiling shades of his three "good" fathers: Ben, Yoda, and Vader in the human guise of Annakin Skywalker. Throughout, the fantasy balances contradictory desires and meticulously covers its tracks so that Luke is always guilt-free and sexually innocent even as he acts out aggressive and sexual impulses against var-ious parent figures. One "good" father dies in each film; and the two less satisfactory father figures, Owen and the Emperor, die at the beginning and end of the saga. No wonder the *Star Wars* epic is so popular among children!

Yet the unconscious content of this fantasy bears still closer scrutiny. Luke Skywalker is first presented as being kept "down on the farm" by his Uncle Owen and Aunt Beru. That they are his actual aunt and uncle is questionable, considering what is learned later about Luke's parentage. In any case, these farmers appear to have adopted and raised the boy and to have lied to him about the identity of his father out of fear he will leave the farm to follow in the Jedi Knight father's footsteps. In the family romance fantasy suffusing the trilogy, however, Owen is the real father—ordinary and repressive, hardworking, harsh, and petty bourgeois—while the Knight is the idealized image of the father.

The call to adventure arrives fortuitously for Luke; in fact, everything happens fortuitously for him, as if designed by fate or wish fulfillment. A little robot appears, delivering a plea for rescue from a beautiful princess. Rescuing the princess offers

Luke the opportunity to fulfill simultaneously erotic, ambitious, and rebellious desires. He might win her favor romantically by rescuing her; he will be acclaimed a hero; he can leave behind the boring farm and his tedious adoptive parents; and he can join the ongoing rebellion against the Empire. According to Rank, "Besides the excuse of the hero for his rebellion, the myth contains also the excuse of the individual for his revolt against the father."[17] At the same time that Luke is rebelling against his adoptive father, it at first appears, he will be vindicating his biological father; Ben Kenobi implies that by joining the rebellion Luke can avenge the slain father and assume his former glory by becoming a Jedi himself—that is, by abandoning his "real" parents, he can become a version of the idealized father.

Luke's decision is conveniently made for him when Imperial troops, following Darth Vader's orders, burn the farm and kill his aunt and uncle. Again, as Rank explains, "the myth throughout reveals an endeavor to get rid of the parents." However, by a process of reversal or projection, the son's hostility against the parents, particularly against the father, is seen both as the hostility of outside forces—the Empire slays Owen—and as the father's hostility against the son. This illuminates the paradox of Luke rushing to avenge a slain father even as the father, Darth Vader, still alive, rushes to slay Luke.[18]

As in a dream, all the characters in a myth are extensions of the central character's fears and desires. Vader is thus, all at once, a monster from Luke's id (the tyrannical ogre father—he even looks phallic), Luke's own parricidal desires projected back against him, and an archetype of villainy so potent that every viewer can see in him a custom-made figure of absolute evil. In contrast, the grandfatherly Ben Kenobi represents the father's good side, the superego in opposition to Vader's id. Like the conscience, he becomes the remnant of parental guidance that persists as a voice inside the mind.

Han Solo is an older brother figure who performs a number of functions for Luke. As his name implies, Solo is an apparently amoral loner who acts out Luke's antisocial desires for total independence. He is also a sexual surrogate for Luke, acting out Luke's passion for Leia, the forbidden sister/mother figure, to allow Luke to remain apparently asexual and guilt-free throughout the trilogy. Solo is punished for Luke's forbidden passion by being frozen and later suffering temporary blindness. Freezing is a symbolically appropriate way to cool down sexual heat, and blindness is a traditional literary symbol for castration that, quite appropriately, alludes to *Oedipus Rex*.

As really the only woman in the series (aside from Aunt Beru, who is quickly dispatched, and some extras and walk-ons), Leia too must serve multiple functions. However, those functions are sometimes incompatible, so she becomes a confusing figure. Luke comes to know his father, but not his mother. The kindly Aunt Beru tries to shield young Luke from his uncle's patriarchal sternness, but she is not entirely successful. Later, Leia assumes this maternal function. Yet there is throughout the series a deliberate ambiguity in Luke's relationship with Leia—is she to be substitute mother, friend, or lover?—that is only resolved at the end. When he first comes to rescue her from the Death Star, he seems to be trying to impress her with his impulsive, boyish derring-do. One naturally expects the dashing Knight to woo and win the fairy princess after he rescues her, but that never happens due to Luke's sexual innocence, Leia's maternal attitude toward Luke, and Han's sexual aggressiveness. It is clear in *Jedi* that all these plot devices are merely convenient ways of avoiding the incest taboo.

Leia is also in some ways a "phallic woman," which makes her a forbidding character. In *Star Wars*, by far the best and most well-integrated of the films, the bifurcation in Leia's personality becomes another of the film's comic incongruities: This white-robed goddess belittles her rescuers, seizes a gun, and resourcefully blasts a way out for them. But the contradictions in her character are no longer humorous in *Jedi*, in which she makes her first appearance disguised as a man but, as a consequence, is soon degraded as a harem girl bound by a chain to Jabba. From one extreme, the tough, mannish woman, she is reduced to the other extreme, a shapely sex slave. Finally, she frees herself by strangling Jabba with her own chain. The garroting, detailed through gruesome close-ups, is ghastly, and casts Leia in a repellent light. Previously, it was Darth Vader who had been the strangler. Leia is temporarily made into a fearsome killer, and the strangulation in its context suggests a castration.

The widened split in *Jedi*'s depiction of Leia may be due to the increasing psychological tension created as the series nears its conclusion. As the hero approaches the destruction of the father, the goal of union with the mother also draws closer. Anxiety increases because this union is desired yet feared. Thus Leia becomes both more "feminine," erotic and emotional, and more "masculine," strong and deadly.

In fact, the entire saga is drenched in castration anxiety, which is constantly being aroused only to be allayed. This anxiety takes many forms: fear of being swallowed up or dismembered, of being suffocated or strangled, and of falling. In the first film, Vader strangles a man with one hand and nearly strangles another using his mental powers. Leia's rescuers are sucked by a tractor beam into the Death Star, as if swallowed alive, and later fall down a chute into the garbage room, where Luke is almost strangled and drowned by a tentacled creature and the entire group is nearly crushed to death. One alien in the cantina has an arm sliced off by Ben's light saber, and C3PO loses an arm during the attack by the Sandpeople.

In *Empire*, Luke is almost eaten by an ice creature, R2D2 is swallowed but then regurgitated by a swamp creature, and the *Millennium Falcon* is swallowed by a gigantic space slug. Vader meditates on board his ship in a chamber that resembles an enormous jaw with clenching metal teeth, an image repeated in *Jedi* in the gates of Jabba's palace. Also, Luke learns that the Dark Side of the Force can "consume" him if he is not careful. C3PO is dismantled but later reassembled. Luke crash-lands twice and later plunges into an abyss, a fall he miraculously survives. Darth Vader strangles another victim, and Chewbacca tries to strangle Lando Calrissian. Han Solo's ship won't even go into warp drive, afflicted temporarily with mechanical impotence. And, most significantly, Luke suffers the loss of his right hand to Vader's light saber only to avenge himself in the next film by severing Vader's right hand.

In *Jedi* the images of symbolic castration continue to multiply. A slave girl falls into a pit and is eaten alive by the Rancor. Later, one of Jabba's guards meets the same fate, and Luke narrowly escapes it. Jabba also eats live creatures, and the Ewoks at first prepare to roast and eat the heroes. But the connection between being eaten alive and being emasculated is made blatantly clear in the Sarlacc, the man-eating pit in the desert into which Luke is to be cast, which several critics have pointed out resembles the mythical *vagina dentata*.[19] Such repeated evocations of castration anxiety are appropriate in a rites-of-passage film: Initiation rituals are intended to serve as a passage to manhood through symbolically tempting and defying castration; that is the purpose of the circumcision rites of primitive tribes.[20] The *Star Wars* saga evokes such anxieties to create either suspense or, in the case of the robots, comedy.

But the *Star Wars* saga exhibits yet another, related sexual undercurrent: the attraction to, yet fear of, the homosexual alternative to the passage to heterosexual adulthood. Just as homoerotic elements are implicit in *American Graffiti*, a buddy film in which the boys are more in love with each other (as in Terry's hero worship of John) or with their cars than with the girls, so too is the *Star Wars* epic another series of buddy films in which the closest relationships, aside from Luke's ties to his three male mentors (Ben, Yoda, and Vader), are between male partners— Luke and Han, Han and Chewbacca, Han and Lando, R2D2 and C3PO. Dale Pollock even sees a homosexual strain in Lucas's first film, *THX–1138*: "The most unsettling relationship . . . is the one between THX and SEN, the supervisor who has designs on THX. As played by Donald Pleasance, SEN displays homosexual characteristics."[21] SEN's intervention in the growing sexual love between THX and his female roommate, LUH, could be interpreted as a son's nightmare of a father's revenge for an Oedipal crime. Other critics have mentioned that the relationship in *Star Wars* between C3PO and R2D2 "is a caricature (though not a hostile one) of that of two male homosexuals. . . . The presentation of the droids as mechanical men is a great assistance in allowing the theme of homosexual resolution . . . to emerge in a form which is not anxiety-producing."[22]

Just as SEN tries to seduce THX, so do Darth Vader in *The Empire Strikes Back* and the Emperor in *Return of the Jedi* try to seduce Luke. The hero's ambivalent love and hate toward paternal authority is projected as that authority's attempt to seduce and destroy the hero. The Emperor is played in a campy style like a repulsive, aging queen. He has already seduced Vader to "the Dark Side of the Force," and now he intends to replace the aging Vader with Vader's handsome young son, who has more of "The Force" in him. The sexual implications are blatant as the Emperor fondles Luke's light saber. And the temptation he offers Luke is implicitly homosexual: He expresses his delight as Luke "swells" with anger before him, and he dares Luke to grab his light saber and overpower him. The Emperor then stages a sadomasochistic pageant between father and son. Either way, he wins: The more potent man survives the phallic saber duel and becomes his. Since Luke is such a threat, he must either be seduced or killed.

As the servant of the Emperor, Vader is finally perceived as a feminized father, and Luke fears he will become just like him. By *Jedi*'s climax, both have already suffered symbolic castration through the loss of their right hands. Giving in to the Emperor, being seduced by "the Dark Side," represents for Luke total submission to all the primal forces he most fears inside himself, including the desire to make love to and kill his father. Luke's refusal is an assertion of his virtue in more than one sense, but it is a foregone conclusion—and thus, finally, dramatically un-satisfying—since he is always shown as outwardly so pure that the audience never believes in his internal struggle. Sexuality is only for Han and Leia or the villains, not for Luke.

There are a number of ways to interpret the homosexual am-bivalence in the *Star Wars* trilogy: It may stem in part from an underlying fear of strong, "castrating" women; it may represent a desire to retain the father's love and avoid punishment by submitting to him; or it may be a projection back against himself of the hero's own ambivalent love and hate toward father fig-ures. These alternatives are not mutually exclusive. As psycho-analysis has so abundantly demonstrated, a single fantasy or defense may simultaneously fulfill a number of functions.[23]

The multiple functions performed by the most interesting new character in the final film, Jabba the Hutt, illustrate the over-determined nature of the characters, situations, and archetypes in the *Star Wars* series. Jabba, as one critic has suggested, is the Devil; his palace is a dark, underground Hell.[24] He is also Herod cum Pontius Pilate, ordering Solo crucified. On another level, he is the archetypal gangster, the bloated criminal mastermind like so many characters portrayed by Sydney Greenstreet, or the fat, jaded sultan of countless Hollywood films, with his harem and his unspeakable depravity. Physically, he is a giant toad or slug or reptile. This plays on the audience's instinctive revulsion at coldblooded or slimy creatures, and the viewer is also morally repelled by Jabba's greed, his gluttony, his drooling lust, his voyeurism, and his sadistic cruelty.

On a psychosexual level, Jabba represents total oral regression: With his giant eyes and mouth, he leers at and ogles his victims, enjoys watching them being eaten alive, or pops live bait into his own mouth. Sexually, he is an ambiguous figure who seems both phallic (his swollen, froglike appearance) and vaginal (his all-devouring mouth and eyes). The camera dwells a long time on Jabba, as if delighting in all his regressive qualities. It is precisely because Jabba, like Darth Vader, is so psychosexually primitive that he is so powerful an archetype, at once terrifying and secretly appealing. Each viewer in the audience plays in part the role of Jabba the Hutt: immobile, dwelling in the dark, stuffing oneself with popcorn, voyeuristically devouring the images on the screen, delighting in the explosions.

Despite its surface morality, the *Star Wars* trilogy provides something for everyone, on one psychosexual level or another. First, it overwhelms the eyes and ears and satisfies a craving for action and speed. Next, through its mythic framework, it allows the viewer to triumph vicariously over fears of incest, castration, and homosexuality in the ultimate victory of Luke, who overcomes all these perils and remains chaste to the end. The audience is distracted from noticing that Luke's righteous fulfillment of his destiny is achieved at the expense of a series of mentor or father figures (Uncle Owen, Ben Kenobi, Yoda, and the redeemed Darth Vader), all of whom die that Luke may live. In the first film, both after the deaths of Uncle Owen and Aunt Beru and after the death of Ben, someone comforts Luke with the identical words—"There was nothing you could have done"— as though absolving him of blame. To finally resolve this problem, all the fathers (except Uncle Owen, whom Luke never liked anyway) are resurrected at the finale, at least in ectoplasmic form!

Although it may not be safe to keep living fathers around,

brothers or male buddies are less threatening; so all these masculine partners (Luke, Han, Chewbacca, Lando, and the two robots) are reunited in the flesh, fur, or metal at the conclusion, allowing the survival of an innocent, muted homoeroticism that is less fraught with neurotic conflict than homoeroticism between father and son. Sister survives too in this family romance, but she is no longer sexually tempting because she has been married off to a surrogate, best buddy Han. Meanwhile, all those villains who were permitted to act out the audience's hidden desires so blatantly—hence the popularity of Darth Vader and Jabba—have been burned to ashes or blown to bits to reassure the viewer that they have been totally eliminated.

Is there sex in the *Star Wars* saga? Certainly, in the same way sex is present in the stories of the Brothers Grimm. Lucas's films simply could not command their overwhelming appeal to a mass audience without drawing on "the power of the Force."

NOTES

1. Dale Pollock, *Skywalking: The Life and Films of George Lucas* (New York: Harmony, 1983), pp. 17, 101, 142, 165. For comparisons between the "Flash Gordon" serials, *Forbidden Planet*, and *Star Wars*, see the author's "*Star Wars*: A Myth for Our Time," *Literature/Film Quarterly* 6, 4 (Fall 1978): 317.

2. Jonathan Rosenbaum, "The Solitary Pleasures of *Star Wars*," *Sight and Sound* 46 (Autumn 1977): 209.

3. On *Star Wars* as family romance, see Dan Rubey, "*Star Wars*: Not So Far Away," *Jump Cut* 18 (August 1978): 12; Martin Miller and Robert Sprich, "The Appeal of *Star Wars*: An Archetypal-Psychoanalytic View," *American Image* 38, 2 (Summer 1981): 209; and the author's "*Return of the Jedi*: The End of the Myth," *Film Criticism* 8, 2 (Winter 1984): 49.

4. James M. Curtis, "From *American Graffiti* to *Star Wars*," *Journal of Popular Culture* 13, 4 (Spring 1980): 592.

5. Rubey, p. 11.

6. Curtis, p. 594.

7. Ibid., p. 593.

8. See Miller and Sprich, pp. 216–217.

9. See Donald Palumbo, "Loving that Machine; or, the Mechanical Egg: Sexual Mechanisms and Metaphors in Science Fiction Films," in *The Mechanical God: Machines in Science Fiction*, eds. Thomas P. Dunn

and Richard D. Erlich (Westport, Conn.: Greenwood Press, 1982), pp. 124–125; and Curtis, p. 596.

10. Sigmund Freud, "Family Romances," *The Standard Edition of the Complete Psychological Works of Sigmund Freud*, vol. 9 (1906–1908), ed. James Strachey (London: Hogarth, 1959), pp. 237, 238–239.

11. Ibid., pp. 240–241.

12. Phyllis Greenacre, "The Family Romance of the Artist," *Psychoanalytic Study of the Child*, vol. 13 (New York: International Universities Press, 1958), pp. 10–11.

13. Freud, p. 239.

14. Otto Rank, *The Myth of the Birth of the Hero*, ed. Philip Freund (New York: Vintage, 1959), pp. 84, 85.

15. Freud, p. 238.

16. Miller and Sprich, p. 206.

17. Rank, p. 85.

18. Ibid., pp. 71, 78–89.

19. Harlan Jacobson, "Thunder on the Right," *Film Comment* (August 1983): 10, and the author's "*Return of the Jedi*: The End of the Myth," p. 51.

20. Bruno Bettelheim, *Symbolic Wounds: Puberty Rites and The Envious Male*, rev. ed. (New York: Collier Books, 1962).

21. Pollock, p. 95.

22. Miller and Sprich, p. 213.

23. See, for example, Robert Waelder, "The Principle of Multiple Function: Observations on Over-Determination," *Psychoanalytic Quarterly* 5 (1936): 45–62.

24. Anne Lancashire, "*Return of the Jedi*: Once More with Feeling," *Film Criticism* 8, 2 (Winter 1984): 58–59.

17

Sexism in Space: The Freudian Formula in "Star Trek"

MARY JO DEEGAN

Space, the final frontier. These are the voyages of the starship
Enterprise, its five year mission to explore strange new worlds, to
seek out new life and new civilizations, to boldly go where no
man has gone before.

These words, spoken at the beginning
of each televised "Star Trek" episode, set the stage for the fantastic future. Although the "Star Trek" series was cancelled in
1969 after only three years of production, it generated a large
cult following that flourishes still today. One reason for the
series' remarkable longevity is its depiction of the future as a
Freudian fantasy. This Freudian vision draws on cultural myths
embedded in the patriarchal dominance of men over women
characteristic of Western civilization.

According to Freud, both sexes are driven by three instincts—
sex, aggression, and the death wish—but men have the most
powerful instincts, and they are most driven by their desire to
have power over other men. This Freudian worldview is dra-
matized aboard the starship *Enterprise*, where women are secondary figures who either provide romance or reveal that any
woman's desire for power is "abnormal." But men "normally"

struggle for power, and the men of "Star Trek" usually strive for control over the starship. Sometimes, however, all human life is threatened by nonsexed "things," such as viruses or living energy, and the men struggle to defeat these alien forces. Yet in all cases this fantasy of space travel involving a deeply bonded, essentially male group is linked to everyday discrimination against women in contemporary society.

Freud's concept of personal development and its instinctual basis is one of the most influential interpretations of social behavior accepted today. Based on the idea that men are physiologically, psychologically, and mentally superior to women, Freudian thought has been strongly criticized by many feminists (e.g., Friedan, 1963; Miller, 1975; Firestone, 1971). Their critiques interpret Freud's worldview as a legitimization of sexism and, therefore, antithetical to feminism. Mitchell, however, developed in 1975 an innovative feminist critique that sees Freud as an accurate observer of a sexist society. Freud's ideas can thus be seen from a feminist perspective to illuminate rather than perpetuate sexism.

Each Freudian instinct—involving sex, aggression, and the struggle to live or die—is enacted differently by each sex, and each instinct is unconscious and symbolically hidden. The male body, defined as superior to the female's, drives the male to seek power in the social order. Yet each male's quest for power conflicts with that of other males, and this especially threatens each father's control over his sons. Freudians discuss the central theme of males seeking to overthrow the power of other males as either the "Oedipal myth" or the theory of the "primal horde." The "Oedipal myth" involves the son overthrowing the power of the father. This senario is reenacted in every father-son relationship; it is the major developmental state for generating "normal" behavior in men and determines their adult capacity to "love and work." The "primal horde" theory is a large scale reenactment of the Oedipal myth in which control over society is achieved by challengers, usually younger men, who overthrow once powerful older men. Females who "properly" recognize their physical and emotional inferiority to males want only to love men and bear their children.

Freudian concepts form a network of ideas, a formula, for

organizing action in a dramatic script. This particular, patriarchal formula segregates the world into spheres of "male" and "female" control; but the female sphere is dependent upon the male sphere for knowledge, access to material and emotional resources, and power. The male sphere is governed by rational rules that generate and maintain the social order (e.g., the rules governing the military, education, business, and politics). The female sphere is governed by emotions and relations within the family and home. Love links these separate spheres. For women, sex is defined as an emotional and material connection necessary for establishing paternity as well as financial and emotional security. For men, sex is a physical, animal instinct that explains why men temporarily succumb to the power of women. Women gain power and protection through men; their world is mediated through men, and this explains their need to "capture" men.

There are three major variations of this Freudian formula in "Star Trek," and each variation corresponds to a cultural myth associated with a Freudian instinct. The first myth involves the sexual instinct. In this romantic scenario, women want to love the men of "Star Trek" in order to find meaning and happiness. While the men find these women attractive, women must be forsaken in favor of the men's higher mission on the starship. The second myth involves the aggression instinct. In this power scenario, men want dominance over other men; women are not seen as appropriate opponents. The third myth involves the struggle between life and death. In this death struggle, the men fight living but asexual "things"; the success of the patriarchal leaders in these struggles literally determines the survival or extinction of all humans, and usually prevents a potential Armageddon. Each "Star Trek" episode contains components of each myth and echoes of each instinctual battle, but the most prominent and engaging scenario involves the Oedipal struggle for power.

Together, the *Enterprise*'s male leaders face the dangerous unknown. They share fear and excitement, laughter and tears, the conquest of internal and external challenges. This male bond is the emotional focus of the series and determines the fate of all dependents. Captain James T. Kirk has absolute command of the *Enterprise*. In every episode, Kirk makes crucial decisions affecting the lives of his crew, and he usually seeks the advice of Mr. Spock (the half-human, half-Vulcan First Officer and Science Officer) and Dr. "Bones" McCoy (the Chief Medical Officer). Since Spock identifies with his Vulcan heritage, he bases his decisions on logic and rationality, and is so threatened by emotionality that expressing emotion can be fatal for him; he is the most popular member of the crew, surpassing the Captain in fan appeal (Marsano, 1977). Dr. McCoy, the voice of concern and nurturance, is Spock's foil; he is concerned with the emotional effects on the crew of Kirk's decisions. Outspokenly opposed to Spock's reliance on logic, McCoy repeatedly insists that people are not essentially rational and that the application of reason alone to a human situation is destructive and short-sighted.

Symbolically, Spock represents the extreme embodiment of masculine traits, and McCoy represents the feminine. They externalize respectively the voices of reason and emotion in the Captain's continual struggle to decide the fate of the ship and its crew. Both gender poles are integrated in the patriarchal leader, Kirk. While in some ways Kirk thus seems to be psychologically androgynous, to combine both male and female traits, his decisive masculinity is nonetheless established through his conspicuous heterosexuality, the frequent display of his chest and biceps, and his exaggerated, even swaggering "macho" air. Kirk is a "real man"; and all men on the *Enterprise* are distanced from the "female" concerns of our culture, bearing and rearing children and performing domestic labor (Mitchell, 1966). Instead, they live in a rarefied, masculine sphere dedicated to an abstract, rational ideal that is accomplished through their nurturant starship. These men love each other and the ship; however, any hint of homosexual overtones in their characterizations would destroy this vision of heterosexual male bonding. Thus, women are constantly introduced as attractive temptations that are resisted for the sake of the "higher," male mission. In this way, "normal" heterosexuality is constantly reaffirmed, but assigned an inferior status and thus controlled.

The starship, an idealized womb, is home to 430 crew members for whom it provides defense and mobility as well as life support. It handles all the crew's needs quickly, efficiently, and quietly: Wall slots deliver food and drink, doors automatically slide open when approached, and all rooms are kept constantly spotless without the appearance of any human intervention. The *Enterprise* is emphatically female. She is the target of men's ambitions, greed, lust for power, and love. Usually referred to by feminine pronouns, "she" is Kirk's love, his "mistress." No mortal woman can compete successfully with "her." While all the male leaders, as well as Chief Engineer Scotty, "love" her, McCoy because she nurtures her human inhabitants and Spock because she embodies his duty, only Kirk admits to his emotional bond and need to deny himself sexually in order to have "her." Because she enables the men to fulfill their life's mission but makes no emotional demands on them, she cannot ask too much. Only human females can do that.

The only female character who appears regularly in the series is Lieutenant Uhuru, the black Communications Officer who fills the traditional female role of translating linguistic meaning. She is the high-tech telephone operator of the future. She is never the primary focus of an episode, however, and one of her largest roles occurs in "The Trouble with Tribbles," in which she "adopts" the very affectionate, furry little title creatures, which are unable to control their reproductive functions.

It is as romantic figures that other women ordinarily occupy their most significant, although individually short-lived, roles (see Table 1). Instead of struggling against men for power, women try to associate with powerful men who represent and protect "their women." For "Star Trek" men, romantic involvement is a distracting and threatening emotion. They want but do not need romantic love, and their sexual desires are awakened by the female presence. Women, however, do need love and must trick men into giving it to them. Therefore, romantic love in this patriarchal formula is an exploitative device used by women to gain some control over specific men. The only exception occurs when a perfect, sacrificing female attracts the higher emotions as well; one such female appears, in "The City on the Edge of Forever," but she dies at the end of the episode.

In the very first episode, "The Man Trap," McCoy is lured into protecting and loving a being he believes is an old flame. Unfortunately, she is a disguised alien who kills men by draining their bodies of salt. Undisguised, she is quite ugly; her face is

Table 1.
Episodes Structured around the Romantic Myth—
The Struggle for Love

	Episodes Involving Human Females	Episodes Involving Alien Females
First Year of TV Series	"Mudd's Women" "Miri" "The City on the Edge of Forever"	"The Man Trap" "What Are Little Girls Made of?" "The Menagerie," Parts I & II "The Devil in the Dark"
Second Year of TV Series		"Catspaw" "The Metamorphosis" "Friday's Child"
Third Year of TV Series	"Is There in Truth No Beauty?" "The Paradise Syndrome"	"The *Enterprise* Incident" "Spock's Brain" "For the World Is Hollow and I Have Touched the Sky" "Wink of an Eye" "The Empath" "Elaan of Troyius" "The Mark of Gideon" "That Which Survives"

dominated by a large, salt-sucking mouth. McCoy accurately perceives her only after he is no longer in love with her. In "For the World is Hollow and I Have Touched the Sky," McCoy "allows" himself to fall in love when he believes he is fatally ill and decides to spend his last year of life with the high priestess of a doomed planet. When he recovers and the planet is saved, both return to their "duties." In "This Side of Paradise" McCoy falls in love due to the influence of alien spores; when the spores' effects are counteracted, McCoy returns to "normal."

Kirk is frequently seduced by women. In his one "true love" affair, in "The City on the Edge of Forever," he goes back in time with Spock to the Earth of the 1930s to rescue a drug-crazed McCoy, who is being aided by a beautiful twentieth-century social worker. Kirk falls in love with her, but must finally let her die rather than alter the course of history by saving her. In "Shore Leave," Kirk imagines that he meets an old lover while on a planet whose alien inhabitants make the thoughts of humans appear to be reality. In "Elaan of Troyius," Kirk falls hopelessly in love with a warrior princess who is bound to a loveless marriage agreement designed to settle a war between two planets. The episode's title suggests she is, like Helen of Troy, the most beautiful woman of all times. In "The Paradise Syndrome," Kirk is lured into marriage with another high priestess and proclaimed a god after he develops amnesia. Spock must destroy the mythical paradise ruled by the priestess to extricate Kirk from his "dream-state."

Most of Spock's romantic temptations occur when "he is not himself"—i.e., when he is invaded by spores in "This Side of Paradise" or transported to an earlier, barbaric age when Vulcans had emotions in "All Our Yesterdays." These are unusual, life-threatening states; but even his "normal" period of sexual arousal, when he is driven by libido, severely limits his ability to work. This occurs once every seven years and is called (appropriately, for patriarchs) "Amok Time." During this brief period Vulcans are completely controlled by their sex drive, and it is only then that they marry. To choose his bride, Spock fights—and, through McCoy's ruse, believes he kills—Kirk, his "best friend and commander." Yet Spock's intended love rejects him because he is away from home too much. Thus Spock's "normal" sexuality is satisfied—for at least another seven years.

Human women—for example, the blind telepath of "Is There in Truth No Beauty?" and the woman who loves a Greek god in "Who Mourns for Adonis?"—frequently fall in love with aliens. These women abandon "human" society, preferring their alien lovers over their basic identification with humanity. For women, love overrides any other bond or commitment. In every romantic episode, human women are introduced either as evil temptresses or as culturally and morally superior but sexually unavailable temptresses. Yet they can be legitimately attractive. Female aliens, however, are usually just stupid and vicious, and provide opportunities for the extreme depiction of females as limited and despicable beings. "The Man Trap" is a salt-eating killer. The series' answer to the titular question, "What Are Little Girls Made of?" is "mechanical bodies and brains." In this episode, a male who had previously loved Nurse Chappel controls an "army" of loyal female androids who try to destroy the *Enterprise*.

In "The Metamorphosis," an alien Companion enters the body of an ancient, marooned space pioneer, rejuvenates him, and communicates with him. He is still so lonely, however, that he has the Companion bring Kirk, Spock, and a human female diplomat to his planet of exile. The human woman, a brilliant ambassador who makes constant complaints and demands, has a rare disease. Her dissatisfaction is due to her declining health and her failure to fulfill her life-long ambition, to love and marry a man. The pioneer, on realizing he has been having an alien form of intercourse with the Companion, feels he has been raped and that the immortality conferred through his congress with the alien is not worth this price. Thus, the alien enters the dying body of the diplomat, revivifying it but thereby relinquishing "her" alien immortality, in order to love a mortal man.

In one of "Star Trek" 's most complicated deprecations of women, yet another priestess steals "Spock's Brain" and installs it in the computer that empowers her to act and requires the brain to continue functioning. Kirk and McCoy, with Spock's brainless body in tow, follow the "brain tracks" to descend to, and are captured on, a planet where the native males inhabit a harsh environment and are enslaved by the strange creatures (i.e., females) who give them both pleasure and "pain." The pain derives from a strong electric shock transmitted through bracelets all the men wear. Spock's zombie body is impervious to pain, however, and this circumstance allows Kirk and McCoy to free themselves and retrieve Spock's "brain." This story of a computer-controlled woman stealing a man's brain is an intricate seduction/castration fantasy that dramatizes the evil power of mindless women.

"Friday's Child" exploits deep-seated fears men and women have of touching each other. In this episode's "primitive" world, a man must die if he touches a woman who is not his wife: Every woman, except one's spouse, is both untouchable and deadly to men. "The Empath" is an alien female whose species communicates only through the mind. Her race is incapable of acting generously or unselfishly, and she learns to be generous and selfless from the patriarchal men of the *Enterprise*. Both the

Empath and the *Enterprise* crew, however, are guinea pigs in an experiment conducted by a group of male aliens who are testing the Empath's "altruistic" capacity. In "The *Enterprise* Incident" a female Romulan starship captain captures Spock, falls in love with him, and consequently loses her command, her starship, and her status among her species.

Women are customarily nagging and deceitful in episodes involving Harry Mudd. In "Mudd's Women," this sleazy entrepreneur gives women a fountain-of-youth drug that makes them temporarily beautiful—just long enough for him to use them to separate some foolish miners from their valuable dilithium crystals, which they barter for the ersatz beauties. In "I, Mudd," the intergalactic con man creates an army of female androids that participate in his scheme to trap the crew of the *Enterprise* and steal their ship. Mudd's punishment is to endure an endless toungue-lashing from a platoon of androids created in the image of his nagging, unattractive wife.

Although they might become encumbrances as wives, "good women" in "Star Trek" wish only to serve men. They will forsake their species, give up immortality, and practice any deceit to trap one. But they are always put in their place. The real danger to the men of "Star Trek" is not women, however; the serious threat is the loss of power, which only other men can usurp.

Patriarchal authority is threatened by other men, and Kirk is constantly confronted by this Oedipal challenge (see Table 2.). "Charlie X," a seventeen-year-old boy with superhuman powers who is picked up by the *Enterprise* after having been raised by aliens, tries to take control of the ship but is subdued by Kirk in a face-to-face confrontation. In "The Doomsday Machine" a mad starship captain temporarily gains command of the *Enterprise* while Kirk is stranded aboard another starship, but again Kirk ultimately defeats his challenger. Likewise, in "Dagger of the Mind," the inmates of a model penal colony lure Kirk into their fortification, only finally to lose their bid for control also.

In "The Space Seed," Khan, a selectively bred "superman" who ruled a quarter of the Earth in the 1990s, is saved along with his followers from an eternal exile of suspended animation in deep space by the *Enterprise* crew. Khan immediately tries to

Table 2
Episodes Structured around the Oedipal Myth

	Episodes Involving Human Males	Episodes Involving Alien Males
First Year of TV Series	"Charlie X" "Where No Man Has Gone Before" "The Enemy Within" "Dagger of the Mind" "The Conscience of a King" "The Galileo Seven" "Tomorrow Is Yesterday" "Court-Martial" "The Space Seed" "A Taste of Armageddon" "The Alternative Factor"	"The Carbomite Maneuver" "Balance of Terror" "Shore Leave" "The Squire of Gothos" "The Arena" "The Return of the Archons" "Errand of Mercy"
Second Year of TV Series	"Mirror, Mirror" "The Doomsday Machine" "I, Mudd" "A Piece of the Action" "A Private Little War" "Patterns of Force" "The Omega Glory" "Bread and Circuses" "Assignment: Earth"	"Amok Time" "Who Mourns for Adonis?" "The Changeling" "Journey to Babel" "Wolf in the Fold" "The Gamesters of Triskelion" "Return to Tomorrow" "By Any Other Name" "The Ultimate Computer"
Third Year of TV Series	"Whom Gods Destroy" "Let This Be Your Last Battlefield" "Requiem for Methuselah" "The Way to Eden" "The Cloud Minders" "All Our Yesterdays"	"And the Children Shall Lead" "Spectre of the Gun" "The Tholian Web" "Plato's Stepchildren" "The Savage Curtain"
Films	*Star Trek II: The Wrath of Khan*	*Star Trek III: The Search for Spock*

take over the starship through enlisting the aid of a female officer who falls in love with him, but Kirk regains control of his vessel and banishes the "superpeople" to a rough but habitable planet. Khan returns in the movie sequel, *Star Trek II: The Wrath of Khan*, for another unsuccessful Oedipal conflict. In this second failed bid for power Khan is motivated by revenge, for the planet on which Kirk deposited him and his followers was rendered un-inhabitable by a cosmic catastrophe soon after colonization.

Kirk is occasionally challenged by "male" computers that have run amok. When "The Ultimate Computer" is selected to replace Kirk as captain of the *Enterprise*, it subsequently refuses to re-linquish control. This conflict reveals that the "female" ship is helpless without a human male to command her. In "By Any Other Name," a computer that has been tampered with "proves" that Kirk is responsible for the death of a former rival and friend. The fact that false information had been planted in the computer by Kirk's enemy is discovered before the challenging male and his computer "accomplice" can permanently strip Kirk of his rank through a court martial.

In "The Changeling" an ancient space-probe's programming is altered by collisions in deep space, and the probe proceeds to destroy all imperfections, including "flawed" humans. Kirk pretends to be the probe's Maker to reactivate the central direc-tives embedded in the program that require the probe to destroy itself rather than harm people. *Star Trek: The Motion Picture* bor-rows from "The Changeling" plot: an ancient space probe is granted near-infinite power by a race of supermachines and returns to Earth to pose a potential threat to "parasitic" organic life. It, too, searches for its Maker. In this movie, two female aliens are allowed to be officers on the bridge, but only after the "romantic" threat they pose is cancelled: Ilia, a Deltan, has taken a vow of chastity regarding humans because intercourse with a member of her race is fatal to them; Savak is incapable of "falling in love" due to her Vulcan ancestry. This adventure begins when Admiral Kirk wrests command from the new, young captain, Decker. It concludes with the "merging" of Decker, Ilia's former platonic lover, with a robot duplicate of Ilia created by the space probe. Symbolic sex with a machine replaces the deadly inter-course with a female specifically forbidden early in the film.

Male aliens also vie with Kirk for power. In "The Arena," Kirk successfully fights a lizardlike alien commander in a battle of "champions" to settle a territorial dispute. In "And the Children Shall Lead," another male alien, an incarnation of evil, uses children he has traumatized with fear to enter and take control of the *Enterprise*. However, Kirk revives the children's memories of their loving parents, and thus breaks the "evil father's" spell. Kirk is temporarily the "wise" patriarch who cares for the abused and exploited children.

Of course, the series' principal alien antagonists are the Federation's traditional foes, the Romulans and Klingons. Romulans, who appear in "Balance of Terror" and "The *Enterprise* Incident," play more fairly than Klingons; as long as Federation representatives stay in their "territories," the Romulans do not attack. Klingons are a different breed altogether. Gerrold observes:

Klingons are professional villains. They are nasty, vicious, brutal and merciless. They don't bathe regularly, they don't use deodorants or brush their teeth. They don't even visit the dentist twice a year. They sharpen their fangs by hand because they think pain is fun. They eat Blue Meanies for breakfast.[1]

In "Errand of Mercy," their first appearance, the Klingons attack a pacifist planet, Organia, that Kirk mistakenly feels it is his duty to protect. Kirk fights the Klingon captain but is stopped by the Organians, who are actually more powerful than both the Federation and The Klingon Empire. The Organians force the antagonists to stop fighting, thus setting the precedent for their surreptitious conflicts in subsequent episodes. Klingons also appear in "The Trouble with Tribbles." These little fur balls screech and tremble in the presence of Klingons, and this behavior leads to the unmasking of Klingon spies who are sabotaging precious food stores. In both "A Private Little War" and "Friday's Child," Kirk fights Klingon spies who pretend to be helping unsophisticated natives on primitive planets. And in "The Day of The Dove," an alien being that feeds on hatred tries to use and destroy both species. Kirk foils this scheme by establishing a temporary truce with the Klingons that lasts until their mutual enemy is defeated.

Finally, the most serious threat to the ship is internal treachery. This is a major "Star Trek" theme, and a favorite variation is Kirk's vulnerability to "the dark side" of his human nature. "The Enemy Within" appears when a transporter malfunction splits Kirk into two personas, one good and one evil. Neither facet can survive without the other, and both aspects of Kirk finally reintegrate to preserve their shared existence. In "Mirror, Mirror" Kirk finds a counterpart universe in which the parallel Kirk and *Enterprise* crew are evil instead of good. Evil doubles replace Kirk and McCoy, who are transported to the "wicked" *Enterprise*. The good Kirk wins the day by convincing the evil Kirk's woman—apparently, only an evil Kirk would have one—to join forces with him.

Since all men vie for power, human and alien males have a common bond. In their lust for power even male Klingons behave more like human men than human women do. Only the very last televised episode, "Turnabout Intruder," presents a woman as a serious threat to Kirk's power, and she is mad. The Freudian assumption behind "Turnabout Intruder" is that a "normal" woman would never desire a starship captain's authority. Janice Lester and Kirk had once been lovers, but Janice's jealousy over Kirk's chance to be a starship captain, a chance that a mere female could never have, destroyed their relationship. Later, while conducting an archeological dig, she discovers a machine that lets her exchange bodies with another human. This provides her with the opportunity to "adopt" a male body and end her "penis envy," so she murders the members of her expedition, lures Kirk to her dig, and swaps bodies with him.

Once on board the *Enterprise*, however, Janice-Kirk does not act "correctly." Despite her male body, she does not have the psychological and moral superiority to succeed with the masquerade. The crew senses that something is wrong, and a court martial is initiated. Spock finally deduces that only a woman in Kirk's body would act so strangely—i.e., be so incompetent, so easily angered, and so irrational. Kirk-Janice, however, acts "just like a man," even though he inhabits a female body. Kirk-Janice overcomes Janice-Kirk in a struggle of personalities, and each personality returns to his/her "natural" body. Speculating on Janice's behavior, Kirk and Spock conclude that "Her life could have been as rich as any woman's if only . . . she had ever been able to take pride in *being* a woman."[2] She would have been "sane" and "lovable" had she accepted her place.

A few episodes revolve around the possible extinction of all human life, an Armageddon myth, by asexual things, often chemicals and viruses (see Table 3). In "Operation Annihilate!" a batlike thing attaches itself to the human body and causes excruciating, fatal pain. After killing the inhabitants of an entire planet, it is finally destroyed by massive doses of ultraviolet light. Spock plays a crucial role here because only his "extra Vulcan eyelid" saves his eyesight and life when he is exposed to the ultraviolet radiation. McCoy sometimes saves humanity through his medical knowledge. In "The Naked Time" a mutated form of water reduces everyone to his or her most "animal" nature. Spock, of course, experiences emotions while others exhibit various forms of "madness" stereotypically appropriate for their sex and ethnicity. McCoy finds the antidote in the nick of time. When the spores in "This Side of Paradise" infect his body, only Kirk's love of the *Enterprise* enables him to persevere and prevail. In "The Apple," Kirk, Spock, and McCoy successfully battle a "snake-like" computer that controls humanoids. They "disarm" it to prevent a planet from colliding with a comet.

This familiar trio also rids the galaxy of Zetars, a form of living light. The Zetars invade Mira, a female crew member who is especially open to new experience. Ultimately, they are forced out of her body by air pressure. The malevolent cloud of Kirk's "Obsession" is similarly removed by air pressure and forced out of the *Enterprise's* conduits. In "The Immunity Syndrome," Kirk, Spock, and McCoy fight a mega-amoeba that threatens to "eat" the whole galaxy. Spock's superior scientific training and physical endurance make him the most "logical" pilot of an exploratory shuttle sent to examine the "thing." Kirk uses the craft as a "hypodermic needle" to innoculate the virulent "virus" with antimatter just before it is ready to form more "little" megathings! Another energy "thing" meddles in space conflicts in "The Day of the Dove," when Klingons and Earthmen form a temporary truce to save their lives. The "aging virus" of "The Deadly Years" almost causes the *Enterprise* crew to perish due to the ineptness of a commander who governs in Kirk's absence.

Table 3
Episodes Structured around the Armageddon Myth

	Episodes with Nonsexed Things
First Year of TV Series	"The Naked Time" (alien water)
	"This Side of Paradise" (spores)
	"Operation Annihilate!" (single cell that attacks nerves)
Second Year of TV Series	"The Apple" (snake-image computer)
	"The Deadly Years" (aging virus)
	"Obsession" (chemical creature)
	"The Immunity Syndrome" (mega-amoeba)
Third Year of TV Series	"The Day of the Dove" (entity that lives off hatred)
	"The Lights of Zetar" (energy entity)
Films	*Star Trek: The Motion Picture* (V'ger)
	Star Trek II: The Wrath of Khan (Project Genesis)
	Star Trek III: The Search for Spock (Project Genesis)

Only Kirk, after recovering from the virus, can guide the ship to safety.

"Star Trek" was originally conceived as a less sexist entertainment than it finally turned out to be in the majority of its televised episodes.[3] Yet the Freudian formula is a successful one, emotionally and commercially, because it provides a consistent view of women as "aliens" who know their proper place. Powerless in political, military, and economic spheres, these women of the future still resort to stereotypical feminine wiles and snares to lure unsuspecting men into emotional traps. Although they may sometimes, often through subterfuge, gain a temporary advantage, women are always subdued by the men of the *Enterprise*. Sexually stimulating women may only temporarily distract these men from their higher duty to their feminized machine, their starship. Emotional attachments between men and to a machine are depicted as normal; however, commitment to women is not only traitorous but—in the instance of the masculine ideal embodied in Spock—can even be fatal.

"Star Trek" dramatizes patriarchy, male control over women. Its audience identifies with the characters and their struggles and has installed the TV series and subsequent films in an enduring niche in the sexist culture it reflects. The "Star Trek" formula thus supports and is supported by other partriarchal formulas. Each one echoes the others in providing models of submissive roles for women and dominant roles for men.

NOTES

1. David Gerrold, *The World of Star Trek* (New York: Ballantine Books, 1974), p. 32.

2. James Blish, *Star Trek 5* (New York: Bantam Books, 1972), p. 338.

3. See Stephen E. Whitfield and Gene Roddenberry, *The Making of Star Trek* (New York: Ballantine Books, 1968).

18

Sexual Freaks and Stereotypes in Recent Science Fiction and Fantasy Films: Loathing Begets Androgyny

SAM UMLAND

As the mass art of a culture reveals something about the culture that produces and consumes it, a look at the treatment of sex and sexuality in some recent Anglo-American science fiction and fantasy films should reveal something about the sexual ambience in Anglo-American culture. A plethora of contemporary films either ridicule heterosexual relationships or present such relationships as having their bases in mutual exploitation, oppression, or sheer delusion. Moreover, these films treat the freakish sexuality of alien beings and the thoroughly mundane sexuality of instantly recognizable cultural stereotypes identically, with an unprecedented disgust; there is no middle ground, no contrapuntal hint in these films of what the healthy expression of human sexuality might be. In treating both the most bizarre and the most trivial of sexual encounters so similarly and so negatively, while presenting no "romantic" sexual alternative, do these films mirror some new disenchantment in Anglo-American culture with heterosexuality?

Science fiction and fantasy films often articulate a generation's particular sexual tensions, but they have just as often in the past defined that generation's image of healthy sexuality, perhaps in contrast to what was considered perverse. Howard Hawks's *The Thing* (1951) provides a good example from an earlier era. The film's subtext, often ignored by the critics, is suggested in the first scene, in which a group of bachelors in an Officer's Club flippantly discuss their experiences—and lack of experiences—with women. Captain Hendry is the butt of some good-natured kidding from Lt. Sykes and Lt. McPherson, who chide Hendry about his recent, well-known fling with "a pin-up girl," Nikki, who is currently working at the North Pole. When Hendry later seeks a few moments alone with Nikki, after flying a group of soldiers and reporters to her polar station, Lts. Sykes and McPherson tag along to tell her that her previous treatment of Hendry was "an awful way to treat our Captain." The ensuing second courtship between Hendry and Nikki (who eventually considers Hendry's proposal to "start over"), far from being a matter unrelated to the main plot, is the early 1950s image of healthy sexuality that counterpoints the sick concept of sexuality underlying that plot.

It is a healthy contrast to the asexuality embodied in the Thing itself, which arctic base scientist Dr. Carrington praises. Dr. Carrington is quite favorably, even jealously, impressed that the Thing's evolutionary "development was not handicapped by emotional or sexual factors." He proudly exhibits to all present a "seed pod" he has removed from the Thing's detached forearm (torn off by one of the sled dogs), and announces that the seed pod is an example of the "neat and unconfused reproductive technique of vegetation. No pain or pleasure as we know it. No emotions, no heart. Far superior—far superior in every way." The asexual and unmarried scientist, who wants desperately to preserve this viscous life-form that the others plot to destroy, ardently preaches to the others the virtues of being a nonsexual creature. Hendry's and Nikki's hesitant courtship, urged on by Sykes and McPherson, is the healthy 1950s alternative to the bizarre, threatening asexuality of the Thing. The Thing perishes, but the courtship is revived.

A similar sexual subtext also informs Don Siegel's *Invasion of the Body Snatchers* (1956), a film that is commonly compared to *The Thing* as another example of 1950s Cold War paranoia. *The Thing*'s motif of the seed pod representing "a neat and unconfused reproductive technique" is clearly present in Siegel's film, in which the seed pods are an alien presence that threatens to duplicate each human host "cell for cell, atom for atom." While the duplicate will have the same life, the same memories, the same body as before, it will be devoid of any emotional capacity whatsoever. In the context of the film, the pod "takeover" specifically terrorizes the familial unit—sons fear mothers, nieces fear uncles, sisters fear sisters—yet the sprouting of the duplicated humans is most directly a threat to Dr. Miles Bennell and Becky Driscoll, a couple in the embryonic stages of a heterosexual relationship. Both are recently divorced, a point made much of early in the film, and they are attempting to renew an old romance. Their courtship is continually thwarted by the paranoia spreading among the citizens of the small community of Santa Mira, however, and theirs is a doomed romance. Becky Driscoll's duplication towards the end of the film is a betrayal; her falling asleep and being "snatched" prevents any further exchange of love with Miles.

Philip Kaufman's remake of *Invasion of the Body Snatchers* (1978) repeats the same sexual subtext. While this film is overtly a story of dehumanization through bureaucratic depersonalization and oppression, it is implicitly a story of depersonalization and repression as well. Kaufman's casting of Leonard Nimoy—who will never shake the persona of the asexual, unemotional Mr. Spock of "Star Trek"—is a shrewd declaration of this sexual subtext. Nimoy plays Dr. David Kibner, a contemporary manifestation of *The Thing's* Carrington and one of the leaders of the alien conspiracy to dehumanize humankind. Kibner suggests that his kind are "evolving into a new life form," that those who have undergone the transformation are "born again" into an untroubled world "free of anxiety," free of the urge to hate, but also free of love. It is also a de-sexed world; the last scenes of the film suggest there will be no personal relationships in it, and that reproduction via seed pods—asexual, "neat and unconfused"—will be maintained and controlled by the State. The remake of *Invasion of the Body Snatchers* views such a world of asexual, "vegetative" reproduction—the totalitarian expropriation of the means of reproduction, if you will—with horror. Elizabeth Driscoll's duplication is, in this context, not a betrayal, as in the original film, but an utter abomination. Her prototype is the "false" Maria of Fritz Lang's *Metropolis* (1926), the soulless mechanical duplicate of a loving woman.

While the remake of *Invasion of the Body Snatchers* borrows the characterization of a Dr. Carrington-like seed-pod-sympathizer, Dr. Kibner, from the original *The Thing*, the 1982 remake of *The Thing* borrows the paranoid horror of the alien life form replicating the appearance of its victims from the original *Invasion of the Body Snatchers*. This cross-borrowing highlights the original film's sexual subtext in the case of the remake of *Invasion of the Body Snatchers*, but it obscures the original film's sexual subtext in the case of the remake of *The Thing*, in which the romantic subplot involving Nikki and Hendry is completely removed. Elizabeth Driscoll's duplication is, similarly, not so much a betrayal as an abomination in the 1978 *Invasion of the Body Snatchers* because she and Matthew (the remake's Miles) are merely friends, not lovers; she is living with another man, Geoffrey. The healthy counterimage of heterosexual courtship found in both 1950s films—one successful and one thwarted—is absent in both contemporary remakes. Perhaps this is due to the increased stress placed on contemporary heterosexual relationships. This absence of an affirmation of heterosexuality, an assertion of normalcy that counterbalances the asexual horror in the earlier movies, is also a characteristic of recent, original science fiction and fantasy films.

David Lynch's *Eraserhead* (1976) is a "midnight movie" or "cult" film that has received critical praise. Critics laud its dark imagery, view it as a perfectly filmed "nightmare," and note that its perverse sexual imagery is linked with a Swiftian notion of degenerate matter. The central character, Henry, is the "ultimate schlemiel" inhabiting a dreary industrial wasteland of filth and squalor, a world in which matter is all-powerful; and the film itself is a comically grotesque portrayal of teenage courtship.[1]

The Dark Woman Across the Hall (a prostitute) tells Henry that his girlfriend, Mary, has called, is at her parents, and expects him for dinner. Henry's and Mary's relationship is clearly strained: This is revealed when Henry pulls a photograph of Mary from his bedside bureau, but the picture is torn in two. Later, when Mary berates him for being late for dinner, Henry responds that he wasn't even sure she wanted him to come; he tells her, "You never come around anymore." The dialogue here is characteristic of the role-reversal between Henry and Mary. The dinner conversation with Mary's parents, like all the dialogues between Henry and Mary, is intentionally trite, banal, and clichéd. Mary's family, a perverse parody of the nuclear family, contributes to the relationship's morbidity. "Henry, isn't it?" Mary's mother asks with undisguised displeasure. Bill, Mary's father, is dressed in a garage attendant's jumpsuit and is capable only of the banal banter that betrays an uneducated dullness. A catatonic grandma appears to be very close to death. The dinner turns into a nightmare: The main course, "man-made" squab, oozes fluid when it is about to be cut, and its thighs "start to move rhythmically . . . suggesting at once the pelvic movements of intercourse and childbirth."[2] Finally, Mary's mother, after coercing Henry to confess that he and Mary have had sex, announces that their baby is at the hospital.

The couple's child is hideously deformed, however; it looks more like a turtle removed from its shell than like anything recognizably human. Tired of the child's incessant whining and of the squalor in which she lives, Mary soon begins to reject Henry's amorous advances; she eventually leaves him to tend the "child" himself. Predictably, Henry turns to the dark, alluring woman across the hall, but she too rejects him because of the nauseating, now sickly child. Finally, Henry begins a fantasy relationship with the Woman in the Radiator. Utterly repulsive, the Woman in the Radiator is a gross caricature of the All-American Girl: She possesses bulging, distorted dimples, a perpetual smile, starched blonde hair, and wide, plump hips suggestive of horrific fecundity. In her shy, impish fashion, however, she at one point deliberately squashes one of the many spermlike objects that proliferate in the film; the All-American Girl is too refined for vulgar sex.

Eraserhead satirizes traditional courtship procedures and presents procreation as something totally repulsive. If Henry represents "a naive adolescent with a strict, puritanical upbringing," as one critic suggests,[3] the child can be interpreted as a justly nightmarish product of illicit, premarital sex. But this implies acceptance of a conservatism linked with puritanical repression and guilt that is entirely at odds with the tone and perverse mood of the film. This interpretation is no more likely than is one that assumes the film represents a cultural expression of fear and unmitigated horror at the responsibility of impending parenthood. *Eraserhead* does view the responsibility of parenthood as a horrible prospect, and the courtship ritual that precedes parenthood is intentionally caricatured to expose it to ridicule.

Nicolas Roeg's *The Man Who Fell to Earth* (1976) concerns the ironic victimization of an alien visitor (played by David Bowie) through human exploitation and greed. The alien, even in his human disguise as Thomas Jerome Newton, is thin and frail and has odd, orange hair and the pale, pasty-white skin of someone who avidly avoids sunlight. Yet it is not Newton's strange features but his alien sexual "freakishness" that causes his victimization. While the initial, poignant love scene between Newton and his human lover, Mary Lou, is a direct contrast to the exploitative and vicious sex between Newton's traitorous friend, Nathan Bryce, and his student maidens, Newton's and Mary Lou's relationship degenerates into sheer intentional perversity by the end of the film. This happens, in part, because Newton has been corrupted by his mission and by his years on Earth, and has become sexually exploitative himself; like Bryce and Mary Lou, he comes to view sex as sublimated aggression. His original mission—to manipulate Earth's economy and technology towards the end of transporting Earth's water to his own dry and dying planet—is in itself essentially exploitative, sublimated economic aggression, and ends in failure.

While Newton's alienness, which in itself suggests sexual ambiguity, is determined in part by his unearthly features, the characterization is given an additional perverse twist in being portrayed by David Bowie, the rock star who was notorious in the mid-1970s for his alleged bisexuality and androgynous public image. Bowie's "off-screen" persona, like Nimoy's Mr. Spock persona in *Invasion of the Body Snatchers*, is transferred to the "on-screen" role of Newton. This "person-role confusion"[4] encourages the viewer to speculate on Newton's potential sexual ambivalence, and this is specifically exploited in a scene near the end of the film in which Newton confesses that when he drinks he hallucinates about men. Not only is he an alien, but he might also be a homosexual alien.

Ridley Scott's *Blade Runner* (1982) provides an especially aesthetic treatment of the violence in films directed against sexually active women. The two renegade female Replicants, Zhora and Pris, are both portrayed as sexually aggressive killers who have murdered humans off-screen in order to escape a brief life of slavery on the "Off-World" colony. They are "retired" (executed) far more graphically than are their male counterparts. Zhora, who works as a nude "snake charmer" in a Los Angeles nightclub and is referred to as "beauty and the beast," is shot twice in the back by detective antihero Deckard as she careens, in slow motion, through wall after wall of shattering plate glass. Pris, a "basic pleasure model" (i.e., an android hooker), also experiences an aesthetic demise in balletic slow motion. She too is shot twice. The first shot only sends her into a violent seizure that is either the result of internal mechanisms short-circuiting, so to speak, or of her own blind fury. But Deckard's second shot sends her into orgasmic oblivion: Her hips and buttocks arch off the floor in a slow-motion parody of the pelvic thrust, and then she is dead, a bloody, gaping wound in her abdomen. In contrast, the death of the male Replicant, Leon, whom the audience sees commit a murder on-screen, is clean and swift: He is shot once through the back of the head by Rachel, a non-renegade but illegal Replicant who is attracted to Replicant hunter Deckard, whose life she thus saves. The females' retirements are ethically gratuitous and also have far less immediate dramatic justification, yet they are far more elaborate, protracted, and spectacular than Leon's.

Deckard, who manages to kill both females but neither of the male renegade Replicants he pursues, seems to see women as either objects of lust or objects of revulsion. This ambivalence is revealed in his treatment of the apparently virginal Rachel, a distinctly passive, inexperienced Replicant who believes she is human and is a foil to the sexually fallen Zhora and Pris. Nevertheless, her latent sexuality is threatening to Deckard. Seemingly attracted to her against his sense of what is taboo, Deckard slaps Rachel into submission to both excite and tame her already repressed sexuality. Sexually submissive rather than sexually aggressive, Rachel is not murdered by Deckard, but escapes from Los Angeles with him at the film's conclusion.

A symbolic *vagina dentata* in the form of the gaping mouth of a female panther is the last image of Paul Schrader's *Cat People* (1982), in which the emergence of feminine sexuality is linked to the eruption of havoc and mayhem. In *Cat People* a young orphan girl, Irena, discovers both her unusual feline ancestry and her sexuality simultaneously, the dual discovery of her fundamental bestial and sexual natures. While Irena initially appears to be the stereotypically shy, withdrawn teenager (i.e., normal), the viewer learns that she is descended from a race of humans who, in the mythic past, had mated with black panthers. Moreover, her kind can now only mate safely with siblings, for the act of intercourse with a human will end in the human's ugly death; as her lecherous brother Paul tells her, theirs is "an incestuous race." Irena tries for as long as possible to deny both her emerging sexuality and her feline heritage; but when it appears she is going to lose her human suitor, Oliver, to another woman, Alice, and after Paul is killed, she opts to seduce and devour the suitor and accept her true sexual/bestial nature.

Cat People's implicit puritanism also informs many other contemporary science fiction and fantasy films. It is implicit as well, for example, in Brian De Palma's *Dressed to Kill* (1980), in which Kate Miller (Angie Dickinson, is still another instance of person-role confusion) is severely punished for an illicit sexual affair by her sexually conservative psychiatrist, Dr. Elliot, a man afflicted with a murderous sense of biblical morality. Kate Miller is an archetype of the sexually alluring yet threatening woman of the Hollywood popular film. Ostensibly the stereotypical frustrated housewife who dreams incessantly of the Ultimate Orgasm, Kate is sultry, sexually insatiable, manipulative, and promiscuous; i.e., this woman is dangerous, and her brutalization is a not-too-subtle punishment for her too-menacing sexuality. She is finally cut to ribbons with a straight razor and bleeds to death. While not a fantasy in the sense that *Cat People* (or De Palma's *Carrie*) is fantastic, *Dressed to Kill* is a soft-core sexual fantasy of the type contained in *True Confessions* that dwells on the graphic sexual fantasies of the unfulfilled heroine.

In some cases the filmmaker exploits the audience's puritanical expectation and uses it as a structuring device. In John Carpenter's *Halloween* (1978), sexually promiscuous (i.e., "bad") teenage girls and boys are viewed as sinners in the hands of an angry god; hence, their punishment at the hands of Michael Myers, God's agent, is inevitable and inexorable. Whereas *Halloween* is arguably a rather wry and witty commentary on Puritan sexual morality, its sequel, *Halloween II* (1981), is an indiscriminate bloodbath in which characters are killed without rhyme or reason. A similar absence of logic—even if the logic in *Halloween* is misogynistic—mars *Friday the 13th* (1980) and its imitative sequels, *Friday the 13th, Part 2* (1981) and *Friday the 13th, Part 3-D* (1982). These "stalk and slash" films simply portray the brutalization of teenagers for the sake of portraying brutalization; they use teenage promiscuity as a mere formulaic justification. The link here between illicit sex and retributive violence is not consistent: "Nice" girls and boys, those who haven't engaged in premarital sex, are punished along with the "bad" teenagers. There is some possibility, of course, that these unlucky stereotypes of teenage virtue represent a despised, anachronistic sexual morality that is only presented so that it can be ritualistically brutalized.

Joe Dante's *The Howling* (1981) and David Cronenberg's *Videodrome* (1983) illustrate a new trend in the treatment of sexuality in science fiction and fantasy film, a movement towards androgyny. *The Howling* is a clever parody of the "werewolf" film, a subgenre that trades on the same "beast within" theme as does *Cat People*. The two are similar also in that the male protagonist in each is confronted with a choice between two distinct types of women, two modes of feminine sexuality. In *Cat People*, Oliver must choose between the safe, submissive, motherly Alice and the dark, mysterious, dangerous Irena. In *The Howling* the alternatives are Karen White, a blonde, sexually timid, professional woman from the city, and Marsha Quist, a dark, inscrutable, sexually aggressive woman from the country. Marsha is sexually attracted to Bill, Karen's husband. Though Bill tries to reject Marsha's blatant and aggressive advances, he is eventually "bitten" by Marsha while she is in werewolf form and thus "infected" with werewolf blood. Any man who is bitten by a werewolf and lives becomes a werewolf himself, and the werewolf's bite quite naturally arouses Bill's bestial (sexual) nature. Later, while on a midnight stroll, Bill meets Marsha in the woods and loses his individual identity as he and Marsha merge in the fellowship of bestiality. As Bill changes into a beast, saliva drools from his mouth, and he howls in sensual delight. Marsha is no less repulsive during her transformation: She undoes the bandage covering a wound on Bill's arm and begins to lick the sore. In effect, both lose their human sexual identities, and any distinction between male and female, to become unisexual beings covered with hair, totally indistinguishable from one another, and equally revolting.

Videodrome is more difficult to interpret. A narrative labyrinth in which the audience is left to wander, it is superficially a detective story. Max Renn, Toronto cable television entrepreneur, discovers an underground television program called "Videodrome" that specializes in telecasting torture and mayhem, "Snuff" film fare. Because he thinks it is exactly the kind of show his station needs—something "tough" to replace the soft-core pornography he is currently airing—Max embarks on a quest to find the program's creators. He finds instead, however, that he is himself the dupe and guinea pig in a ramifying conspiracy involving mind control via television. The film's presupposition is that television has become "the retina of the mind's eye," a device for exhibiting the darkest, innermost desires and perversities that lurk in the human mind. It takes the "beast within" theme of films such as *Cat People* and *The Howling* one step farther and depicts sexuality, not so much as an indication of man's bestial nature, but as evidence of man's utter depravity.

While the film's imagery associates perversity with sexuality, it too suggests androgyny. As a result of exposure to the "Videodrome" signal, Max grows a vaginal opening in his stomach. The function of this pudendal organ is not entirely clear, though it may be linked to the film's apocryphal preoccupation with the "New Flesh." The theme of the "New Flesh" is introduced by Bianca O'Blivion, the leader of the feminine faction that is vying with a masculine counterforce for Max's heart and mind (and gonads). Although the precise meaning of the term, "New Flesh," is never made explicit, the vaginal opening in Max's stomach suggests that it concerns androgyny. This conclusion is supported by the fact that Max is caught in the middle of an ideological struggle between masculine and feminine forces. Robin Wood writes that "the 'New Flesh' could only be androgynous."[5]

As a cultural phenomenon, this emerging interest in androgyny may be the result of a disenchantment with, or a confusion about, male and female roles or heterosexual relationships in general. Some other recent films that portray androgynous sexuality, in addition to *The Man Who Fell to Earth*, are the works of Andy Warhol, *Heavy Metal*, *Terror Train*, *Performance* (featuring Mick Jagger), *Purple Rain* (featuring Prince), and *The Rocky Horror Picture Show*. In recent years the political use of psychoanalytic research has promulgated the notion that it is humankind's natural state for either sex to be a combination of both sexes. This turn towards androgyny in some films may reflect the same uneasy attitude towards heterosexual relationships that is revealed in others by the holding of such relationships up to ridicule and the implication that they are based on mutual exploitation, oppression, or sheer delusion.

NOTES

1. Jack Kroll's review in *Newsweek*, September 11, 1978, pp. 95, 97; Eric Braun's review in *Films and Filming* 25, 7 (April 1979): 32–33; J. Hoberman and Jonathan Rosenbaum, *Midnight Movies* (New York: Harper & Row, 1983), pp. 214–251.

2. Hoberman and Rosenbaum, p. 237.

3. Ibid., p. 236, citing Veronica Geng.

4. Erving Goffman, *Frame Analysis: An Essay on the Organization of Experience* (New York: Harper Torchbooks, 1974), pp. 269–286, and especially p. 275.

5. Robin Wood, "Cronenberg: A Dissenting View," in *The Shape of Rage: The Films of David Cronenberg*, ed. Piers Handling (New York: Zoetrope, 1983), p. 135.

List of Artworks, Filmography, and Bibliography

Following is a listing of works relevant to the study of sexuality in fantastic art and film. While extensive and eclectic, the listing is certainly not exhaustive. It is the editor's compilation of suggestions provided by each contributor to this volume, augmented by additional information gathered from those reference works on science fiction and fantasy film listed in Section I. The list contains information on all artworks and films discussed by the contributors and on all secondary sources consulted. Each entry for a film or artwork refers the reader to the essay or essays in this volume in which that work is discussed. For an extensive bibliography relevant to the study of sexuality and the fantastic in literature, see *Erotic Universe: Sexuality and Fantastic Literature*, a companion volume in Greenwood Press's series of Contributions to the Study of Science Fiction and Fantasy.

The listing is divided into the following sections:

I. Reference Works Relevant to the Study of Science Fiction and Fantasy Film
II. List of Fantastic Artworks
III. Filmography and Television Listing
IV. Scholarship on Fantastic Art
V. Scholarship on Science Fiction and Fantasy Film and Television

VI. Studies on Sexuality

VII. Other Studies Relevant to Perspectives Offered in This Volume

Works are arranged alphabetically within each section. Section II is arranged by artist. Section III is arranged by title. All other sections are arranged by author or editor. Some scholarship appearing in anthologies is cross-listed.

The following abbreviations are used in the listing.

coll.   collected, collection
dir.   director
ed(s).   editor(s), edition(s)
et al.   and others
scr.   screenplay, screenwriter, script
trans.   translator, translation
v.   volume

The editor is grateful for the advice on compiling a bibliography offered him by Roger Schlobin, Richard Erlich, Thomas Dunn, Donald Morse, and Marshall Tymn, for the extensive bibliographical information supplied by the contributors to this volume, and for the excellent example provided by Dunn's and Erlich's "List of Works Useful for the Study of Machines in Science Fiction," *The Mechanical God: Machines in Science Fiction* (Westport, Conn.: Greenwood Press, 1982).

I. REFERENCE WORKS RELEVANT TO THE STUDY OF SCIENCE FICTION AND FANTASY FILM

Baxter, John. "Selected Filmography." *Science Fiction in the Cinema*. NY: A.S. Barnes, 1970.

Johnson, William, ed. "Select Filmography." *Focus on the Science Fiction Film*. Englewood Cliffs, NJ: Prentice-Hall, 1972.

II. LIST OF FANTASTIC ARTWORKS

Aachen, Hans von. *Bacchus, Ceres and Cupid*, 1585. Kunsthistorisches Museum, Vienna. Discussed by Cheney.

Anonymous. *Demons Dancing Around "Magic Circle" of Satan*, n.d. Woodcut. In *Historia da Gentibus Septentrionalibus* by Olaus Magnus. Rome: 1555. Discussed by Grootkerk.

Anonymous. *Devil Blowing a Cornetto*, n.d. Woodcut. In *Lectionum An-*

tiquarum by Ludovicus Caelius Rhodiginus Ricchierius. Basel: 1517. Discussed by Grootkerk.

Anonymous. *The Devil Tempting St. Jerome*, n.d. Engraving. In *Histoires prodigieuses* by Pierre Boaistuau. Paris: 1597. Discussed by Grootkerk.

Anonymous. Indian Mughal Miniature Painting, Bazaar Style, c. 1830. Victor Lownes collection. Discussed by Layne ("Victorian Illustration").

Anonymous. *Kiss of Shame*, n.d. Woodcut. In *Compendium Maleficarum* by Francesco-Maria Guazzo. Milan: 1626. Discussed by Grootkerk.

Anonymous. *Kiss of Shame*, 15th century. French manuscript painting. Bodleian Library, Oxford. Discussed by Grootkerk.

Anonymous. *Mirdukht's Escape from Dangerous Men* c. 16th century. From the *Hamza Nama*. Museum für Angewandte Kunst, Vienna. Discussed by Layne ("Subliminal Seduction").

Anonymous. *Of Adultery*, n. d. Woodcut. In *Ship of Fools* by Sebastian Brant. Basel: 1494. Discussed by Grootkerk.

Anonymous. *Rebaptism by the Devil*, n. d. Woodcut. In *Compendium Maleficarum* by Francesco-Maria Guazzo. Milan: 1626. Discussed by Grootkerk.

Anonymous. *Transvection to the Sabbat*, n. d. Woodcut. In *Compendium Maleficarum* by Francesco-Maria Guazzo. Milan: 1626. Discussed by Grootkerk.

Artzybasheff, Boris. "Miss Birdsong in Arcadia." Illustration in Charles G. Finney's *The Circus of Dr. Lao*. N.Y.: Viking Penguin, 1935. Discussed by Layne ("Subliminal Seduction").

Banderoles, Master of the. *The Pool of Youth*, c. 1460. Engraving. Discussed by Grootkerk.

Batten, John Dickson. "The Lambton Worm." Illustration in *More English Fairy Tales*. London: David Nutt, 1890. Discussed by Layne ("Victorian Illustration").

Beardsley, Aubrey. "Lysistrata." Frontispiece for *The Lysistrata of Aristophanes*, 1896. Discussed by Layne ("Victorian Illustration").

———. "Salome with the Head of John the Baptist." Illustration in Oscar Wilde's *Salome*, 1894. Discussed by Layne ("Subliminal Seduction").

Beham, Sebald. *The Nose Dance at Gumpelsbrunn*, 1534. Woodcut. Discussed by Grootkerk.

Bernini, Lorenzo. *The Ecstasy of St. Theresa*, 1645. S. Maria della Vittoria, Rome. Mentioned by Cheney.

Blake, William. *The Great Red Dragon and the Woman Clothed with the Sun*, n.d. Collection of A. Edward Newton. Discussed by Russo.

Borcht, Pieter van der. *Peasant Kermis*, 16th century. Engraving. Discussed by Grootkerk.

Bosch, Hieronymus. *The Garden of Earthly Delights*, c. 1500. Panel. Prado, Madrid. Discussed by Grootkerk, mentioned by Layne.

———. *The Haywain*, c. 1485. Panel. Prado, Madrid. Discussed by Grootkerk.

———. *Hermit Saints*, n.d. Panel. Palace of the Doges, Venice. Discussed by Grootkerk.

———. *The Last Judgement*, c. 1500. Panel. Akademie Bildenden Kunste, Vienna. Discussed by Grootkerk.

———. *The Ship of Fools*, c. 1485. Panel. Louvre, Paris. Discussed by Grootkerk.

———. *The Temptation of St. Anthony*, c. 1500. Panel. Museu Nacional de Arte Antiga, Lisbon. Discussed by Grootkerk.

———. *The Wayfarer*, c. 1500. Panel. Boymans-van Beuningen Museum, Rotterdam. Discussed by Grootkerk.

Bosch, Hieronymus (after). *The Concert in the Egg*, n. d. Panel. Palais des Beaux Arts, Lille. Discussed by Grootkerk.

Bosch, Hieronymus (copy and variation). *The Temptation of St. Anthony*, n.d. Panel. Rijksmuseum, Amsterdam. Discussed by Grootkerk.

Bosch, Hieronymus (workshop of). *The Last Judgement*, n.d. Panel. Groeninge Museum, Bruges. Discussed by Grootkerk.

Boucher, Francois. *The Boyish Prank*, n. d. Discussed by Russo.

Brauner, Victor. *La Ville*. Discussed by Pantalacci.

Bronzino, Agnolo. *Allegory of Luxuria* (also, *Venus, Cupid, Time and Folly*), 1545. National Gallery, London. Discussed by Cheney.

Bruegel, Pieter. *The Feast of Fools*, c. 1568. Engraving. All Bruegel works discussed by Grootkerk.

———. *The Peasant Kermis*, c. 1567. Panel. Kunsthistorisches Museum, Vienna.

———. *Peasant Wedding Dance*, 1566. Panel. Detroit Institute of Arts.

———. *St. James and the Magician Hermogenes*, 1565. Engraving.

Bruegel, Pieter (after). *Kermis at Hoboken*, 1559. Engraving. Discussed by Grootkerk.

Burnett, Virgil. Illustration for *Sir Gawain and the Green Knight. A Comedy for Christmas*. Trans. from Middle English by Theodore Silverstein. Chicago and London: University of Chicago Press, 1974. Discussed by Layne ("Victorian Illustration").

Cock, Jan Wellens de. *The Temptation of St. Anthony*, 1522. Woodcut. Discussed by Grootkerk.

Correggio, Antonio Allegri da. *Danae*, 1530. Borghese Gallery, Rome. All Correggio paintings discussed by Cheney.

———. *Jupiter and Antiope*, 1530. Louvre, Paris.

———. *Jupiter and Io*, 1532. Kunsthistorisches Museum, Vienna.

Dali, Salvador. *The Great Masturbator*, 1929. Private collection, Paris. Discussed by Koslow.

———. *Minotaure #8*, cover. Discussed by Pantalacci.

Delvaux, Paul. *Pygmalion*, 1939. Musées Royaux des Beaux Arts de Belgique, Brussels. Discussed by Koslow.

Doyle, Richard. Illustrations in *The Doyle Fairy Book*, 1890. Trans. by Anthony R. Montalba. Discussed by Layne ("Victorian Illustration").

Dürer, Albrecht. *Adam and Eve*, 1504. Engraving. All Dürer engravings discussed by Grootkerk.

———. *Four Witches*, 1497. Engraving.

———. *Witch Riding on a He-Goat*, n.d. Engraving.

Ernst, Max. *L'Ange du foyer*, 1937. Discussed by Pantalacci.

———. *Men Shall Know Nothing of This*, 1923. Tate Gallery, London. Discussed by Koslow.

Fiorentino, Rosso. *Leda and the Swan* after Michelangelo, 1530. National Gallery, London. Mentioned by Cheney.

Floris, Frans. *Feast of the Gods*, 1546. National Museum, Stockholm. Discussed by Cheney.

Fontainebleau, School of. *Venus at her Toilette* (also, *After the Bath*), 1535. Louvre, Paris. Discussed by Cheney.

Foster, Robert. Cover for John Norman's *Outlaw of Gor*. N. Y.: Ballantine Books, 1967. Discussed by Layne ("Subliminal Seduction").

Fragonard, Jean-Honoré. *The Swing*, 1766. The Wallace Collection, London. Discussed by Russo.

Freas, Frank Kelly. Illustration for *Door into Summer* by Robert A. Heinlein. *Magazine of Fantasy and Science Fiction*, October 1956. In *Frank Kelly Freas: The Art of Science Fiction*. Norfolk, Va.: Donning, 1977. Discussed by Layne ("Victorian Illustration").

———. Illustration for *Plus X* by Eric Frank Russell. *Astounding Science Fiction*, June 1956. In *Frank Kelly Freas: The Art of Science Fiction*. Norfolk, Va.: Donning, 1977. Discussed by Layne ("Subliminal Seduction").

Fuseli, Henry. *Ezzelin Bracciaferro Musing Over Meduna, Slain by Him for Disloyalty During His Absence*, 1779. Sir John Soane Museum, London. All Fuseli works discussed by Russo.

———. *Half Length Figure of a Courtesan*, c. 1800–1810. Kunsthaus, Zurich.

———. *The Nightmare*, 1781. Detroit Institute of Arts.

———. *Symplegma of a Man with Two Women*, 1770–1778. Museo Horn, Florence.

Giger, H. R. "Necronom II" and "Necronom IV." In *Necronomicon*. Mentioned by Ambrogio ("Alien").

Greuze, Jean-Baptiste. *The Broken Pitcher*, 1773. Louvre, Paris. Discussed by Russo.

Grün, Hans Baldung. *The Bewitched Groom*, n. d. Engraving. All Grün works discussed by Grootkerk.

———. *Three Excited Witches*, n. d. Drawing.

———. *Witches' Sabbat*, 1514. Woodcut.

———. *Young Witch and Demon*, 1515. Drawing.

Grün, Hans Baldung (ascribed to). *Witches Preparing to Embark for the Sabbat*, n. d. Drawing. Discussed by Grootkerk.

Heintz, Joseph. *Adonis Leaving Venus*, 1590. Kunsthistorisches Museum, Vienna. Discussed by Cheney.

Hill, Vernon. Illustrations for *Ballads Weird and Wonderful* by Richard Chope, 1912. Discussed by Layne ("Victorian Illustration").

———. "The Personality." Illustration for *The New Inferno* by Stephen Phillips, Jr. London: John Lane, 1911. Discussed by Layne ("Victorian Illustration").

Hogarth, William. *After*, 1798. Tate Gallery, London. All Hogarth paintings discussed by Russo.

———. *Before*, 1798. Tate Gallery, London.

———. *Harlot's Progress*.

———. *Rake's Progress*.

Hogenberg, Frans. *The Feast of Fools*, c. 1550–1560. Etching. Discussed by Grootkerk.

Iwerks, Ub. Cover for *Flip the Frog Coloring Book*. Akron, Ohio: Saalfield Publishing, 1932. Discussed by Layne ("Subliminal Seduction").

Kaluta, Michael. *The Sacrifice*, 1976. Discussed by Layne ("Subliminal Seduction").

———. *Why He Doesn't Sleep at Night*, 1976. Discussed by Layne ("Victorian Illustration").

Knowles, Reginald Lionel. Frontispiece for *Tales from the Norse*. London: George Routledge and Sons, Ltd, 1910. Discussed by Layne ("Victorian Illustration").

Leyden, Lucas Van. *The Prodigal Son*, 1519. Woodcut. Discussed by Grootkerk.

Magritte, René. *L'Esprit de la géométrie*, 1937. Tate Gallery, London. Discussed by Pantalacci.

———. *La Dame*. Discussed by Koslow.

———. *L'Invention collective*, 1934. Collection of Konrad Klapheck. Discussed by Pantalacci.

———. *La Gâcheuse*, 1935. Private collection, London. Discussed by Pantalacci.

———. *The Rape*, 1934. Menil Foundation, Houston. Discussed by Pantalacci and Koslow.

Massys, Quentin. *Ill-Matched Lovers*, c. 1520. Panel. National Gallery of Art, Washington, D.C. Discussed by Grootkerk.

Mieris, Frans van. *Oyster Meal*, 1661. Mauritshuis Museum, The Hague. Discussed by Cheney.

Miro, Joan. *Tête de femme*, 1938. Pierre Matisse Gallery, N.Y. Discussed by Pantalacci.

Ochtervelt, Jacob. *The Oyster Meal*, Boymans-van Beuningen Museum, Rotterdam. Discussed by Cheney.

Oostsanen, Jacob Cornelisz. van. *The Witch of Endor*, 1526. Panel. Rijksmuseum, Amsterdam. Discussed by Grootkerk.

Patinir, Joachim and Quentin Massys. *The Temptation of St. Anthony*, c. 1520. Panel. Prado, Madrid. Discussed by Grootkerk.

Picasso, Pablo. *Woman in an Armchair: The Dream*, 1932. Collection of Mr. and Mrs. Victor W. Ganz, N. Y. Discussed by Layne ("Subliminal Seduction").

Rembrandt van Rijn. *Danae*, 1636. Hermitage, Leningrad. Discussed by Cheney.

Rossetti, Dante Gabriel. Illustrations to Christina Rossetti's *Goblin Market and Other Poems*, 1862. Discussed by Layne ("Victorian Illustration").

Rubens, Peter Paul. *Adbuction of the Daughters of Leucippus*, 1617. Alte Pinakotek, Munich. Mentioned by Cheney.

Sergel, Johan Tobias. *Abduction Scene*, c. 1770–1780. National Swedish Art Museums, Stockholm. All Sergel works discussed by Russo.

———. *Nymph and Satyr*, 1710.

———. *Passionate Lovers*, c. 1770–1780.

———. *Satyr Attacking a Nymph*, n. d.

———. Untitled, n. d.

Spranger, Bartholomeus. *Hermaphroditus and the Nymph*, 1580. Kunsthistorisches Museum, Vienna. Discussed by Cheney.

Steen, Jan. *The Dissolute Household*, 1661. Wellington Museum, London. Discussed by Cheney.

Titian, Tiziano Vecellio. *The Rape of Europa*, 1562. Isabella Stewart Gardner Museum. Mentioned by Cheney.

———. *The Rape of Lucretia*, 1570. Musée des Beaux Arts, Bordeaux. Discussed by Cheney.

Vallejo, Boris. Cover for John Norman's *Outlaw of Gor*. N. Y.: Ballantine Books, 1977. Discussed by Layne ("Subliminal Seduction").

Vasari, Giorgio. *Venus at her Toilette*, 1555. National Museum, Stockholm. Mentioned by Cheney.

Velazquez, Diego Rodriguez de Silva y. *Venus at her Mirror*, 1651. National Gallery, London. Mentioned by Cheney.

Veneziano, Agostino. *Lo Stregozzo*, 16th century. Engraving. Discussed by Grootkerk.

Weiditz, Hans. *Witches Celebrating*, 16th century. Woodcut. Discussed by Grootkerk.

III. FILMOGRAPHY AND TELEVISION LISTING

Alien. Ridley Scott, dir. USA: 20th Century Fox, 1978. Dan O'Bannon and Ronald Shusett, scr. Discussed by Ambrogio (*"Alien"*), mentioned by Kilgore.

American Graffiti. George Lucas, dir. USA: Universal, 1973. Discussed by Gordon.

An American Werewolf in London. John Landis, dir. UK: Lycanthrope Films, 1981. Discussed by Heldreth.

Attack of the 50-Foot Woman. Nathan Juran, dir. USA: Allied Artists, 1958. Mentioned by Ambrogio ("Fay Wray").

Barbarella. Roger Vadim, dir. USA/France/Italy: De Laurentis/Marianne/Paramount, 1967. Based on Jean-Claude Forest's comic strip. Mentioned by Clemens.

Battle Beyond the Stars. Jimmy T. Murarami, dir. USA: Roger Corman Productions, 1980. Mentioned by Clemens.

The Beginning of the End. Bert I. Gordon, dir. USA: Republic, 1957. Fred Freiberger and Lester Gorn, scr. Mentioned by Clemens.

Black Moon. Roy William Neill, dir. USA: Columbia, 1934. Mentioned by Ambrogio ("Fay Wray").

Blade Runner. Ridley Scott, dir. USA/UK: The Ladd Co., 1982. Hampton Fancher and David Peoples, scr. Discussed by Umland, mentioned by Gordon.

Brainstorm. Douglas Trumbull, dir. USA: MGM/UA, 1983. Stitzel, Rubin, and Messina, scr.

Bride of Frankenstein. James Whale, dir. USA: Universal, 1935. William Hurlbut, scr. From *Frankenstein*, a novel by Mary Wollstonecraft Shelley. Discussed by Norden, mentioned by Heldreth.

Carrie. Brian de Palma, dir. USA: United Artists, 1976. Lawrence Cohen, scr. Mentioned by Umland.

Cat People. Val Lewton, dir. 1941. USA: RKO, 1942. Mentioned by Heldreth.

Cat People. Paul Schrader, dir. USA: Universal, 1982. Alan Ormsby, scr. Discussed by Umland, mentioned by Heldreth.

Charly. Ralph Nelson, dir. USA: Cinerama, 1968. Stirling Silliphant, scr. From *Flowers for Algernon*, a novel by Daniel Keyes.

The Clairvoyant (also, *The Evil Mind*). Maurice Elvey, dir. USA: Gaumont, 1935. Mentioned by Ambrogio ("Fay Wray").

A Clockwork Orange. Stanley Kubrick, dir. UK: Warner, 1971. Kubrick, scr. From the novel by Anthony Burgess.

Close Encounters of the Third Kind. Stephen Spielberg, dir. USA: Columbia/EMI, 1977. Mentioned by Ambrogio (*"Alien"*).

The Creature from the Black Lagoon. Jack Arnold, dir. USA: Universal, 1954. Harry Essex and Arthur Ross, scr.

Curse of the Werewolf. Terrence Fisher, dir. UK: Universal International, 1961. Mentioned by Heldreth.

Day of the Triffids. Steve Sekely, dir. UK: United Artists, 1963. Philip Yordan, scr. From the novel by John Wyndham. Mentioned by Kilgore and Clemens.

The Day the Earth Stood Still. Robert Wise, dir. USA: 20th Century Fox, 1951. Edmund H. North, scr. From "Farewell to the Master," a story by Harry Bates. Mentioned by Ambrogio (*"Alien"*) and Clemens.

The Day the World Ended. Roger Corman, dir. USA: Golden Gate, 1955. Lou Rusoff, scr. Mentioned by Clemens.

Demon Seed. Donald Cammell, dir. USA: MGM, 1977. From the novel by Dean Koontz.

The Discreet Charm of the Bourgeoisie. Louis Buñuel, dir. France/Spain/Italy: Greenwich Film/Jet Film/Dean Film, 1972. Mentioned by Heldreth.

Dr. Jekyll and Mr. Hyde. Rouben Mamoulian, dir. USA: Paramount, 1932. From the story by Robert Louis Stevenson. Mentioned by Ambrogio ("Fay Wray").

• *Dr. Jekyll and Mr. Hyde*. Victor Fleming, dir. USA: MGM, 1941. Mentioned by Ambrogio ("Fay Wray").

Dr. Strangelove: Or How I Learned to Stop Worrying and Love the Bomb. Stanley Kubrick, dir. UK: Columbia, 1964. Kubrick, scr. From *Red Alert* (also, *Two Hours to Doom*), a novel by Peter George.

Dr. X. Michael Curtiz, dir. USA: Warner Brothers, 1932. Earl Baldwin and Robert Tasker, scr. From a play by Howard Comstock and Allen Miller. Discussed by Ambrogio ("Fay Wray").

Dracula. Tod Browning, dir. USA: Universal, 1931. Mentioned by Heldreth.

Dragstrip Riot. David Bradley, dir. USA: American International, 1958. Mentioned by Ambrogio ("Fay Wray").

Dressed to Kill. Brian de Palma, dir. USA: Filmways, 1980. De Palma, scr. Discussed by Umland.

The Empire Strikes Back. Irvin Kershner, dir. USA: 20th Century/Lucasfilms, 1980. Discussed by Gordon.

Eraserhead. David Lynch, dir. USA: AFI, 1976. Lynch, scr. Discussed by Umland.

E.T.: The Extraterrestrial. Stephen Spielberg, dir. USA: Universal, 1982. Mentioned by Ambrogio ("Alien").

Fire Maidens from Outer Space. Cy Roth, dir. USA: Criterion Films, 1955. Mentioned by Clemens.

Forbidden Planet. Fred McLeod Wilcox, dir. USA: MGM, 1956. Cyril Hume, scr. From a story by Irving Block. Discussed by Holte, mentioned by Gordon and Clemens.

Frankenstein. James Whale, dir. USA: Universal, 1931. From the novel by Mary Wollstonecraft Shelley. Mentioned by Norden, Kilgore, Heldreth, and Ambrogio ("Fay Wray").

Friday the 13th. Sean S. Cunningham, dir. USA: Paramount, 1980. Victor Miller, scr. Discussed by Umland.

Friday the 13th, Part 2. Steve Miner, dir. USA: Paramount, 1981. Ron Kurz, scr. Discussed by Umland.

Friday the 13th, Part 3-D. Steve Miner, dir. USA: Paramount, 1982. Martin Kitrosser, scr. Discussed by Umland.

Futureworld. Richard T. Hefron, dir. USA: AIP, 1976. Sequel to *Westworld*.

Galaxina. William Sachs, dir. USA: Marimark, 1980. Mentioned by Clemens.

Game of Death. Robert Wise, Dir. USA: RKO, 1945. Remake of *The Most Dangerous Game*. Mentioned by Ambrogio ("Fay Wray").

Halloween. John Carpenter, dir. USA: Universal, 1978. Carpenter and Debra Hill, scr. Discussed by Umland.

Halloween II. Rick Rosenthal, dir. USA: Universal, 1981. John Carpenter and Debra Hill, scr. Discussed by Umland.

Heavy Metal. Gerald Potterton, dir. USA: Columbia, 1981. Dan Goldberg and Len Blum, scr. Animated. Mentioned by Umland.

The Howling. Joe Dante, dir. USA: Avco Embassy, 1981. John Sayles and Terence Winkless, scr. Discussed by Umland.

I Married a Monster from Outer Space. Gene Fowler, Jr., dir. USA: Paramount, 1958. Louis Vittes, scr.

Ingagi. Grace McKee, dir. USA: Congo Pictures, 1930. Mentioned by Ambrogio ("Fay Wray").

Invasion of the Body Snatchers. Don Siegel, dir. USA: Allied Artists, 1956. Daniel Mainwaring, scr. From *The Body Snatchers*, a novel by Jack Finney. Discussed by Umland.

Invasion of the Body Snatchers. Philip Kaufman, dir. USA: United Artists, 1978. Discussed by Umland.

It! The Terror from Beyond Space. Edward L. Cahn, dir. USA: United Artists, 1958. Mentioned by Ambrogio ("*Alien*").

King Kong. Merian C. Cooper and Ernest B. Schoedsack, dirs. USA: RKO, 1933. James Creelman and Ruth Rose, scr. From a story by Edgar Wallace and Cooper. Discussed by Ambrogio ("Fay Wray"), mentioned by Kilgore and Clemens.

Liquid Sky. Slava Tsukerman, dir. USA: Z Films, 1983. Tsukerman, Anne Carlisle, and Nina Kerova, scr.

The Man Who Fell to Earth. Nicolas Roeg, dir. USA: Cinema 5, 1976. Paul Mayersberg, scr. From the novel by Walter Tevis. Discussed by Umland.

Mars Needs Women. Larry Buchanan, dir. USA: Asylum Films, 1968.

Metropolis. Fritz Lang, dir. Germany: Ufa, 1926. Lang and Thea von Harbou, scr. From the novel by von Harbou. Mentioned by Umland.

The Most Dangerous Game. Ernest B. Schoedsack and Irving Pichel, dir. USA: RKO, 1932. From a story by Richard Connell. Discussed by Ambrogio ("Fay Wray").

Murders in the Rue Morgue. Robert Florey, dir. USA: Universal, 1932. Mentioned by Ambrogio ("Fay Wray").

The Mysterians. Inoshiro Honda, dir. Japan: Toho, 1954.

Mystery of the Wax Museum. Michael Curtiz, dir. USA: Warner Brothers, 1933. Discussed by Ambrogio ("Fay Wray").

1984. Michael Anderson, dir. UK: Columbia, 1956. William P. Templeton, scr. From the novel by George Orwell.

Outland. Peter Hyam, dir. USA: Ladd Company/Warner Bros., 1980. Discussed by Holte.

Performance. Donald Cammell and Nicolas Roeg, dirs. UK: Warner Brothers, 1970. Cammell, scr. Mentioned by Umland.

Purple Rain. Albert Magnoli, dir. USA: Warner Bros., 1984. Mentioned by Umland.

Psycho. Alfred Hitchcock, dir. USA: Paramount, 1960. Mentioned by Ambrogio (*"Alien"*).

Q. Larry Cohen, dir. USA: Larco, 1982. Mentioned by Clemens.

Return of the Jedi. Richard Marquand, dir. USA: 20th Century/Lucasfilms, 1984. Discussed by Gordon, mentioned by Clemens.

Revenge of the Creature. Jack Arnold, dir. USA: Universal, 1955. Martin Berkely, scr. Mentioned by Clemens.

The Rocky Horror Picture Show. Jim Sharman, dir. UK: 20th Century Fox, 1975. Sharman and Richard O'Brien, scr. From *The Rocky Horror Show*, a play by O'Brien. Discussed by Ruble and Kilgore, mentioned by Umland and Heldreth.

Saturn 3. Stanley Donen, dir. UK: Lew Grade/Shepperton Studios, 1980. Mentioned by Gordon.

Sign of the Cross. Cecil B. deMille, dir. USA: Paramount, 1932. Mentioned by Ambrogio ("Fay Wray").

Sleeper. Woody Allen, dir. USA: Jack Rollins-Charles H. Joffe Productions/United Artists, 1973.

Son of Kong. Ernest B. Schoedsack, dir. USA: RKO, 1933. Ruth Rose, scr. Mentioned by Ambrogio ("Fay Wray").

"Star Trek" Episodes—Television. All are discussed by Deegan.

"All Our Yesterdays." March 14, 1969. Jean Lissette Aroeste, scr.

"The Alternative Factor." March 30, 1967. Don Ingalls, scr.

"Amok Time." September 15, 1967. Joseph Pevney, dir. Theodore Sturgeon, scr.

"And the Children Shall Lead." October 11, 1968. Edward J. Lasko, scr.

"The Apple." October 13, 1967. Max Ehrlich and Gene L. Coon, scr.

"The Arena." January 19, 1967. Gene L. Coon, scr. From a story by Frederick Brown.

"Assignment: Earth." March 29, 1968. Art Wallace, scr. From a story by Gene Roddenberry and Wallace.

"Balance of Terror." December 15, 1966. Paul Schneider, scr.

"Bread and Circuses." March 15, 1968. Gene L. Coon and Gene Roddenberry, scr.

"By Any Other Name." February 23, 1968. D. C. Fontana and Jerome Bixby, scr.

"Catspaw." October 27, 1967. Robert Bloch, scr.

"The Changeling." September 29, 1967. John Meredyth Lucas, dir.

"Charlie X." September 15, 1966. D. C. Fontana, scr. From a story by Gene Roddenberry.

"The City on the Edge of Forever." April 6, 1967. Joseph Pevney, dir. Harlan Ellison, scr.

"The Cloud Minders." February 28, 1969. Margaret T. Armen, scr.

"The Conscience of a King." December 8, 1966. Barry Trivers, scr.

"The Corbomite Maneuver," November 10, 1966. Jerry Sohl, scr.

"Court-Martial." February 2, 1967. Don M. Mankiewicz and Stephen W. Carabatsos, scr.

"Dagger of the Mind." November 3, 1966. Shimon Wincelberg (S. Bar-David), scr.

"The Day of the Dove." November 1, 1968. Jerome Bixby, scr.

"The Deadly Years." December 8, 1967. David P. Harmon, scr.

"The Devil in the Dark." March 9, 1967. Gene L. Coon, scr.

"The Doomsday Machine." October 27, 1967. Norman Spinrad, scr.

"Elaan of Troyius." John Meredyth Lucas, scr.

"The Empath." December 6, 1968. Joyce Muskat, scr.

"The Enemy Within." October 6, 1966. Richard Matheson, scr.

"The *Enterprise* Incident." September 27, 1968. D. C. Fontana, scr.

"Errand of Mercy." March 3, 1967. Gene L. Coon, scr.

"For the World is Hollow and I Have Touched the Sky." November 11, 1968. Rick Vollaerts, scr.

"Friday's Child." December 1, 1967. D. C. Fontana, scr.

"The Galileo Seven." January 5, 1967. Oliver Crawford and S. Bar-David, scr.

"The Gamesters of Triskelion." January 5, 1968. Margaret T. Armen, scr.

"The Immunity Syndrome." January 19, 1968. Robert Sabaroff, scr.

"I, Mudd." March 3, 1967. Stephen Kandel and David Gerrold, scr.

"Is There in Truth No Beauty?" October 11, 1968. Jean Lissette Aroeste, scr.

"Journey to Babel." November 17, 1967. D. C. Fontana, scr.

"Let This Be Your Last Battlefield." January 10, 1969. Oliver Crawford scr. From a story by Lee Cronin.

"The Lights of Zetar." January 31, 1969. Jeremy Tarcher and Sharie Lewis, scr.

"The Man Trap." September 8, 1966. George Clayton Johnson, scr.

"The Mark of Gideon." January 17, 1969. George F. Slavin and Stanley Adams, scr.

"The Menagerie," Parts I and II. November 17 and 24, 1966. Gene Roddenberry, scr.

"Metamorphosis." November 10, 1967. Gene L. Coon, scr.

"Miri." October 27, 1966. Adrian Spies, scr.

"Mirror, Mirror." October 6, 1967. Jerome Bixby, scr.

"Mudd's Women." October 13, 1966. Stephen Kandel, scr. From a story by Gene Roddenberry.

"The Naked Time." September 29, 1966. John F. Black, scr.

"Obsession," December 15, 1967. Art Wallace, scr.

"The Omega Glory." March 1, 1968. Gene Roddenberry, scr.

"Operation Annihilate!" April 4, 1967. Stephen W. Carabatos, scr.

"The Paradise Syndrome." October 4, 1968. Margaret T. Armen, scr.

"Patterns of Force." February 16, 1968. John Meredyth Lucas, scr.

"A Piece of the Action." January 12, 1968. David P. Harmon and Gene L. Coon, scr.

"Plato's Stepchildren." November 22, 1968. Meyer Dolinsky, scr.

"A Private Little War." February 2, 1968. Gene Roddenberry, scr. From a story by Judd Circus.

"Requiem for Methuselah." February 14, 1969. Jerome Bixby, scr.

"The Return of the Archons." February 9, 1967. Boris Sobelman, scr.

"Return to Tomorrow." February 9, 1968. Gene Roddenberry, scr.

"The Savage Curtain." March 7, 1969. Gene Roddenberry and Arthur Heinemann, scr.

"Shore Leave." December 29, 1966. Theodore Sturgeon, scr.

"The Space Seed." February 16, 1967. Gene L. Coon and Carey Wilbur, scr.

"Spectre of the Gun." October 15, 1968. Lee Cronin, scr.

"Spock's Brain." September 20, 1968. Lee Cronin, scr.

"The Squire of Gothos." January 12, 1967. Paul Schneider, scr.

"A Taste of Armageddon." February 23, 1967. Robert Hamner and Gene L. Coon, scr.

"That Which Survives." January 24, 1969. John Meredyth Lucas, scr. From a story by Michael Richards (pseud.).

"This Side of Paradise." March 2, 1967. D. C. Fontana, scr.

"The Tholian Web." November 15, 1968. Ralph Senensky, dir. Judy Burns and Chet Richards, scr.

"Tomorrow is Yesterday." January 26, 1967. D. C. Fontana, scr.

"The Trouble with Tribbles." December 29, 1967. David Gerrold, scr.

"The Ultimate Computer." March 8, 1968. D. C. Fontana, scr. From a story by Lawrence N. Wolfe.

"Turnabout Intruder." June 3, 1969. Herb Wallerstein, dir. Gene Roddenberry, story. Arthur Singer, scr.

"The Way to Eden." February 21, 1969. Arthur Heinemann, scr. From a story by Michael Richards.

"What Are Little Girls Made of?" October 20, 1966. Robert Block, scr.

"Where No Man Has Gone Before." September 22, 1966. Samuel A. Peeples, scr.

"Wink of an Eye." November 29, 1968. Arthur Heinemann, scr. From a story by Lee Cronin.

"Who Mourns for Adonis?" September 22, 1967. Gilbert Ralston and Gene L. Coon, scr.

"Whom Gods Destroy." January 3, 1969. Lee Erwin, scr.
"Wolf in the Fold." December 22, 1967. Robert Bloch, scr.

Star Trek: The Motion Picture. Robert Wise, dir. USA: Paramount, 1979. Harold Livingston, Alan Dean Foster, and Gene Roddenberry, scr. Discussed by Deegan.

Star Trek II: The Wrath of Khan. Nicholas Meyer, dir. USA: Paramount, 1982. Jack Sowards, scr. Discussed by Deegan.

Star Trek III: The Search for Spock. Leonard Nimoy, dir. USA: Paramount, 1984. Harve Bennett, scr. Discussed by Deegan.

Star Wars. George Lucas, dir. USA: Lucas Film and 20th Century Fox, 1977. Lucas, scr. Discussed by Gordon and Holte, mentioned by Clemens.

The Stepford Wives. Bryan Forbes, dir. USA: Columbia, 1975. From the novel by Ira Levin.

Summer Love. Charles Haas, dir. USA: Universal, 1958. Mentioned by Ambrogio ("Fay Wray").

The Tenth Victim. Elio Petri, dir. Italy/France: Avco/CC Champion/Concordia, 1965. Petri, Ennio Flaiano, Tonino Guerra, and Giorgio Salvione, scr. From "The Seventh Victim," a story by Robert Sheckley.

Terror Train. Roger Spottiswoode, dir. USA: 20th Century Fox, 1980. T. Y. Drake, scr. Mentioned by Umland.

The Thing (also, *The Thing from Another World*). Christian Nyby, dir. USA: RKO, 1951. Charles Lederer, scr. From "Who Goes There?" a story by John W. Campbell, Jr. Discussed by Umland, mentioned by Ambrogio ("*Alien*").

The Thing. John Carpenter, dir. USA: Universal, 1982. Bill Lancaster, scr. Discussed by Umland.

THX–1138. George Lucas, dir. USA: Warner, 1971. Lucas and Walter Murch, scr. Mentioned by Gordon.

The Time Machine. George Pal, dir. USA: MGM, 1960. From the novel by H. G. Wells. Mentioned by Clemens.

Tobor the Great. Lee Sholem, dir. USA: Republic Pictures, 1954. Mentioned by Clemens.

2001: A Space Odyssey. Stanley Kubrick, dir. UK: MGM, 1968. Kubrick and Arthur C. Clarke, scr. From "Sentinel," a story by Clarke. Discussed by Holte, mentioned by Ambrogio ("*Alien*").

Vampire Bat. Frank Strayer, dir. USA: Majestic, 1932. Discussed by Ambrogio ("Fay Wray").

Videodrome. David Cronenberg, dir. Canada: Universal, 1983. Cronenberg, scr. Discussed by Umland.

Village of the Damned. Wolf Rilla, dir. UK: MGM, 1960. Rilla, Stirling

Silliphant, and George Barclay, scr. From *The Midwich Cuckoos*, a novel by John Wyndham.

Warlords of Atlantis. Kevin Connor, dir. UK: EMI, 1978. Mentioned by Clemens.

Werewolf of London. Stuart Walker, dir. USA: Universal, 1935. Discussed by Heldreth.

Westworld. Michael Crichton, dir. USA: MGM, 1973. Crichton, scr.

When Dinosaurs Ruled the Earth. Val Guest, dir. UK: Warner Brothers, 1970. Mentioned by Clemens.

The Wolfman. George Waggner, dir. USA: Universal, 1941. Discussed by Heldreth, mentioned by Kilgore and Ambrogio ("Fay Wray").

Young Frankenstein. Mel Brooks, dir. USA: 20th Century Fox, 1974. Brooks and Gene Wilder, scr. Mentioned by Ambrogio ("Fay Wray").

IV. SCHOLARSHIP ON FANTASTIC ART

Abastado, Claude. *Introduction au Surréalisme*. Paris: Bordas, 1971.

Ades, Dawn. *Dada and Surrealism Reviewed*. London: Arts Council of Great Britain, 1978.

———. *Dali and Surrealism*. N. Y.: Harper and Row, 1982.

Alexandrian, Sarane. *Dali Paintings*. N. Y.: Tudor Publishing Council, 1969.

———. *Le Surréalisme et le rêve*. Paris: Gallimard, 1974.

Allentuck, Marcia. "Henry Fuseli's 'Nightmare': Eroticism or Pornography." In *Woman as Sex Object: Studies in Erotic Art 1730–1797*. Eds. Thomas B. Hess and Linda Nochlin. N. Y.: Newsweek, 1972.

Alquie, Ferdinand, ed. *Entretiens sur le Surréalisme*. Paris and La Hague: Mouton, 1968.

———. *The Philosophy of Surrealism*. Ann Arbor: University of Michigan Press, 1965.

Apra, Nietta. *Eighteenth Century French Art*. Trans. Terry Peppiott. Milan: Arti Grafiche Ricordi, 1963.

Arms, J. T. "The Groom Bewitched." *Print* 6 (1950): 22–24.

Audouin, Philippe. *Les Surréalistes*. Paris: Seuil, 1973.

Ballantine, Betty, ed. *The Fantastic Art of Frank Frazetta*. N. Y.: Rufus Publications, 1975.

———, ed. *Frank Frazetta: Book Four*. N. Y., Toronto, London: Peacock Press/Bantam Books, 1980.

Balakian, Anna. *Surrealism: The Road to the Absolute*. N. Y.: Dutton, 1970.

Bancquart, Marie Claire, ed. *Permanence du Surréalisme*. Paris: Klincksieck, 1975.

Barr, Alfred. *Fantastic Art, Dada and Surrealism*. N. Y.: Museum of Modern Art, 1936.

Bataille, Georges. *L'Érotisme*. Paris: Ed. de Minuit, 1957.

———. *Les Larmes d'Éros*. Paris: Pauvert, 1971.

Bauer, G. *Bernini in Perspective*. Englewood Cliffs, N.J.: Prentice-Hall, 1976.

Becker, Jochen J., ed. *Incogniti Scripturis Nova Poemata*. Soest, Holland: Davaco, 1972.

Bédouin, Jean-Louis, ed. *La Poésie surréaliste*. Paris: Seghers, 1964.

Benayoun, Robert. *Érotique du Surréalisme*. Paris: Pauvert, 1965.

Bentley, Richard. *Erotic Art*. N. Y.: Gallery Books, 1984.

Bigsby, C. W. E. *Dada and Surrealism*. London: Methuen, 1972.

Bjurstrom, Per. *Drawings of Johan Tobias Sergel*. Chicago: University of Chicago Press, 1979.

Bland, David. *A History of Book Illustrations: The Illuminated Manuscript and the Printed Book*. Cleveland and N. Y.: World Publishing Co., 1958.

Blankert, A., ed. *Gods, Saints and Heroes*. Washington, D. C.: National Gallery of Art, 1980.

Boase, T. S. R. *Giorgio Vasari: The Man and the Book*. Princeton: Princeton University Press, 1979.

Bonnet, Marguerite. *André Breton: naissance de l'aventure surréaliste*. Paris: José Corti, 1975.

Bowie, Theodore, and Cornelia Christenson, ed. *Studies in Erotic Art*. N. Y.: Basic Books, 1970.

Brant, Sebastian. *The Ship of Fools*, trans. Edwin H. Zeydel. N. Y.: Dover Publications, 1962.

Breton, André. *Manifestes du Surréalisme*. Paris: Pauvert, 1962. Rpt. as *Manifestoes of Surrealism*. Trans. Richard Seaver and Helen R. Lane. Ann Arbor: University of Michigan Press, 1977.

———. *Position politique du Surréalisme*. Paris: Ed. du Sagittaire, 1935.

———. *Le Surréalisme et la peinture*. Paris: Gallimard, 1965. Rpt. as *Surrealism and Painting*. Trans. Simon W. Taylor. N. Y.: Harper and Row, 1972.

———. *What is Surrealism?* N. Y.: Pathfinder Press, 1978. Rpt. in *Selected Writings of Breton*. Ed. Franklin Rosemont. London: Pluto Press, 1978.

Bréchon, Robert. *Le Surréalisme*. Paris: A. Collin, 1971.

Brion, Marcel. *Art Fantastique*. Paris: Editions Albin Michel, 1961.

Brochier, Jean-Jacques. *L'Aventure des Surréalistes: 1914–1940*. Paris: Stock, 1977.

Brookner, Anita. *Greuze*. London: Paul Elek, Ltd., 1972.

Browder, Clifford. *André Breton, Arbiter of Surrealism*. Geneva: Droz, 1967.

Bussy, Christian. *Anthologie du Surréalisme en Belgique*. Paris: Gallimard, 1972.

Carrouges, Michel. *André Breton et les Données fondamentales du Surréalisme*. Paris: Gallimard, 1967.

Cats, Jacob. *Howelich*. Amsterdam: M. de Groot, 1661.

———. *Silenus Alciabiadis, Sive Proteus*. Middelburg: I. Hellenij, 1618.

Chastel, André. *La Crise de la Renaissance, 1520–1600*. Geneva: Skira, 1968.

Clark, Kenneth. *Rembrandt and the Italian Renaissance*. London: Murray, 1966; N. Y.: New York University Press, 1966.

Crastre, Victor. *Le Drame du Surréalisme*. Paris: Ed. du Temps, 1963.

Cuttler, Charles D. "Witchcraft in a Work by Bosch." In *Bosch in Perspective*. Ed. James Snyder, Englewood Cliffs, N. J.: Prentice-Hall, 1973.

Dali, Salvador. *La Conquête de l'irrationnel*. Paris: Editions Surréalistes, 1935.

Duplessis, Yvonne. *Le Surréalisms*. Paris: Presses Universitaires de France, 1978.

Durozoi, Gerard, and Bernard Charbonnier. *Le Surréalisme: théories, thémes, techniques*. Paris: Larousse, 1972.

Easson, Roger R., and Robert N. Essick. *William Blake: Book Illustrator. A Bibliography and Catalogue of the Commercial Engravings*. Vol. I. Normal, Ill.: The American Blake Foundation, 1972.

Edwards, Hugh, comp. *Surrealism and Its Affinities: A Bibliography Compiled by Hugh Edwards*. Chicago: Art Institute, 1973.

Erasmus, Desiderius. *The Praise of Folly*. Trans. John Wilson. Ann Arbor: University of Michigan Press, 1971.

Ferguson, George. *Signs and Symbols in Christian Art*. N. Y.: Oxford University Press, 1966.

Finkelstein, H. *Surrealism and the Crisis of the Object*. Ann Arbor, Mich.: UMI Research Press, 1979.

Fischel, Lilli. "Hans Baldung Grien: The Flesh and the Devil." *Art News* 58 (September 1959): 18–24 + .

Fowlie, Wallace. *Age of Surrealism*. N. Y.: Swallow Press, 1950.

Freas, Frank Kelly. *The Art of Science Fiction*. Introduction by Isaac Asimov. Norfolk, Va.: The Donning Company, 1977.

Freas, Polly and Kelly, eds. *Wonderworks: Science Fiction and Fantasy Art*. Virginia Beach, Va.: The Donning Co., 1979.

Freedberg, Sydney. *Painting in Italy; 1500–1600*. Baltimore: Penguin Books, 1971.

Friedlander, Max J. *Early Netherlandish Painting*. Vols. 5 and 7. Trans. Heinz Norder, N. Y.: Praeger, 1971.

Gascoyne, David. *A Short Survey of Surrealism*. London: F. Cass, 1970.

Gaunt, William. *The Surrealists*. N. Y.: Putnam, 1972.

Gauthier, Xaviére. *Surréalisme et sexualité*. Paris: Gallimard, 1971.

Gerhard, Poul. *Pornography in Fine Art from Ancient Times to the Present*. Los Angeles: Elysium, 1969.

Gershman, Herbert. *The Surrealist Revolution in France*. Ann Arbor: University of Michigan Press, 1969.

Gibson, Walter S. *Brueghel*. N. Y.: Oxford University Press, 1977.

―――. *Hieronymus Bosch*. N. Y.: Praeger, 1973.

Givry, Grillot de. *Witchcraft, Magic and Alchemy*. Trans. J. Courtenay Locke. N. Y.: Dover Publications, 1971.

Glum, Peter. "Divine Judgement in Bosch's *Garden of Earthly Delights*." *Art Bulletin* 57 (March 1976): 45–54.

Gould, Cecil. *The Paintings of Correggio*. Ithaca, N. Y.: Cornell University Press, 1976.

Grigson, Geoffrey. "Painters of the Abyss." *Architectural Review* (October 1950): 215–220.

Groot, Cornelis Wilhelmus de. *Jan Steen, Beeld en Woord*. Utrecht: Dekker & Van de Vegt, 1952.

Hackford, Terry Reece. "Fantastic Visions: British Illustration of the *Arabian Nights*." In *The Aesthetics of Fantasy Literature and Art*. Ed. Roger C. Scholbin, Notre Dame, Ind.: University of Notre Dame Press and Harvester Press, 1982.

Hammacher, Abraham Marie. *Phantoms of the Imagination: Fantasy in Art and Literature from Blake to Dali*. Trans. Tony Langhan and Plym Peters, N. Y.: Harry W. Abrams, 1981.

Haslam, Malcolm. *The Real World of the Surrealists*. London: Weidenfeld & Nicholson; N. Y.: Rizzoli, 1978.

Hauser, Arnold. *Mannerism*. London: Routledge and Kegan Paul, 1965.

Held, J. S. *Rubens and His Circle*. Princeton: Princeton University Press, 1982.

Henkel, Arthur, and Albrecht Schöne. *Emblemata*. Stuttgart: J. B. Metzler, 1967.

Hess, Thomas, and Linda Nochlin, ed. *Woman as a Sex Object: Studies in Erotic Arts, 1730–1970*. N. Y.: Newsweek, 1972.

Hope, Charles. *Titian*. London: Jupiter Books, 1980.

Huizinga, Johan. *The Waning of the Middle Ages*. London: E. Arnold and Co., 1924.

Janis, Sidney. *Abstract and Surrealist Art in America*. N. Y.: Reynal & Hitchcock, 1944.

Jannini, P. A., ed. *Surréalisme*. Paris: Nizet, 1974.

Janover, Louis. *Surréalisme, arts et politique*. Paris: Galilée, 1980.

Jason, Horst Woldemar. "Fuseli's Nightmare." *Arts and Sciences* 2 (Spring 1963). Rpt. in *Sixteen Studies*. N. Y.: Harry N. Abrams, 1974.

Jean, Marcel. *Autobiographie du Surréalisme*. Paris: Seuil, 1978. Rpt. as *The Autobiography of Surrealism*. N. Y.: Viking Press, 1980.

———. *Histoire de la peinture surréaliste*. Paris: Seuil, 1959.

Johnson, Diane L. *Fantastic Illustration and Design in Britain, 1850–1930*. Providence: Rhode Island School of Design, 1979.

Jones, Henri. *Le Surréalisme ignoré*. Montreal: Centre Educatif et Culturel, 1969.

Jones, Jeffrey, Michael Kaluta, Barry Windsor-Smith, and Berni Wrightson. *The Studio*. Holland: Dragon's Dream Ltd., 1979.

Jongh, E. de. *Die Sprache der Bilder*. Braunschweig: Herzog Aton Ulrich Museum, 1978.

———. "Erotica in volgenperspectief." *Simiolus* 3 (1968–1969): 22–74.

Kahmen, Volker. *Erotic Arts Today*. Greenwich, Conn.: New York Graphic Society, 1972.

Kahr, M. M. *Velazquez*. N. Y.: Harper and Row, 1976.

Kauffmann, Hans. "Die funf Sinne in der Niederlandisher Malerie des 17 Jahrhunderts." *Kunstgeschchtliches Studien*. Ed., Hans Tintelnot. Breslau: Gauverlag-NS-Schlesien, 1943.

Keane, Patrick. "The Human Entrails and the Starry Heavens: Some Fantasies in the Visual Arts as Patterns for Yeats' Mingling of Heaven and Earth." *Bulletin of Research in the Humanities* (Autumn 1981): 366–391.

Klein, H. Arthur. *Graphic Worlds of Peter Bruegel the Elder*. N. Y.: Dover Publications, 1963.

Kock, Robert A. *Joachim Patinir*. Princeton: Princeton University Press, 1968.

Kronhausen, Phyllis and Eberhard, eds. *Erotic Art*. N. Y.: Grove Press, 1968; Bell Publishing, 1978.

Kuretsky, S. D. *The Paintings of Jacob Ochtervelt: 1634–1682*. London: Phaidon, 1979.

Landow, George P. "And the World Became Strange: Realms of Literary Fantasy." *Georgia Review* 33, no.1 (1979): 7–42.

Landwehr, John. *Enblem Books in the Low Countries: 1554–1949*. Utrecht: Haentjens, Dekker & Gumbert, 1970.

Langdon, Helen. "Salvator Rosa in Florence 1640–49." *Apollo* 100 (September 1974): 190–197.

Larkin, David. *Fantastic Art*. N. Y.: Ballatine Books, 1974.

———. *The Fantastic Kingdom*. N. Y.: Ballatine Books, 1974.

Laughlin, J., ed. *Surrealism Pro and Con*. N. Y.: Gotham Book Mart, 1973.

Larousse Encyclopedia of Renaissance and Baroque Art, ed. René Huyghe. N. Y.: Prometheus Press, 1964.

Légoutière, Edmond. *Le Surréalisme*. Paris: Masson, 1972.

Leher, Ernst and Johanna. *Devils, Demons, Death and Damnation*. N. Y.: Dover Publications, 1971.

Lehrs, Max. *Late Gothic Engravings of Germany and the Netherlands*. N. Y.: Dover Publications, 1969.

Levy, Julien, ed. *Surrealism*. N. Y.: Black Sun Press, 1936.

Linfert, Carl. *Hieronymus Bosch*. N. Y.: Harry N. Abrams, N. D.

Lippard, Lucy, ed. *Surrealists on Art*. Englewood Cliffs, N. J.: Prentice-Hall, 1970.

Lo Duca, Guiseppi von. *Die Erotick in der Kunst; die Welt des Eros*. Munich, Vienna, and Basel: Verlag Kurt Desch, 1965.

———. *Histoire de l'érotisme*. Paris: La Jeune Parque, 1969.

Lucie-Smith, Edward. *Eroticism in Western Art*. N. Y.: Oxford University Press, 1972.

McCorquodale, Charles. *Bronzino*. N. Y.: Harper and Row, 1981.

Mahle, Hans. "Zu Hans Baldung Grien." *Pantheon* 11 (June 1933): 169–177.

Matthews, J. H. *The Imagery of Surrealism*. Syracuse: Syracuse University Press, 1977.

———. *An Introduction to Surrealism*. University Park: Pennsylvania State University Press, 1965.

Mariën, Marcel. *L'Activité surréaliste en Belgique: 1924–1950*.Bruxelles: Ed. Lebeer-Hossman, 1979.

Melville, Robert. *Erotic Art of the West*. London: Weidenfeld & Nicolson, 1973.

Moffitt, J. F. "*Fuseli: The Nightmare* by Nicolas Powell." *Burlington Magazine* (July 1976): 526–527.

Morris, Cyril Brian. *Surrealism and Spain. 1920–1936*. Cambridge: Cambridge University Press, 1972.

Mountfield, D. *Greek and Roman Erotica*. N. Y.: Crescent Books, 1982.

Moxey, Keith P. F. "Pieter Brueghel and The Feast of Fools." *Art Bulletin* 64, no. 4 (December 1982): 640–646.

Muir, Percy. *Victorian Illustrated Books*. N. Y. and Washington: Praeger, 1971.

Nadeau, Maurice. *Histoire du Surréalisme, suivie de documents surréalistes*. Paris: Seuil, 1964. Rpt. as *The History of Surrealism*. Trans. Richard Howard. N. Y.: Macmillan, 1965.

Naumann, O. "Frans van Mieris as a Draughtsman." *Master Drawings* 16, no. 1 (Spring 1978): 3–34.

Peckham, Morse. *Art and Pornography*. N. Y.: Harper and Row, 1971.

Peppin, Brigid. *Fantasy: The Golden Age of Fantastic Illustration*. N. Y.: Watson-Guptill, 1975.

Picon, Gaétan. *Surrealists and Surrealism: 1919–1939*. N. Y.: Rizzoli International, 1977.

Pierre, José. *A Dictionary of Surrealism*. London: Methuen, 1974.

———. *Surrealism*. London: Heron Books, 1970.

Posner, Donald. "The Swinging Women of Watteau and Fragonard." *The Art Bulletin* 64 (March 1982): 75–88.

Powell, Nicholas. *The Drawings of Henry Fuseli*. London: Faber & Faber, 1951.

———. *Fuseli: The Nightmare*. N. Y.: Viking Press, 1972.

Praz, Mario. "Painter Ordinary to the Devil." *Art News* (January 1953): 333–354.

———. *Studies in Seventeenth Century Imagery*. Rome: Edizioni di storia e letteratura, 1964.

Pressly, Nancy L. *The Fuseli Circle in Rome: Early Romantic Art of the 1770's*. New Haven: Yale Center for British Art, 1979.

Pritzer, Pamela. *Ernst*. N. Y.: Leo Amiel, 1975.

Puppi, Lionello. "Eroticismo e osismo nella produzione artistica del Manierismo." *Rivista Internazional di Architettura* 8–9 (Fall 1976): 142–146.

Rawson, Philip. *Erotic Art of India*. N. Y.: Universe Books, 1977.

Ray, Gordon. *The Illustrator and the Book in England from 1790 to 1914*. N. Y.: The Pierpont Morgan Library, 1976.

Ray, Paul. *The Surrealist Movement in England*. Ithaca: Cornell University Press, 1971.

Raymond, Marcel. *De Baudelaire au Surréalisme*. Paris: Corti, 1963.

Read, Herbert, ed. *Surrealism: Contributions by Antré Breton and Others*. N. Y.: Praeger, 1971.

Reade, Brian. *Aubrey Beardsley*. London: Victoria and Albert Museum, 1966.

Reid, Forrest. *Illustration of the Sixties*. London: Faber and Gwyer, 1928.

Robbins, Rossell Hope. *Encyclopedia of Witchcraft and Demonology*. N. Y.: Bonanza Books, 1981.

Rodriquez Prampolini, Ida. *El Surrealismo y el arte Fantástico de México*. México: Universitad Nacional Autónoma de México, Instituto de Investigaciones Estéticas, 1969.

Rosenberg, J., and S. Slive. *Dutch Art and Architecture*. Baltimore: Penguin Books, 1972.

Rosenthal, Raymond, trans. *Aretino's Dialogues*. N. Y.: Stein and Day, 1971.

Ross, Roberto. *Aubrey Beardsley*. New York: Jack Brussel, 1967.

Rottensteiner, Franz. *The Fantasy Book: An Illustrated History from Dracula to Tolkien*. N. Y.: Collier Books, Macmillan, 1978.

Rudolph, H. "Vanitas." In *Festschrift Wilhelm Pinder Zum Sechzigsten Geburtstage, Überreicht von Freunden und Schülern*. Leipzig: Verlag E. H. Seemann, 1938.

Runeberg, Arne. *Witches, Demons, and Fertility Magic.* Helsingfors, England: 1947.

Salaman, M. C. *Modern Book Illustrators and Their Work.* London, Paris, N. Y.: The Studio, 1914.

Schiff, Gert, "Fuseli, Lucifer and the Medusa." *Tate Gallery* (1975): 9–20.

———. *Images of Horror and Fantasy.* N. Y.: Harry N. Abrams, 1978.

———. *Johan Heinrich Fuseli, 1741–1825.* 2 vols. Zurich: Verlag Berichthaus; Munich: Prestel-Verlag, 1973.

Schiff, Gert, and Werner Hofman. *Henry Fuseli 1741–1825.* London: Tate Gallery, 1975.

Schlobin, Roger, ed. *The Aesthetics of Fantasy Literature and Art.* Notre Dame, Ind.: University of Notre Dame Press and Harvester Press, 1982.

Schneede, Uwe. *Surrealism.* N. Y.: Harry N. Abrams, 1974.

Schneider, Luis Mario. *México y el Surrealismo (1925–1950).* Mexico: Arte y Libros, 1978.

Shoemaker, Innis H., and Elizabeth Brown. *The Engravings of Marcantonio Raimondi.* Lawrence, Kan.: Allen Press, 1982.

Short, Robert. *Dada and Surrealism.* London: Octopus, 1980.

———. "Eros and Surrealism." In *The Erotic Arts.* Ed. Peter Webb. Boston: New York Graphic Society, 1975.

Smith, Bradley. *Erotic Art of the Masters: The 18th, 19th, and 20th Centuries.* Secaucus, N. J.: Lyle Stuart, 1974.

———. *Twentieth Century Erotica.* N. Y.: Crown, 1980.

———. *Twentieth Century Masters of Erotic Art.* N. Y.: Crown, 1980.

Summers, Ian, ed. *Tomorrow and Beyond: Masterpieces of Science Fiction Art.* N. Y.: Workman Publishing Co., 1978.

Taylor, Gordon. *Sex in History.* N. Y.: Ballantine Books, 1962.

Timm, Werner, ed. *Albrecht Dürer Kupferstiche.* Leipzig: Insel Verlag, 1971.

Tomory, Peter. *The Life and Art of Henry Fuseli.* N. Y.: Praeger, 1972.

Tzara, Tristan. *Le Surréalisme et l'après-guerre.* Paris: Ed. Nagel, 1966.

Velde, Carl van de. *Frans Floris.* Brussels: Paleis der Academien, 1975.

Visscher, Roemer. *Sinnepoppen.* Amsterdam: Willem Iansz, 1614.

Voraigne, Jacobus de. *The Golden Legend.* Trans. Granger Ryan and Helmut Ripperger. N. Y.: Arno Press, 1969.

Vovelle, José. *Le Surréalisms en Belgique.* Bruxelles: A. de Roche, 1972.

Waldberg, Patrick. *Surrealism.* N. Y.: McGraw-Hill, 1971.

———. *Le Surréalisme. 1922–1942.* Paris: Musée des Arts Décoratifs, 1972.

Walton, Paul H. *Dali/Miro.* N. Y.: Tudor Publishing Co., 1967.

Webb, Peter. *The Erotic Arts.* Boston: New York Graphic Society, 1975; N. Y.: Farrar Giroux, 1984.

Wechsler, Jeffrey. *Surrealism and American Art. 1931–1947.* New Brunswick, N. J.: Rutgers, 1976.

Welch, Stuart Cary. *Imperial Mughal Painting.* N. Y.: George Braziller, 1978.

———. *Persian Painting. Five Royal Safavid Manuscripts of the Sixteenth Century.* N. Y.: George Braziller, 1976.

White, Terence Hanbury, ed. and trans. *The Bestiary, A Book of Beasts.* N. Y.: Putnam's, 1960.

White, T. W. Gleeson. *English Illustration: The Sixties.* London: Constable, 1897; reprinted Kingsmead, 1970.

Wölfflin, Heinrich. *The Art of Albrecht Dürer.* Trans. Alastair and Heide Grieve. N. Y.: Phaidon Publishers, 1963.

V. SCHOLARSHIP ON SCIENCE FICTION AND FANTASY FILM AND TELEVISION

"*Alien* from the Inside Out, Part I." *Fantastic Films*, no. 11 (October 1979): 8–21+.

"*Alien* from the Inside Out, Part II." *Fantastic Films*, no. 12 (November 1979): 22–30+.

"*Alien* Pre-Production: The Artists." *Fantastic Films*, no. 11 (October 1979): 15–17.

"An Interview with Gordon Carroll and David Giler, Producers of *Alien.*" *Fantastic Films*, no. 12 (November 1979): 38–39+.

"An Interview with Sigourney Weaver." *Fantastic Films*, no. 12 (November 1979): 33–35.

"An Interview with Tom Skerritt." *Fantastic Films*, no. 12 (November 1979): 36–37.

"An Interview with Veronica Cartwright." *Fantastic Films*, no. 12 (November 1979): 37–39.

Anger, Kenneth. *Hollywood Babylon.* Phoenix, Ariz.: Associated Professional Services, Inc., 1965.

Anobile, Richard, Richard O'Brien, and Jim Sharman. *The Official Rocky Horror Picture Show Movie Novel.* N. Y.: A & W Publishers, 1980.

Atkins, Thomas R., ed. *Sexuality in the Movies.* Bloomington: Indiana University Press, 1975.

Bailey, Margaret. *Live Long and Prosper.* New Brunswick: Graduate School Library Service, 1976.

Battcoch, Gregory. *The New American Cinema.* N. Y.: Dutton, 1967.

Baumgarten, Marge. "*Bride of Frankenstein.*" *CinemaTexasFilm Notes* 13 (7 September 1977): 21–25.

Baxter, John. *Science Fiction in the Cinema.* N. Y.: A. S. Barnes, 1970.

Beauvoir, Simon de. *Brigitte Bardot and the Lolita Syndrome*. Trans. Bernard Fretchman, N. Y.: Beynal, 1960; Arno, 1972.

Bell-Metereau, Rebecca. "Woman: The Other Alien in *Alien*." Unpublished paper presented at "Women Worldwalkers: New Dimensions of Science Fiction and Fantasy." The Sixteenth Annual Comparative Literature Symposium, Texas Tech University, Lubbock, Texas, 28 January 1983.

Blish, James. *Star Trek 5*. N. Y.: Bantam Books, 1972.

Bold, Rudolph. "*Rocky Horror*: The Newest Cult." *The Christian Century* 12 (September 1979): 861.

Britton, Andrew, Richard Lippe, Tony Williams, and Robin Wood. *The American Nightmare: Essays on the Horror Film*. Toronto: Festival of Festivals, 1979.

Brosnan, John. *Future Tense: The Cinema of Science Fiction*. N. Y.: St. Martin's Press, 1978.

———. *The Horror People*. N. Y.: St. Martin's Press, 1976.

Bruno, Michael. *Venus in Hollywood: The Continental Enchantress from Garbo to Loren*. N.Y.: Lyle Stuart, 1970.

Brusendorff, Ove, and Paul Henningsen. *Erotica for the Millions: Love in the Movies*. Los Angeles: Book Mart, 1960.

Cameron, Ian and Elisabeth. *Broads*. N. Y.: Praeger, 1969.

———. *Dames*. London: Studio Vista, 1969.

Canham, Kingsley. *The Hollywood Professionals, Volume One: Michael Curtiz, Raoul Walsh, Henry Hathaway*. N. Y.: A. S. Barnes & Co., 1973.

Carducci, Mark. "Making *Alien*: Behind the Scenes." *Cinefantastique* 9, no. 1 (Fall 1979): 10–39.

Changas, Estells. "Slut, Bitch, Virgin, Mother: The Role of Women in Some Recent Films." *Cinema* 6, no. 3 (Spring 1971): 43–47.

Clarens, Carlos. *An Illustrated History of the Horror Film*. N. Y.: Capricorn Books, 1967.

Cook, Pam. "Exploitation Films and Feminism." *Screen* 17, no. 2 (Summer 1976): 122–127.

Crawley, Tony. *Screen Dreams: The Hollywood Pinup*. N. Y.: Putnam, 1982.

Crowther, Bosley. *The Great Films*. N. Y.: G. P. Putnam's Sons, 1967.

Curtis, James. "From *American Graffiti* to *Star Wars*." *Journal of Popular Culture* 13, no. 4 (Spring 1980): 590–601.

———. *James Whale*. Metuchen, N. J.: The Scarecrow Press, 1982.

De Coulteray, George. *Sadism in the Movies*. Trans. Steve Hult. N. Y.: Medical Press, 1965.

Durgnat, Raymond. *Eros in the Cinema*. London: Calder and Boyars, 1966.

———. *Sexual Alienation in the Cinema*. London: Studio Vista, 1972.

Dyer, Richard. *Gays and Film*. London: British Film Institute; N. Y.: Zoetrope, 1977.

Early, Steven. *An Introduction to American Movies*. N. Y.: New American Library, 1978.

Edwards, Roy. "Movie Gothick: A tribute to James Whale." *Sight and Sound* 27 (Autumn 1957): 95–98.

Eisen, Ken. "The Young Misogynists of American Cinema." *Cineaste* 13, no. 1 (1983): 31–35.

Eisenstein, Alex. "*Alien* Dissected." *Fantastic Films*, no. 13 (January 1980): 51–63.

Erens, Patricia. *Sexual Stratagems: The World of Women in Film*. N. Y.: Horizon, 1979.

Evans, Walter. "Monster Movies: A Sexual Theory." In *Sexuality in the Movies*. Ed. Thomas R. Atkins. Bloomington: Indiana University Press, 1975.

Everson, William K. *Classics of the Horror Film*. Secaucus, N. J.: Citadel Press, 1974.

Farber, Stephen. "Violence and the Bitch Goddess." *Film Comment* 10, no. 6 (November-December 1974): 2 + .

Fitzgerald, Michael G. *Universal Pictures: A Panoramic History in Words, Pictures, and Filmographies*. New Rochelle, N. Y.: Arlington House, 1977.

Flora, Paul. *Viva Vamp! A Book of Photographs in Praise of Vamps from Mae West to Marilyn Monroe, from Marlene Dietrich to Brigitte Bardot*. N. Y.: David McKay, 1959.

Foster, Alan Dean. *Alien*. N. Y.: Warner Books, 1979.

French, Brandon. *On the Verge of Revolt: Women in American Films of the Fifties*. N. Y.: Frederick Ungar, 1978.

Gerrold, David. *The World of Star Trek*. N. Y.: Ballantine Books, 1974.

Gianetti, Louis. *Understanding Movies*, 3d ed. Englewood Cliffs, N. J.: Prentice-Hall, 1982.

Golemba, Henry. "Not Quite So Alien." Unpublished paper presented at the First International Conference on the Fantastic in the Arts, Boca Raton, Florida, March 1980.

Gordon, Andrew. "*Return of the Jedi*: The End of the Myth." *Film Criticism* 8, no. 2 (Winter 1984): 45–54.

————. "*Star Wars*: A Myth for Our Time." *Literature/Film Quarterly* 6, no. 4 (Fall 1978): 314–326.

Gough-Yates, Kevin. "The Heroine." *Films and Filming* 12 (May-August 1966): 8–11.

Gould, Louis. "Pornography for Women." *The New York Times Magazine*, 2 March 1975; pp. 10–11 + .

Greenberg, Harvey R. *The Movies on Your Mind*. N. Y.: Saturday Review Press, 1975.

Grove, Martin A., and William S. Ruben. *The Celluloid Love Feast: The Story of Erotic Movies*. N. Y.: Lancer, 1971.

Handling, Piers, ed. *The Shape of Rage: The Films of David Cronenberg*. Toronto: General Publishing; N. Y.: Zoetrope, 1983.

Hanson, Gillian. *Original Skin: Nudity and Sex in Cinema and Theatre*. London: Tom Stacey, 1970.

Haskell, Molly. *From Reverence to Rape: The Treatment of Women in the Movies*. N.Y.: Holt, Rinehart and Winston, 1974.

Hoberman, J., and Jonathan Rosenbaum. *Midnight Movies*. N. Y.: Harper and Row, 1983.

"How Wray Met Kong, or the Scream That Shook the World." *New York Times*, September 21, 1969, II, 17:1.

Hurwood, Bernhardt J., ed. *The Whole Sex Catalog*. N. Y.: Pinnacle, 1975.

Huss, Roy. "Almost Eve: The Creation Scene in *The Bride of Frankenstein*." In *Focus on the Horror Film*. Eds. Roy Huss and T. J. Ross. Englewood Cliffs, N. J.: Prentice-Hall, 1972.

Jacobson, Harlan. "Thunder on the Right." *Film Comment* 19 (August 1983): 9–11 + .

Jarvie, I. C. *Movies as Social Criticism: Aspects of Their Social Psychology*. Metuchen, N. J.: Scarecrow, 1980.

Kane, John. "Beauties, Beasts, and Male Chauvinist Monsters." *Take One* 4, no. 4 (July 1974): 8–10.

Kay, Karyn. "*The Beguiled*: Gothic Misogyny." *The Velvet Light Trap*, no. 16 (Fall 1976): 32–33.

Kay, Karyn, and Gerald Peary, eds. *Women and the Cinema: A Critical Anthology*. N. Y.: Dutton, 1977.

Kennedy, X. J. "Who Killed King Kong?" *Dissent* (Spring 1960). Rpt. in *The Girl in the Hairy Paw: King Kong as Myth, Movie, and Monster*. Eds. Ronald Gottesman and Harry Geduld, N. Y.: Avon Books, 1976.

Kiron, Adonis. *Le Surréalisme au cinéma*. Paris: Arcanes, 1953.

Knight, Arthur. *Playboy's Sex in Cinema (A Series)*. Chicago: Playboy Press, 1974.

Knight, Arthur, and Hollis Alpert. *Playboy's Sex in Cinema, 1970*. Chicago: Playboy Press, 1970.

———. *Playboy's Sex in Cinema 2*. Chicago: Playboy Press, 1972.

———. *Playboy's Sex in Cinema 3*. Chicago: Playboy Press, 1973.

Kobal, John. *Gods and Goddesses of the Movies*. N. Y.: Crescent, 1973.

Koenigil, Mark. *Movies in Society: Sex, Crime and Censorship*. N. Y.: Robert Speller and Sons, 1962.

Kovacs, Steven. *From Enchantment to Rage: The Story of Surrealist Cinema*. Cranbury, N. J.: Associated Universities Press, 1979.

Kronhausen, Phyllis and Eberhard. *The Sex People: Erotic Performers and Their Bold New Worlds*. Chicago: Playboy Press, 1975.

Kuhn, Annette. *Women's Pictures: Feminism and Cinema*. London: Routledge and Kegan Paul, 1982.

Lancashire, Anne. "*Return of the Jedi*: Once More with Feeling." *Film Criticism* 8, no. 2 (Winter 1984): 55–66.

Lavalley, Albert J. "The Stage and Film Children of *Frankenstein*: A Survey." In *The Endurance of Frankenstein*. Eds. George Levine and U. C. Knoepflamacher, Berkeley: University of California Press, 1979.

Lee, Raymond. *A Pictorial History of Hollywood Nudity*. Chicago: Camerarts, 1964.

Lee, Walt. *Reference Guide to Fantastic Films: Science Fiction, Fantasy, and Horror*. Los Angeles: Chelsea and Lee Books, 1972–1974.

Levine, George. "The Ambiguous Heritage of *Frankenstein*." In *The Endurance of Frankenstein*. Eds. George Levine and U. C. Knoepflamacher, Berkeley: University of California Press, 1979.

Levine, George, and U. C. Knoepflamacher, eds. *The Endurance of Frankenstein*. Berkeley: University of California Press, 1979.

Lo Duca, Giuseppi von. *Technique of Eroticism*. Trans. Alan Hull Walton, London: Eros Library, 1963.

McVay, Douglas. "The Goddesses." *Films and Filming* 11, no. 11 (August-September 1965): 5–9.

Malone, Michael. *Heroes of Eros: Male Sexuality in the Movies*. N. Y.: Dutton, 1979.

Manchel, Frank. *Women on the Hollywood Screen*. N. Y.: Franklin Watts, 1977.

Manvell, Roger. *Love Goddesses of the Movies*. London: Hamlyn, 1975.

Marsano, William. "Groking Mr. Spock." *TV Guide*, March 25, 1976. Rpt. in *The Making of the Trek Convention*. Ed. Jean Winston. Garden City, N. Y.: Doubleday, 1977.

Mast, Gerald. *A Short History of the Movies*. Indianapolis: Bobbs Merrill, 1976.

Mast, Gerald, and Marshall Cohen. *Film Theory and Criticism*. N. Y.: Oxford University Press, 1979.

Matthews, J. H. *Surrealism and American Feature Films*. Boston: Twayne Publishers, 1979.

Mellon, Joan. *Big Bad Wolves: Masculinity in the American Film*. N. Y.: Pantheon, 1977.

———. *Women and Their Sexuality in the New Film*. N. Y.: Horizon, 1973.

Meyers, Richard. *For One Week Only: The World of Exploitation Films*. N. Y.: New Century Publishers, 1983.

Miller, Martin, and Robert Sprich. "The Appeal of *Star Wars*: An Archetypal-Psychoanalytic View." *American Image* 38, no. 2 (Summer 1981): 203–220.

Milne, Tom. "One Man Crazy: James Whale." *Sight and Sound* 42 (Summer 1973): 166–170.

Milner, Michael. *Sex on Celluloid*. N. Y.: McFadden, 1964.

Modleski, Tania. "Never to Be Thirty-Six Years Old: *Rebecca* as Female Oedipal Drama." *Wide Angle* 5 (1982): 34–41.

Nugent, Frank S. Review of *Bride of Frankenstein*. *New York Times*, May 11, 1935, p. 21.

Palumbo, Donald. "Loving That Machine; or, the Mechanical Egg: Sexual Mechanisms and Metaphors in Science Fiction Films." In *The Mechanical God: Machines in Science Fiction*. Eds. Thomas P. Dunn and Richard D. Erlich, Westport, Conn.: Greenwood Press, 1982.

Pascall, Jeremy, and Clyde Jeavons. *A Pictorial History of Sex in the Movies*. London: Hamlyn, 1975.

Peary, Danny. *Cult Movies: The Classics, the Sleepers, the Weird, and the Wonderful*. N. Y.: Dell, 1981.

Peary, Gerald. "Missing Links: The Jungle Origins of *King Kong*." In *The Girl in the Hairy Paw: King Kong as Myth, Movie, and Monster*. Eds. Ronald Gottesman and Harry Geduld. N. Y.: Avon Books, 1976.

Pollock, Dale. *Skywalking: The Life and Films of George Lucas*. N. Y.: Harmony, 1983.

Prawer, S. S. *Caligari's Children: The Film as Tale of Terror*. N. Y.: Oxford University Press, 1980.

Renan, Sheldon. *An Introduction to the American Underground Film*. N. Y.: Dutton, 1967.

Rosen, Marjorie. "Movies, Mommies, and the American Dream." *American Film* 1, no. 4 (January-February 1976): 10–15.

———. *Popcorn Venus: Women, Movies & the American Dream*. N. Y.: Coward, McCann, Geoghegan, 1973.

Rosenbaum, Jonathan. "The Solitary Pleasures of *Star Wars*." *Sight and Sound* 46 (Autumn 1977): 208–209.

Rotsler, William. *Contemporary Erotic Cinema*. N. Y.: Ballantine, 1973.

Rowe, Carol. *The Baudelairean Cinema: A Trend Within the American Avant-Garde*. Ann Arbor, Mich.: UMI Research Press, 1982.

Rubey, Dan. "*Star Wars*: Not So Far Away." *Jump Cut* 18 (August 1978): 9–14.

Russo, Vito. *The Celluloid Closet: Homosexuality in the Movies*. N. Y.: Harper and Row, 1981.

Samuels, Stuart. *Midnight Movies*. N. Y.: Macmillan, 1983.

Sarris, Andrew. *The American Cinema*. N. Y.: Dutton, 1968.

Schwartz, Nancy. "Coming of Age: A Masculine Myth?" *The Velvet Light Trap*, no. 6 (Fall 1972): 33–35.

Solomon, Stanley J. *Beyond Formula: American Film Genres*. N. Y.: Harcourt Brace Jovanovich, 1976.

Strick, Marv, and Robert Lethe. *The Sexy Cinema*. Los Angeles: Sherbourne, 1975.

Trevelyan, John. *What the Censor Saw*. London: Michael Joseph, 1973.

Turan, Keneth, and Stephen F. Zito. *Sinema: American Pornographic Films and the People Who Make Them*. N. Y.: Praeger, 1974.

Tyler, Parker. *Magic and Myth in the Movies*. N. Y.: Simon and Schuster, 1970.

————. *Screening the Sexes: Homosexuality in the Movies*. N. Y.: Holt, Rinehart and Winston, 1972.

————. *Sex, Psyche, Etcetera in the Film*. N. Y.: Horizon, 1969.

————. *Underground Film: A Critical History*. N. Y.: Grove, 1969.

Tyreel, William Blake. "*Star Trek* as Myth and Television as Mythmaker." *Journal of Popular Culture* 10 (Spring 1977): 711–719.

Ursini, James, and Alain Silver. *The Vampire Film*. South Brunswick: A. S. Barnes & Co., 1975.

Vertlieb, Steve. "In Search of *Alien*." *Cinemacabre* 1, no. 2 (Fall 1979): 25–29.

————. "The Man Who Saved King Kong." *The Monster Times* 1 (January 1972). Rev. and rpt. in *The Girl in the Hairy Paw: King Kong as Myth, Movie, and Monster*. Eds. Ronald Gottesman and Harry Geduld. N. Y.: Avon Books, 1976.

Vogel, Amos. *Film as a Subversive Art*. N. Y.: Random House, 1974.

Von Gunden, Kenneth. "The RH Factor." *Film Comment* 15 (September 1979): 54–56.

Walker, Alexander. *The Celluloid Sacrifice: Aspects of Sex in the Movies*. N. Y.: Hawthorn, 1967.

————. *Sex in the Movies*. Baltimore: Penguin Books, 1968.

Weiss, Marion. "Have We Really Come a Long Way, Baby?" *University Film Association Journal* 26, no. 1 (1974): 11.

Whitfield, Stephen E., and Gene Roddenberry. *The Making of Star Trek*. N. Y.: Ballantine Books, 1968.

Williams, Linda. *Figures of Desire: A Theory and Analysis of Surrealist Films*. Urbana: University of Illinois Press, 1981.

Willis, Donald. *Horror and Science Fiction Films: A Checklist*. Metuchen, N. J.: Scarecrow Press, 1972.

————. *Horror and Science Fiction Films II*. Metuchen, N. J.: Scarecrow Press, 1982.

Wortley, Richard. *Erotic Movies*. London: Studio Vista, 1975.

Zierold, Norman. *Sex Goddesses of the Silent Screen*. Chicago: Henry Regnery, 1973.

VI. STUDIES ON SEXUALITY

Bem, Sandra Lipsitz, et al. "Sex Typing and Androgyny: Further Explorations on the Expressive Domain." *Journal of Personality and Social Psychology* 34 (1976).

Broverman, I. K.; S. R. Vogel; D. Broverman; F. Clarkson; and P. S. Rosenkrantz. "Sex Role Stereotypes and Clinical Judgements of Mental Health." *Journal of Consulting and Clinical Psychology* 34 (1970): 1–7.

Beauvoir, Simone de. *The Second Sex*. N. Y.: Knopf, 1949.

Firestone, Shulamith. *The Dialectics of Sex*. N. Y.: William Morrow, 1970.

Forisha, Barbara E. *Sex Roles and Personal Awareness*. Morristown, N. J.: General Learning Press, 1978.

Freud, Sigmund. "Civilization and Its Discontents." In *The Standard Edition of the Complete Psychological Works of Sigmund Freud*. vol. 21. Ed. James Strachey. London: Hogarth Press, 1961.

——. "The Ego and the Id." In *The Standard Edition of the Complete Psychological Works of Sigmund Freud*. vol. 19. Ed. James Strachey. London: Hogarth Press, 1955.

——. "Family Romances." In *The Standard Edition of the Complete Psychological Works of Sigmund Freud*. vol. 9. Ed. James Strachey. London: Hogarth Press, 1959.

——. "Femininity." In *Introductory Lectures on Psychoanalysis*. 1933; London: Pelican Books, 1974.

——. *The Interpretation of Dreams*. N. Y.: Random House, 1950.

——. *Moses and Monotheism*. Ed. T. K. Jones. N. Y.: Random House, 1950.

——. *New Introductory Lectures on Psychoanalysis*. 1932; London: Pelican books, 1975.

——. "Totem and Taboo." In *The Standard Edition of the Complete Psychological Works of Sigmund Freud*. vol. 13. Ed. James Strachey. London: Hogarth Press, 1935.

Friedan, Betty. *The Feminine Mystique*. N. Y.: Norton, Dell, 1963.

Gelpi, Barbara Charlesworth. "The Politics of Androgyny." *Women's Studies* 2 (1974): 151–160.

Gessain, Robert. "Vagina Dentata dans la Clinique et la Mythologie." *La Psychoanalyse* 3 (1957).

Goffman, Erving. "The Arrangement Between the Sexes." *Theory and Society* 4, no. 3 (Fall 1977): 301–331.

——. "Gender Advertisements." *Studies in the Anthropology of Visual Communication* 3 (Fall 1976): 69–95.

Greenacre, Phyllis. "The Family Romance of the Artist." In *Psychoan-*

alytic Study of the Child 13. N. Y.: International Universities Press, 1958.

Heilbrun, Carolyn G. *Toward a Recognition of Androgyny.* N. Y.: Alfred A. Knopf, 1973.

Kaplan, Alexandra G., and Joan P. Bean. *Beyond Sex-Role Stereotypes: Readings Toward a Psychology of Androgyny.* Boston: Little, Brown, 1976.

Keill, Norman. *Varieties of Sexual Experience: Psychosexuality in Literature.* N.Y.: International Universities Press, 1976.

May, Robert. *Sex and Fantasy: Patterns of Male and Female Development.* N. Y.: Norton, 1980.

Myerhoff, B. "Older Woman as Androgyne." *Parabola: Myth and the Quest for Meaning* 3, no. 4 (November 1978): 74–89.

O'Flaherty, Wendy Doniger. *Women, Androgynes, and Other Mythical Beasts.* Chicago: University of Chicago Press, 1980.

Secor, Cynthia. "Androgyny: An Early Appraisal." *Women's Studies* 2 (1974): 161–169.

Singer, June. *Androgyny: Toward a New Theory of Androgyny.* Garden City, N. Y.: Doubleday, 1976.

Vetterling-Bragin, Mary, ed. *Femininity, "Masculinity," and "Androgyny": A Modern Philosophical Discussion.* Totowa, N. J.: Rowman and Littlefield, 1982.

VII. OTHER STUDIES RELEVANT TO PERSPECTIVES OFFERED IN THIS VOLUME

Apter, T. E. *Fantasy Literature: An Approach to Reality.* Bloomington: Indiana University Press, 1982.

Baudelaire, Charles. *Oeuvres Complètes.* Paris: Editions Gallimard, 1961.

Bercovitch, Sacvan. *The American Self: Myth, Ideology, and Popular Culture.* Albuquerque: University of New Mexico Press, 1981.

Bettelheim, Bruno. *Symbolic Wounds: Puberty Rites and the Envious Male,* rev. ed. N. Y.: Collier Books, 1962.

Cawelti, John G. *Adventure, Mystery and Romance.* Chicago: University of Chicago Press, 1976.

———. "The Concept of Formula in the Study of Popular Literature." *The Journal of Popular Culture* 3 (Winter 1969): 381–390.

Cirlot, J. E. *A Dictionary of Symbols.* N. Y.: Philosophical Library, 1962.

Goffman, Erving. *Asylums: Essays on the Social Situation of Mental Patients and Other Inmates.* Garden City, N.Y.: Doubleday, 1961.

———. *Frame Analysis: An Essay on the Organization of Experience.* N.Y.: Harper and Row, 1974.

Habermas, Jurgen. *Toward a Rational Society.* Boston: Beacon Press, 1970.

Jackson, Rosemary. *Fantasy: The Literature of Subversion*. London and
    N. Y.: Methuen, 1981.
Key, Wilson Bryan. *The Clam-Orgy and Other Subliminal Techniques for
    Manipulating Your Behavior*. Englewood Cliffs, N. J.: Prentice-Hall,
    1980.
————. *Media Sexploitation*. Englewood Cliffs, N. J.: Prentice-Hall, 1976.
————. *Subliminal Seduction*. Englewood Cliffs, N. J.: Prentice-Hall, 1973.
Miller, Jean Baker, ed. *Psychoanalysis and Women*. Baltimore: Penguin
    Books, 1973.
Mitchell, Julliet. *Psychoanalysis and Feminism*. N. Y.: Vintage Books, 1975.
————. "Women: The Longest Revolution." *New Left Review* 40 (No-
    vember 1966): 11–37.
Nietzsche, Friedrich. *On Truth and Lies in a Nonmoral Sense*. Trans. Daniel
    Breazeale. In *Philosophy and Truth*. Atlantic Highlands, N. J.: Hu-
    manities Press, 1979.
Parsons, Talcott, and Robert Bales. *Family, Socialization and Interaction
    Process*. Glencoe, Ill.: The Free Press, 1955.
Rabkin, Eric, ed. *Fantastic Worlds: Myths, Tales, and Stories*. N. Y.: Oxford
    University Press, 1979.
Rank, Otto. *The Myth of the Birth of the Hero*. Ed. Philip Freund. N. Y.:
    Vintage, 1959.
Ries, Al, and Jack Trout. *Positioning: The Battle for Your Mind*. N. Y.:
    McGraw-Hill, 1981.
Slotkin, Richard. *Regeneration Through Violence: The Mythology of the
    American Frontier 1600–1860*. Middletown, Conn.: Wesleyan Uni-
    versity Press, 1973.
Turner, Victor. *Dramas, Fields, and Metaphors: Symbolic Action in Human
    Society*. Ithaca: Cornell University Press, 1974.
————. *The Ritual Process: Structure and Anti-Structure*. Chicago: Aldine,
    1969.
Waelder, Robert. "The Principle of Multiple Function: Observations on
    Over-Determination." *Psychoanalytic Quarterly* 5 (1936).

About the Editor and Contributors

ANTHONY AMBROGIO taught composition and film part-time at Wayne State University, Detroit, for fourteen years and is now a documentation specialist for Maccabees Insurance. His first published article, "In Defense of the Thing That Came and Went Again," a discussion of downbeat endings in horror films, appeared in the first and only issue of *Pukka Afflatus*. He has since published in *Film Criticism* and has nine essays on horror genre figures forthcoming in *Actors and Actresses*, volume 3 of the St. James Press *Films and Filmmakers* series. He has presented papers on horror films and fantasy comics at various national conferences and would like to sell his novel, *The Root of All Evil* (a horror story about dentists), for a lot of money.

LIANA CHENEY is Art Department Chairperson at the University of Lowell, Lowell, Massachusetts. She is an active member of the International Association for the Fantastic in the Arts and has presented papers and chaired sessions on hair as a fantasy object at the association's annual conferences.

SARAH CLEMENS has written and produced many planetarium shows, including a show on astronomical art featuring the work of Chesley Bonestell. She is also art editor for Bar Sinister Press and a designer of "Trial by Pylon," a fantasy adventure game. She has exhibited works in and judged art shows at science fiction conventions and is currently writing a history of fantastic art, tentatively titled *The Painted Dream*, for Greenwood Press.

MARY JO DEEGAN is an Associate Professor of Sociology at the University of Nebraska–Lincoln. She is the author of over forty articles on contemporary theory, history of social science, feminism, and popular culture. She is also the co-editor (with Nancy Brooks) of *Women and Disability* and the author of *Jane Addams and the Men of the Chicago School*, and is currently completing a book on popular culture entitled *American Drama and Ritual*.

ANDREW GORDON is an Associate Professor of English at the University of Florida in Gainesville and has been a Fulbright Lecturer in American Literature in Spain, Portugal, and Yugoslavia. He is the author of *An American Dreamer: A Psychoanalytic Study of the Fiction of Norman Mailer* and of numerous articles on contemporary American Fiction, science fiction, and the science fiction and fantasy films of George Lucas and Steven Spielberg.

PAUL GROOTKERK, an Assistant Professor in the Art Department at Mississippi State University, is an art historian specializing in Renaissance art. He received his B.A. from the State University of New York and his M.A. and Ph.D. from Case Western Reserve University. Professor Grootkerk has an article about satyrs forthcoming in Greenwood Press's *Mythical and Fabulous Creatures: A Source Book and Research Guide*.

LEONARD G. HELDRETH teaches technical writing, literature, and film at Northern Michigan University. He has published articles on E. B. White, William Wordsworth, and Stephen King as well as articles in Greenwood Press's *The Mechanical God*, *Clockwork Worlds*, and *Erotic Universe*, and is editing a volume of critical essays for Greenwood on *Vampires in Literature* as well as writing *The Reader's Guide to Fred Saberhagen*. He lives with his wife and two sons in Marquette, Michigan, where he presents a weekly radio show on current films.

JAMES CRAIG HOLTE received his B.A. from Columbia University and his M.A. and Ph.D. from the University of Cincinnati. He is currently an Assistant Professor at East Carolina University, Greenville, North Carolina, and has taught at the University of Cincinnati, Chatfield College, and the University of New Orleans. Dr. Holte teaches courses in film, popular culture, and writing. He is currently an associate editor of *Melus* and has been a film critic for *NPR* and *Gambit*.

JOHN KILGORE teaches English at Eastern Illinois University. He has published short fiction in *McCall's*, *Nebula*, and elsewhere as well as critical articles in *Modern Language Quarterly* and *Blake: An Illustrated Quarterly*. He recently served as a Fulbright Senior Lecturer in Korea.

FRANCINE AMY KOSLOW received her Ph.D. in Art History from Boston University. A specialist in nineteenth- and twentieth-century European and American art, Dr. Koslow is currently a Professor of Art History at Pine Manor College in Chestnut Hill, Massachusetts. Her work in Art History includes numerous publications and occasional guest curatorships. She is an expert on Henri Gaudier-Brzeska and recently published the *Henry David Thoreau as a Source for Artistic Inspiration* exhibition catalog. Dr. Koslow also serves as Director of Fine Art Tours, a professional art tour company, and lectures on twentieth-century art and literature.

GWENDOLYN LAYNE, an Associate of the Committee on Southern Asian Studies at The University of Chicago, is a Sanskritist (Ph.D., University of Chicago) with interests beyond seventh-century Indian literature. She has taught courses in fantasy and science fiction art and literature and has lectured on subliminal messages in advertising and fantasy art. Currently, she is writing a series of murder mysteries and researching a book on women seers.

MARTIN F. NORDEN received his Ph.D. from the University of Missouri—Columbia in 1977 and currently teaches film as an Associate Professor of Communication Studies at the University of Massachusetts—Amherst. He has published numerous reviews and articles on film and is the co-author of *Movies: A Language in Light*.

DONALD PALUMBO, Language and Humanities Division Chairman at Lorain County Community College, Elyria, Ohio, received his A.B. from The University of Chicago and a Ph.D. in English from The University of Michigan. He had taught composition and literature—including Fantastic Literature—at universities in Michigan and Texas prior to becoming an administrator. He has published over forty articles, including "Fantasy and Sexuality in Homer and Joyce" in *Colby Library Quarterly*; "Loving That Machine; or, The Mechanical Egg: Sexual Mechanisms and Metaphors in Science Fiction Films" in *The Mechanical God*; "Sexuality and the Allure of the Fantastic in Literature" in *Erotic Universe: Sexuality and Fantastic Literature*; and pieces in *Extrapolation* and *Survey of Modern Fantasy Literature*. Dr. Palumbo is currently Treasurer of the International Association for the Fantastic in the Arts and Comic Art and Comics Area Chair for the Popular Culture Association. He has also edited *Erotic Universe*, the companion to this volume, and is presently editing the proceedings volume of the 1985 International Conference on the Fantastic in the Arts, also to be published by Greenwood Press.

SYLVIE PANTALACCI was born and raised in Marseilles, France. She received her Maîtrise de Lettres Modernes at the University of Aix-en-Provence in 1980. She is now a graduate student in Cornell University's Romance Studies Department, where she is researching the image of woman in fantastic literature.

RAYMOND RUBLE received his Ph.D. from the University of Wisconsin and is currently a Professor of Philosophy and Religion at Appalachian State University, Boone, North Carolina. His teaching interests include the Greek classics, the history of philosophy, and contemporary moral and social problems.

KATHLEEN RUSSO, an Assistant Professor of Art at Florida Atlantic University, Boca Raton, is an active member of the International Association for the Fantastic in the Arts and has presented papers on Fuseli at the association's annual conferences.

SAM UMLAND teaches at the University of Nebraska at Lincoln, where he is a doctoral candidate working on the relationship between film and culture.

Index

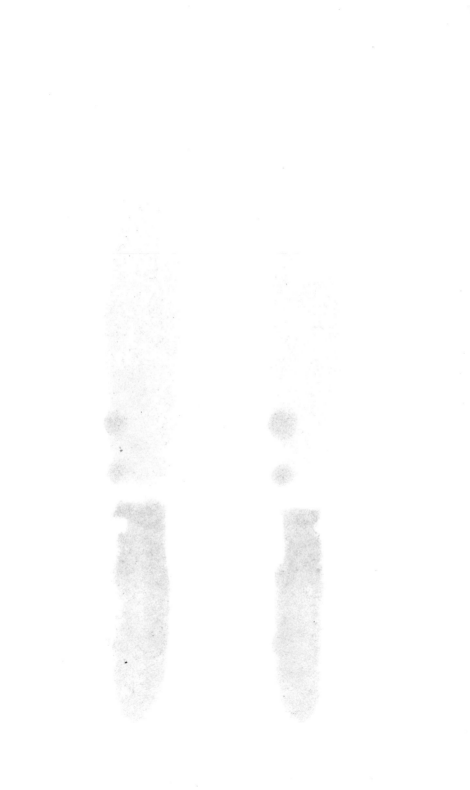